PROBLEMS
FROM LOCKE

BY

J. L. Mackie

CLARENDON PRESS · OXFORD

1976

Oxford University Press, Ely House, London W. 1

GLASGOW NEW YORK TORONTO MELBOURNE WELLINGTON
CAPE TOWN IBADAN NAIROBI DAR ES SALAAM LUSAKA ADDIS ABABA
DELHI BOMBAY CALCUTTA MADRAS KARACHI DACCA
KUALA LUMPUR SINGAPORE HONG KONG TOKYO

CASEBOUND ISBN 0 19 824555 6
PAPERBACK ISBN 0 19 875036 6

*Printed in Great Britain
by Cox & Wyman Ltd
London, Fakenham and Reading*

PREFACE

SEVERAL parts of this book are based on work already published, and I have to thank the editors and publishers in question for permission to use this material. Chapter 2 includes echoes of my lecture 'What's Really Wrong with Phenomenalism?', published in the *Proceedings of the British Academy*, lv (1969), 113–27, and also of my article 'Self-Refutation—a Formal Analysis', published in the *Philosophical Quarterly*, xiv (1964), 193–203. Chapter 3 incorporates my article 'Locke's Anticipation of Kripke', published in *Analysis*, xxxiv (1974), 177–80, and Chapter 4 incorporates a related article, '*De* what *Re* is *De Re* Modality?' published in the *Journal of Philosophy*, lxxi (1974), 551–61. Chapter 7 uses part of my paper 'The Possibility of Innate Knowledge', in *Proceedings of the Aristotelian Society*, lxx (1970), 245–57.

Chapter 6 is a successor to several previous attempts to deal with the problem of personal identity which, though not published, were read at different times and places (first in New Zealand about 1957) and discussed with many people. In many parts of the book I have been greatly helped by criticisms of an earlier draft. I am particularly grateful to Michael Ayers, Gareth Evans, Julie Jack, Derek Parfit, and Oscar Wood for such criticisms. In some places I have gladly adopted their corrections or improved formulations, in others I have reinforced my arguments against their objections, in others again I have simply stood by what I said at first. But I am confident that this process of testing has left the book more defensible than it was before.

I would also like to thank Mrs E. Hinkes for typing this book, as well as its predecessors, *Truth, Probability, and Paradox* and *The Cement of the Universe*.

April 1975   J.L.M.

CONTENTS

CONTENTS

INTRODUCTION

THIS book, as the title indicates, discusses a limited number of problems of continuing philosophical interest which are raised in Locke's *Essay concerning Human Understanding*. It makes no attempt to expound or study Locke's philosophy as a whole, or even that part of it which is to be found in the *Essay*. Then why take the problems from Locke, since none of them in fact originated with him, and all of them have been discussed by many philosophers both before and after Locke? Well, his treatment gave a fresh impetus to these controversies, and much of the later discussion takes his views as its starting-point. I admit that I originally intended to use Locke's presentation of these issues only as a series of pegs on which to hang my arguments about the issues themselves. But as I worked on them, it seemed to me that more of what Locke says is defensible than I had thought. It is always admitted that he displays sturdy good sense and blunt, forceful argument. But I think that he also shows, at a number of points, more acuteness and subtlety than he is commonly given credit for. Locke is frequently accused of muddle and inconsistency. But what gives this appearance is often his very proper realization of the force of arguments on opposite sides. As he himself remarks,

. . . he who will give himself leave to consider freely and look into the dark and intricate part of each hypothesis, will scarce find his reason able to determine him fixedly for or against the soul's materiality: since, on which side soever he views it, either as an unextended substance or as a thinking extended matter, the difficulty to conceive either will, whilst either alone is in his thoughts, still drive him to the contrary side. An unfair way which some men take with themselves, who, because of the unconceivableness of something they find in one, throw themselves violently into the contrary hypothesis, though altogether as unintelligible to an unbiassed understanding.[1]

It is not, of course, only with regard to the materiality of the soul that philosophers have fallen into errors of this sort. On several

---

[1] *An Essay Concerning Human Understanding*, Bk. IV, Ch. 3, Sect. 6. Hereafter all such references to the *Essay* will be given in the form 'IV. iii. 6'; they will be to the Fifth Edition as reprinted in the Everyman Library, edited by J. W. Yolton, except where there is a special reason for referring to an earlier edition.

of the topics discussed in this book, notably the representative theory of perception and the doctrine of substance, Locke has been repeatedly criticized for his readiness to put up with difficulties (of which he was aware) in one view, which his critics have thought fatal; but Locke tolerates them because he is aware of even stronger objections to rival views, which his critics either forget or choose to ignore. It is also one of Locke's merits that he does not think that philosophical questions are easy or straightforward or always capable of being conclusively settled, but yet holds that we need not on that account '. . . . sit still . . . in despair of knowing anything, nor . . . question everything and disclaim all knowledge, because some things are not to be understood'.[2] Nor need we take refuge in mystifications: we should do the best we can. 'It will be no excuse to an idle and untoward servant, who would not attend his business by candlelight, to plead that he had not broad sunshine. The candle that is set up in us shines bright enough for all our purposes.'[3]

It is by finding such strengths actually displayed in Locke's discussions that I have been led to give more space than I originally intended to the exposition and defence, as well as criticism, of his views. Nevertheless, this is still not meant to be a scholarly work on Locke. I hope that I have not misrepresented him. In case readers think that I have done so, I have given fairly full references to the passages in the text of the *Essay* on which my interpretations are based. But I would stress that even as this book has developed its main aim is not to expound Locke's views or to study their relations with those of his contemporaries and near contemporaries, but to work towards solutions of the problems themselves.

In Chapter 1 I defend a distinction between primary and secondary qualities that is close to that which Locke took over from Boyle. This is stated within the framework of something that could be called a representative theory of perception; this also, I argue in Chapter 2, can be defended against objections which many philosophers have thought overwhelming. Chapter 3 examines the notions of substance, substratum, real essence, and nominal essence. I concede that what Locke says about substance is not quite right, but here too a view fairly close to his can be defended, and Berkeley's criticisms are certainly too extreme.

[2] I, i. 6.   [3] I. i. 5.

Locke's account of real and nominal essences has been generally admired, and certainly such a distinction needs to be drawn; but I argue that whereas Locke thought that the meanings of words had to be tied to nominal essences, words can be, and sometimes are, annexed rather to real essences. In Chapter 4 I again defend much of what Locke says about abstraction and abstract general ideas against Berkeleian objections; but I go on to discuss the traditional problem of universals and argue that one part of this problem requires for its solution a version of Aristotelian realism rather than Locke's blend of conceptualism with a resemblance theory. I concede, however, that to some extent universals are the workmanship of the understanding. Chapter 5 deals with the general logical problem of identity, not only identity through time but also the possibility of identifying what are at first sight things of different categories, and the related question whether there are essences of individuals. Chapter 6 deals with personal identity. On these topics I have found it necessary to move quite a long way from Locke's position; yet his chapter on 'Identity and Diversity' has supplied not only the problems but also some of the techniques of discussion and several insights which cannot be ignored.

These six chapters, then, deal with some, but by no means all, of the central aspects of the questions 'What sort of world can we claim to know about?', 'Can we defend our claims to know-ledge?', and 'About what, and how, can we talk meaningfully?' On all these topics there is some conflict or tension between constraints that seem to Locke to be imposed by his empiricist principles (his purpose of explaining knowledge and meaning in terms of 'ideas' which we acquire in understandable ways from experience) and what we in fact seem able to think and say, the sorts of knowledge that both common sense and physical science assure us that we have. As I have said, I think Locke is right to take account of both sides of this conflict, though I do not think that he always finds the right way of reconciling realism with empiricism. In Chapter 7 I take up the question of empiricism itself, particularly in the form in which Locke most explicitly adopted it, the denial of innate principles and innate ideas. I argue that innate knowledge is possible in principle, and that there may actually be some items that merit this description, but I defend the main empiricist theses that innateness is not a source of

necessary truth and that authoritative, autonomous knowledge
of synthetic truths requires empirical support.

It is a natural consequence of this approach that I do not
attempt either to expound or to defend Locke's theory of knowledge as a whole. Indeed, I say comparatively little about Book IV
of the *Essay*, where his explicit account of knowledge is presented.
Nevertheless, I hope that readers who are not already familiar
with Locke's work will be able to follow the discussion of particular controversial topics, and may even acquire in that way a
better understanding of what Locke was concerned about, and of
why he said many of the things he did say, than they could from a
more straightforward exposition. I have deliberately postponed
until my last chapter the discussion of innate ideas and empiricism,
to which Locke more logically devotes his first Book. The issue,
in the form in which he discusses it, is not a live issue for us in
the way that it was for him and his contemporaries. But it acquires
interest for us when we have seen the tension between extreme
empiricism and realism, and the problems to which this gives rise,
in several more specialized areas of Locke's work.

However, one preliminary warning may be in order. Many
difficulties, some real, some imaginary, cluster around Locke's
uses of the word 'idea'. It plays a role both in what I call his
tendency to extreme empiricism and in his tendency towards
Cartesian rationalism. His view that the mind perceives nothing
but its own ideas sets up the problem which the representative
theory of perception has to overcome; his view that words stand
for ideas concentrates in one phrase both what is right and what is
wrong in his theory of meaning; while his definition of knowledge as 'the perception of the connexion and agreement, or
disagreement and repugnancy, of . . . ideas'[4] is hard to reconcile
with the reality of discoveries about the physical world. But he
uses the word 'idea' so broadly and, as he himself admits, so
carelessly that its mere occurrence commits him to very little.
Ideas are sometimes the contents of sensory experiences, what we
are immediately aware of when we are actually perceiving things
through the senses, and again when in 'reflection' we are intro-
spectively aware of our own feelings and thoughts; but they are
also the objects of memory and of imagination, they are what we
use in thinking about things that are not before us; they also in-

[4] IV. i. 2.

clude what we might call concepts; and Locke explicitly warns us
that he sometimes speaks of ideas where he means rather qualities
or collections of qualities of which we may have ideas. In reading
Locke, therefore, we must not be too fussy about the exact words
in which his views are formulated: we must try rather to see past
the words to the substance of the views that he was struggling
to put forward. And while making this plea on Locke's behalf, I
would make a similar one on my own. In several places I have had
to resort to awkward and unnatural ways of speaking. In philosophical discussion, particularly about perception, one needs to
draw attention to things with which in ordinary life we are not
much concerned, and with which ordinary language, therefore, is
not well equipped for dealing. No valid criticism of the views put
forward can be founded merely on such difficulties of formulation,
and I hope that philosophy has got past the stage of trying to
settle substantive issues in metaphysics or theory of knowledge
by appeals to what is alleged to be the ordinary use of language.

I

PRIMARY AND SECONDARY QUALITIES

1. *Locke's distinction and the representative theory of perception*

THE suggestion that primary qualities are to be distinguished from secondary qualities is one that seems to bring science and philosophy into head-on collision. Primary qualities like shape, size, number, and motion have been treated very differently by physicists, at least since the seventeenth century, from secondary qualities like colours, sounds, and tastes. But philosophers have on the whole accepted arguments that would show either that no such distinction can be drawn at all or at least that none can be drawn in the way in which we are initially tempted to draw it. For that way of drawing it presupposes a representative theory of perception, a contrast between percepts or sense-data or ideas as immediate objects of perception and material things which are the more remote or indirect objects of perception, and there are well-known philosophical objections to any such theory.

There is no doubt that Locke asserted, though he did not invent, some distinction between primary and secondary qualities. Whether he adopted a representative theory of perception is a question on which commentators disagree. The two topics cannot be completely separated: in deciding what distinction he drew between the two sorts of qualities we shall also have to decide whether he held something that can be called a representative theory of perception. However, I shall keep these topics as much apart as possible, carrying the discussion of the primary/secondary distinction as far as I can carry it on its own in this chapter, and reserving the discussion of representative theories of perception for Chapter 2.

It is widely believed among philosophers that, whatever Locke said about primary and secondary qualities, it is wrong. It is still more widely believed that, if he held a representative theory, he was wrong there too. He has, indeed, defenders. But they commonly argue either that he did not hold a representative theory or else, conceding that he did hold one, that it is a relatively unimportant part of what he said. For example, Jonathan Bennett, while he speaks of a 'veil-of-perception doctrine', says that the word 'doctrine' is misleading if it suggests something which Locke was 'consciously concerned to expound and defend', and that 'Locke's treatment of the appearance/reality distinction is not prominent in the *Essay*'; he says also that 'something true and interesting is misexpressed' by Locke's thesis about primary and secondary qualities, and goes on to defend a distinction which, though it largely coincides with Locke's, is at least initially quite different in principle.[1]

Similarly, Gilbert Ryle, while utterly condemning the representative theory, admits that one of Locke's uses of the term 'ideas' belongs with that theory: the term is used to denote 'certain supposed entities which exist or occur "in the mind"', certain 'supposed mental proxies for independent realities'; but to have expounded and popularized this theory is no part of Locke's greatness as a philosopher. A. D. Woozley goes further, denying that Locke held what is usually called the representative theory, pointing out that Locke himself criticized that theory as stated by Malebranche, and remarking 'It would be hard to understand why anybody should want to rate Locke an important philosopher if his whole theory rests on errors so elementary that a first-year student has no difficulty in spotting them.'[2]

In opposition to such views, I shall try to show that Locke's own primary/secondary distinction is fairly clear and interesting in its own right, that Locke had good reasons for drawing it, and that something close to it is correct—something closer, for instance, than Bennett's initial distinction. I shall also argue that both Locke's distinction and the one I defend require some sort of representative theory, but that this too is defensible and cannot be refuted by the objections that are so plain to the first-year student.

Locke does, however, present his primary/secondary distinction in a somewhat misleading way, and his use of terms is, as he admits, inconstant. It may therefore be better first to state the substance of his view in somewhat different terms, and only

---

[1] 'Substance, Reality, and Primary Qualities', *American Philosophical Quarterly*, ii (1965), reprinted in *Locke and Berkeley*, ed. C. B. Martin and D. M. Armstrong, esp. pp. 91, 104–5.

[2] G. Ryle, 'John Locke on the Human Understanding', in *Tercentenary Addresses on John Locke*, ed. J. L. Stocks, reprinted in *Locke and Berkeley*; A. D. Woozley, editor's introduction to Fontana edition of Locke's *Essay*, pp. 26–7.

afterwards to show how his words and phrases fit into this picture. Let us, then, suppose that Locke intended to say something like this:

There are material things extended in three-dimensional space and lasting through time. In this room, for example, there are several chairs: each of them has a specific shape and size and position, and is at any time in some definite state of rest or motion. The group of chairs in this room at any time has a certain number. Also, each chair is made up of a great many tiny particles which move about rapidly even when the chair as a whole is at rest. Material things also appear to have many other properties; they differ from one another, we say, in colour, hardness, temperature, and so on. But the real differences which these descriptions reflect consist wholly in the arrangement and motion of the tiny particles of which these material things are composed. Such things are also solid or impenetrable in that each keeps any other out of the place where it is. There are admittedly apparent exceptions: for example, water soaks into or through a sponge or a block of sandstone. But this shows merely that in such large-scale things there may be spaces between the particles: the particles of one thing or quantity of stuff may find their way between the particles of another. But each ultimate particle is completely solid and completely excludes any other particle from the same place. Thus the properties which material things, large or small, have in themselves are shape, size, position, number, motion-or-rest, and solidity. More exactly, each particle has solidity, each large-scale thing has some approximation to solidity, each thing large or small has some determinate shape, some determinate size, is at some place and is in some determinate state of rest or motion, while each group of things has some determinate number.

Material things interact with one another in regular causal ways: hence we can say that each thing has various powers. To say that a certain thing has a certain power is just to say that it would affect or be affected by another thing of a certain sort in some specific manner. A power is not the cause of such an effect; rather to have the power is to be such as to cause the effect. The cause—or, more accurately, a partial cause, since the effect will also depend upon *other* things—will be some set of properties, of the sorts already mentioned, of the thing that has the power: it will generally be, or at least include, some set of such properties of the minute parts of that thing, of the collection of particles of which it is composed. These properties which constitute the cause can be called the ground or basis of the corresponding power.

Material things also interact with our sense-organs and, through them, with our minds in ways that give rise to those states in us which we call the having of sensations and perceptions. That is, material things have powers to produce sensations and perceptions in us, and these powers, like any others, have grounds or bases in the intrinsic properties of the things. Also, our sensations and perceptions have what we can call their experiential content: we have sensations of pain, heat, and cold, and perceptions of coloured shapes, of rough or smooth and variously shaped surfaces, of impacts, pressures, and resistances, of sounds, tastes, smells, and so on. This experiential content is at most times very complex; commonly we do not attend to it or talk about it as such, but rather attend to and talk about the material things, with their properties and what they do, which we take it to reveal to us; but we can attend to the experiential content itself, and it is then most naturally referred to by such phrases as 'how it looks to me' or ' . . . feels to me' or '. . . sounds to me', and so on. This experiential content is partly as of properties of the sorts already noted as belonging to material things—solidity and determinations of shape, size, motion-or-rest, and number. I have a visual perception as of a circular shape in what I take to be a saucer and of which I also have tactual perceptions as of something solid, thin, and concave. But this content is also partly as of other features—colours, sounds, heat, cold, smells, pain, and the like. Shape, size, position, number, motion-or-rest, and solidity, just as they occur as elements in this experiential content, can also belong to material things. The saucer can be circular just as I see it as circular, it can be thin just as I feel it as thin, what I see as a group of three chairs may indeed be three chairs. Of course we can make mistakes, distortions and illusions can occur. I may see as elliptical the saucer which in itself is circular, and it may feel thicker than it is. But we sometimes perceive shapes and so on pretty correctly: material things often have very nearly the shapes etc. that we see or feel them as having. And even when we make mistakes, they have other *shapes*, for example, other determinate properties that belong to the same determinable (that is, shape in general) as those which occur as elements in our experiential content. We also commonly ascribe to material things colours as we see colours, as they occur as elements in our experiential content, and again heat, cold, roughness, and so on as we feel them; we ascribe tastes as we taste them to bits of food and to liquids, smells as we smell them to spatial regions; and I think of the ticking sound as I hear it as coming to me from the clock. But this is all a mistake, a systematic error. All that is out there in reality is the shape, size, position, number, motion-or-rest, and solidity, which occur as properties both of large-scale things and of their minute parts (though perhaps there is also some substance or substratum to which these properties belong; Locke's view about this will be considered in Chapter 3). It is these properties, especially those of the minute parts of things, that cause the corresponding sensations and perceptions whose qualitative content we wrongly ascribe to external things. On the other hand pain as we feel it, though it may be caused by an external object, say by a needle sticking into my finger, is not ascribed to that external object; rather it is commonly ascribed to the part of one's body in which, as we say, the pain is felt.

But how does this view connect with what Locke says? How is it to be translated into his terminology? First, what about 'ideas'? His official definition of 'idea' is very wide: 'whatsoever is the *object* of the understanding when a man thinks'.[3] This could include real, external, independent things considered as objects of thought, and also, as Locke says, what has been meant by such terms as 'phantasm', 'notion', and 'species', or what might now be called concepts—someone's idea of blue, say, or of murder— and again it could include what I have called experiential content. Locke certainly uses it to refer to the elements that form the content of a sensory perception while we are having it, but also to remembered images, imaginary constructions, and concepts, apparently without realizing the difficulty of making a single sort of item do all these jobs. But he does take some care to make his meaning clear. When he is about to introduce the distinction between primary and secondary qualities, he first distinguishes between ideas—the word must here be used in a broad sense—'as they are ideas or perceptions in our minds' and 'as they are modifications of matter in the bodies that cause such perceptions in us', and proposes to call only the former *ideas*.[4] That is, he is introducing

[3] I, i. 8.   [4] II. viii. 7.

a narrow sense of 'ideas' in which these are to be 'perceptions in our minds' and not 'modifications of matter'. One would expect him here to call the latter *qualities*, but in fact this is not what he proposes to do; rather he says that he will give the name *qualities* to the various powers of objects to produce ideas in us. But immediately afterwards his usage is partly inconsistent with this proposal, for what he identifies as *primary qualities* are 'solidity, extension, figure, motion or rest, and number', and these are not powers: rather they are intrinsic properties of things which may be the grounds or bases of powers, and they are 'modifications of matter in the bodies . . .' *Secondary qualities*, however, of which he gives as examples 'colours, sounds, tastes, etc.', he does identify with powers: they are 'nothing in the objects themselves, but powers to produce various sensations in us by their primary qualities, i.e. by the bulk, figure, texture, and motion of their insensible parts'.[5]

In this often-quoted remark 'nothing . . ., but' means (despite the comma) 'nothing except'; but many students and some commentators have read it as if 'but' were the conjunction, and so have taken the first part of the remark as saying that secondary qualities are not in the objects at all. This leads easily to the view that secondary qualities are 'in the mind', that is, that they are a species of what Locke has called ideas in the narrow sense. Other passages, too, lend some colour to this view; but it is clearly a misinterpretation of the doctrine which Locke is trying to expound. It might, indeed, be regarded as a merely verbal distortion of Locke's main way of speaking: obviously we could, quite harmlessly, use the phrase 'secondary qualities' to refer to what Locke would rather have called our ideas of secondary qualities, and find some other term to refer to the powers of things to produce these ideas. But historically it has not been harmless. For example, this distortion was used by Berkeley in constructing a specious argument for his own position (*Hylas*: . . . *secondary qualities*, have certainly no existence without the mind . . . *Philonous*: But what if the same arguments which are brought against secondary qualities, will hold proof against these also? *Hylas*: Why then I shall be obliged to think, they too exist only in the mind.[6]) By 1929, according to Reginald Jackson, this distor-

---

[5] II. viii. 10.
[6] First Dialogue in *Three Dialogues between Hylas and Philonous*.

tion had become the current usage of the term 'secondary qualities'.[7]

But this is not the way in which Locke generally uses the phrase. His official terminology is that while there are ideas both of primary and of secondary qualities, and all such ideas are in our minds, the primary qualities are the intrinsic properties of material things, large or small—that is, shape, size, number, motion-or-rest, and solidity—and the secondary qualities are powers of material things, whose basis is the primary qualities of the minute parts of those things. Locke includes under the heading 'secondary qualities' both powers to produce ideas of colours and so on in us and powers to produce changes in other bodies, for example the power of the sun or of a fire to melt wax.[8]

Locke says that shape, size, etc. 'may be called real, original, or primary qualities, because they are in the things themselves, whether they are perceived or no'. This would seem to suggest, by contrast, that the secondary qualities are neither real nor original, and are not in the things themselves, or perhaps anywhere, unless they are perceived. But to give Locke a consistent view we must read this as meaning merely that the secondary qualities are powers to produce (especially) perceptions, not that they are themselves those perceptions or ideas.

Locke's list of primary qualities varies a little, and often includes 'texture'. But I take it that the texture of, say, the surface of a body is just the way in which the smaller parts at or near that surface are arranged: this, like 'situation', would be covered by the inclusion of position in the original list, with the understanding that this includes both absolute and relative position.

Locke also says that 'the ideas of primary qualities . . . are resemblances of them, and their patterns do really exist in the bodies themselves; but the ideas produced in us by these secondary qualities have no resemblance of them at all'.[9] He means, surely, that material things literally have shapes as we see shapes, feel shapes, and think of shapes, that things move in just the sort of way in which we see, feel, and think of things moving, and so on. But he cannot mean that we never make mistakes, never suffer

[7] 'Locke's Distinction between Primary and Secondary Qualities', in *Mind*, xxxviii (1929), reprinted in *Locke and Berkeley*.
[8] II. viii. 26.   [9] II. viii. 15.

from illusions, with regard to primary qualities. Essentially what he must be claiming is that material things have, for example, shapes which are determinations of the same determinable or category, shape in general, as are the shapes seen, felt, or thought of. Thus I may be wrong in thinking that this table-top is square, and my seeing of it as a non-rectangular parallelogram is indeed distorted (but of course in a standard, familiar way which does not tend to make me judge wrongly, and does not even prevent me from—in another sense—seeing it as square at the same time); but a physical table-top *could* have a shape of either of these sorts, and this one does have some shape that belongs to the same family as these. The contrast that Locke is drawing is with, for example, colours. It is not that we sometimes make mistakes about colours —for example, wrongly match two different shades of blue under artificial light—but that even under ideal conditions, when we are as right as it is possible to be about colours, colours as we see them are totally different not only from the powers to produce such sensations, with which Locke equates the secondary qualities, but also from the ground or basis of these powers in the things that we call coloured. This ground, Locke thinks, will be only some arrangement and motion of the minute parts of the surfaces of these things: no colour as we see colour, no determinate within that category at all, is literally in or on the things, even when they are illuminated, nor is any determinate of that category in the light that comes from the things to our eyes. Similarly, and even more obviously, there is nothing of the same category as a sound as we hear it either in a vibrating gong or around it: sound as we hear it is nothing like a wave motion in the air. It is, of course, a trivial logical point that our ideas of secondary qualities, colours as we see them, sounds as we hear them, and the like, cannot be or resemble powers. But it is not trivial that they do not resemble the grounds of the powers: this is a non-obvious but, Locke thinks, real difference between the secondary qualities and the primary ones.

Someone might argue that primary qualities too should be identified with powers. A square object has the power to produce the idea of squareness in me in favourable conditions of observation. Admittedly there are such powers. But we also need a term to refer to the intrinsic features of things which form the grounds or bases of their various powers, and it is this job that is done by the phrase 'primary quality'. A large part of the basis of a thing's power to produce the idea of squareness will, moreover, be its literally being square, its having a shape-quality which is just like the shape-quality which we find in the experiential content to which the thing gives rise. The ideas of primary qualities resemble the grounds of the powers to produce those ideas.

The inclusion of solidity in the list of primary qualities does, indeed, make it difficult to sustain this distinction between intrinsic qualities and powers, for solidity, as Locke himself explains it, seems to be just the power to keep other things out. Yet after almost conceding that solidity is just impenetrability, which is obviously a power, Locke withdraws and suggests that '*solidity* . . . carries something more of positive in it than *impenetrability*; which is negative, and is perhaps more a consequence of *solidity* than *solidity* itself'.[10] That is, he wants solidity to be the ground of the power, not the power itself.

That this is the distinction which Locke is trying to draw between primary and secondary qualities will, I believe, be evident from a careful and unprejudiced reading of Chapter 8 in Book II of the *Essay* itself. This account agrees also with that given by Reginald Jackson in a classic article which, I think, has never been superseded. And essentially the same view was put forward by Robert Boyle, from whom Locke took the very terms 'primary qualities' and 'secondary qualities'.[11] It is true that Boyle, like Locke himself, shows some tendency to oscillate in his application of the term 'secondary quality': though he usually applies it to the relevant power, he sometimes applies it to the ground of that power, and sometimes to the resulting idea. But the substance of the view does not depend on the decision where a certain label is to be attached, nor need it be undermined by careless inconstancy in labelling. What matters is the claims made about what sorts of entities are or are not there, and what relations hold or do not hold between them.

There is, indeed, a possible objection to part of my interpretation. I have ascribed to Locke the view that there is a systematic error in our ordinary thinking, in that we ascribe colours as we see them, tastes as we taste them, and so on to material things, in

---

[10] II. iv. 1.

[11] For Jackson's article, see note 7 above; for Boyle's view, see 'The Origin of Forms and Qualities according to the Corpuscular Philosophy', *Works*, vol. iii.

effect that we mistake secondary qualities for primary ones. But a primary/secondary distinction could be introduced not as an error theory but as an analysis of what we ordinarily think and say; it could be argued that there are differences already implicit in the ways we handle qualities of the two sorts. Knowing well that a piece of cloth looks a different colour in different lights and even at different angles, and even apart from this may look a different colour to different people, we may already treat 'This is crimson' as the ascription of a power rather than as the claim that there is in the cloth an intrinsic feature that resembles one of our colour ideas. But Locke at least offers his distinction as a correction, not as an analysis, of our ordinary concepts. Whereas the power of the sun to melt wax is recognized as just a power, the secondary qualities 'are looked upon as real qualities in the things thus affecting us', we are 'forward to imagine that those ideas are resemblances of something really existing in the objects themselves'.[12] And on the whole I think he is right. Though we cannot treat secondary qualities in exactly the same way as primary ones, yet our dominant ordinary view gives them much the same status, and if Locke's way of drawing the distinction, at least, is to be defended, it must be in opposition to everyday assumptions.

Diagram (i) may help to make plain both the substance of Locke's distinction and the official terminology which he employs, not quite consistently, in presenting it.

If this is the distinction Locke was trying to draw, it is clear in what way it presupposes a representative theory of perception. It is formulated in terms of a contrast between ideas in minds— here especially elements in the content of a present sensory perception—and intrinsic features of external material things. It is being assumed that the latter are causally responsible for the former, and hence that we can speak of powers, whose grounds are such intrinsic features, to produce those ideas, among other things. The principle of this primary/secondary distinction is that the ideas of primary qualities resemble the grounds of the powers to produce them while the ideas of secondary qualities do not. While our ideas of qualities of both kinds correspond to and systematically represent real differences in external things, it is with the primary qualities alone that our ideas fairly faithfully depict what is there in the things.

[12] II. viii. 24-5.

Intrinsic features of material things = 'P.Q.'	Powers of material things	Items 'in minds'
Shape, size, number, position, solidity, motion-or-rest (i) on large scale = ground of power (i)	(i) Power to produce ideas of P.Q.	Shapes etc. as we see and feel them = 'Ideas of P.Q.'
	(ii) Power to produce ideas of S.Q.	Colours as we see them, sounds as we hear them, etc. = 'Ideas of S.Q.'
(ii) of minute parts = ground of powers (ii) (iii) and (usually) (iv)	(iii) Power to produce pain, sickness, etc.	Pain, Sickness, etc.
	(iv) Power to produce changes in other things	
	Powers (ii), (iii), & (iv) = 'S.Q'	

Diagram (i)

But did Locke have any good reasons for drawing this distinction? Can its coherence be defended against well-known philosophical objections? Should we now accept it, or anything like it, as correct?

2. *Arguments for the distinction*

It is clear that Locke adopted the distinction as part of the 'corpuscularian philosophy' of Boyle and other scientists of the time whose work Locke knew and admired.[13] It had long been known that sound is a vibration in the air, and Hooke, Huygens, and Newton were trying out wave and corpuscular theories of light. In the development of any such theory it is simply superfluous to postulate that there are, in material objects, in the air,

[13] See e.g. the Epistle to the Reader at the beginning of the *Essay*.

or in the light, qualities which are at all like sounds as we hear sounds or colours as we see colours. And though science has changed the details of its accounts since the seventeenth century, the broad outlines of its message on this issue have remained the same: the literal ascription of colours as we see colours, and the like, to material things, to light, and so on, forms no part of the explanation of what goes on in the physical world in the processes which lead on to our having the sensations and perceptions that we have, but, by contrast, the features actually used in the construction of such explanations still include spatial position and arrangement and motions (of various sorts) of items most of which are countable at least in principle. Despite the change from a Newtonian to an Einsteinian space–time framework, physics still recognizes, on a large scale, countable things with at least relative positions and extensions and motions, and despite the Quantum Theory, it still recognizes, on a small scale, particles with something like these spatio-temporal determinations. Solidity, it is true, no longer plays anything like the part it played in Boyle's theory, but is replaced by electromagnetic fields or attractive and repulsive forces; but fairly close relatives of all the other Boyle–Locke primary qualities still figure among the data of physical explanation, whereas no resemblances of our ideas of secondary qualities figure among these data.

But stressing the scientific support for the distinction may invite a facile but mistaken shelving of it as being merely of physical, not philosophical, importance. 'The doctrine of primary and secondary qualities is', says O'Connor '. . . nothing but some scientific truths dangerously elevated into a philosophical doctrine.'[14] It is often suggested that the so-called primary qualities are merely those in which physicists are specially interested, perhaps because they lend themselves more than others to measurement and to use in mathematically formulated theories, but that those of us who have other interests need not defer to such base mechanical preferences. But to say this is to miss the point. The physical considerations do not concern merely features which are scientifically interesting and important; they show that there is no good reason for postulating features of a certain other sort, namely thoroughly objective features which resemble our

[14] 'Locke', by D. J. O'Connor, in *A Critical History of Western Philosophy*, ed. D. J. O'Connor, p. 210.

ideas of secondary qualities. Does this mean that the physicists are telling us that grass is not really green and that blood is not really red, and that we have to take such dogmatism lying down? That would be a misleading way of putting the question. Of course grass and blood differ in some respect which is related to the different colour sensations that we get in looking at them in ordinary conditions in a good light. We could use colour-words in such a way that this, along with some family of similar resemblances and differences, was all that we meant in saying that grass is green, that blood is red, and so on. Over-reliance on the Wittgensteinian thesis that we need 'outward criteria' might lead to the conclusion that this is how we already do and must use colour-words, that only thus can their use form part of a public language. The physicist has nothing to say that would undermine this use. But I have no doubt that most people who use colour-words are commonly inclined to believe something more than is enshrined in this publicly establishable use, something that may be indicated by saying that colours as we see them belong intrinsically to the (illuminated) surfaces of material objects. The physicist (seventeenth- or twentieth-century) can point out that he has no need of this hypothesis. But admittedly physics does not itself tell us that no such properties are there. This denial is a further, philosophical, step; but it is one which is at least prima facie reasonable in the light of the successes of physical theory.

We might further explain and defend the Lockean view about secondary qualities by considering what it would be like for it to be false and for us to have evidence of its falsity—for example, what would be required to justify our taking colours to be primary qualities. For this two steps would be needed. First, we should want a scientific case for postulating the existence of qualities with the spatial structure of colours, either in addition to or instead of the hypothesized micro-structures to which physicists would at present refer in explaining colour phenomena. Secondly, we should need some reason for believing that the postulated surface-covering quality of redness was, qualitatively, as we see it—that is, that different people, and even members of different species, if not colour-blind, all see red alike (it is not the case that you see red as I see green, for example), and that their red-seeing was veridical not only in that they would agree with one another in judgements about what things were red, and not only in that there was some objective feature to which those judgements corresponded, but also in that this feature was just as they all perceived it. But in fact not even the first of these two requirements is satisfied, so the question whether the second is satisfied does not even arise.

Physics, then, gives us no reason for taking colours as primary qualities, and much the same can be said about sound-qualities, tastes, smells, heat, and cold. And the philosophical principle of economy of postulation then supplies a reason for not introducing supposedly objective qualities of kinds for which physics has no need. Perhaps the strongest argument for Locke's distinction, therefore, is based, partly, though not wholly, on physics.

Locke himself, however, was not a physicist, and he says repeatedly that it would be contrary to the design of his essay to 'inquire philosophically into the peculiar constitution of bodies'.[15] Yet he does not merely take over the primary/secondary distinction from Boyle, he argues for it, and his arguments are rather a mixed bag, good, bad, and indifferent.

First, in introducing the distinction, Locke picks out, as what he will call primary, such qualities

as are utterly inseparable from the body, in what estate soever it be; such as, in all the alterations . . . it suffers . . . it constantly keeps; and such as sense constantly finds in every particle of matter which has bulk enough to be perceived, and the mind finds inseparable from every particle of matter, though less than to make itself singly be perceived by our senses.[16]

Locke is here making two points: that when a body is changed or divided it, or its parts, if they are big enough to be seen, can still be seen to have shape, size, and the other primary qualities, and that even if the parts are too small to be seen, we still have to think of them as having shape, size, and so on. But the contrast he is drawing seems to depend on an unfair comparison between determinable qualities on the primary side and determinate ones on the secondary side. The determinate shape, size, and so on of a material thing are as alterable as its determinate colour; and while, no matter how you knock a thing about, cut it up, and so on, either it or its parts will still have some shape, some size, and so on, it seems equally true that so long as the parts are big enough

---

[15] e.g. II. xxi. 73.   [16] II. viii. 9.

to be seen it or they will still have some colour. We can regard heat-or-cold, or temperature, as a determinable analogous to motion-or-rest: a thing's determinate temperature is separable from it, but so is its determinate state of rest or motion, and just as it will always have *some* motion-or-rest, so it will also have *some* temperature. But if we carry division to the point where the separate particles are no longer perceivable by the senses, it seems circular to appeal to the fact that the mind will still give each particle some shape and size, but not, perhaps, any colour or any temperature. If the mind discriminates thus, it will be because it has already adopted the distinction: this cannot be the evidence upon which the distinction itself is based. Despite the prominent place given to it, this is therefore almost worthless as an argument; at best it might provide part of what is meant in calling a quality primary. But even in this respect it is misleading; as we have seen, what is central in the notion of a primary quality is that it is an intrinsic feature of material things, but is also a resemblance of some idea—that is, at least of the same category as some features that figure within the contents of our experience—and that it is something that the best physical theory will find it necessary to use as a starting-point of explanation. But clearly a feature could satisfy all these requirements even if it disappeared when things were divided beyond a certain point.

Secondly, and much more usefully, Locke does refer in outline to the physical considerations which provide the best support for the distinction—the causal processes involved in perception, the likelihood that 'some singly imperceptible bodies' come from seen objects to the eyes, and so convey some motion to the brain. We can conceive, Locke says, that God should annex the ideas of colours to motions to which they have no similitude; but the theology is dispensable: all he needs here is the principle that the sensation-effect need not resemble its cause, as we know it does not when pain is produced by the motion of a piece of steel dividing our flesh. Similarly, we need light to see colours; things have no colour in the dark. But no one, Locke thinks, will suppose that the light produces colours as qualities of what we call coloured objects. It is a much more plausible hypothesis that different surface textures merely reflect different rays of light.[17]

A third argument of the same sort is weaker though more

[17] II. viii. 12–13 and 19, also IV. xvi. 12.

picturesque. If you pound an almond, the taste and colour change, but 'what real alteration can the beating of the pestle make in any body, but an alteration of the texture of it?'[18] Someone might well reply that if there were intrinsic colour-as-we-see-it and taste-as-we-taste-it qualities, the beating could alter them, and that in any case it might easily release differently coloured and differently tasting liquids previously shut up in the cells of the nut. The most that Locke should have said is that the result of this experiment is consistent with his view.

A fourth argument draws an analogy between ideas of secondary qualities and pain and nausea. Everyone will admit that there is nothing like pain or nausea in the materials that produce them in us, so why should we suppose that there must be something like colours as we see them, sounds as we hear them, and so on in the objects that produce these ideas in us? This shows, indeed, that there may well be a pattern of relationships such as Locke describes for secondary qualities, where in virtue of some basis in an object it has the power to produce in us a sensation whose content is quite unlike that basis; but it gives no reason for supposing that colours, sounds, and so on conform to this pattern whereas shapes, sizes, motions, and so on do not. This argument shows that there may be secondary qualities, but not that the line between primary and secondary qualities is to be drawn just where Locke draws it. There is no obvious respect in which colours etc. are more akin to pain and nausea than shapes are.

Fifthly, Locke shows how his theory enables us to explain such illusions as our feeling the same water as hot with one hand but as cold with the other: if our feelings of warmth and cold arise from changes in the motion of minute parts of our 'nerves and animal spirits', it is easy to see how the lukewarm water could produce these different feelings by speeding up the relevant motions in the one hand and slowing down those in the other.[19] In itself this is a good argument, though of course just part of the 'corpuscularian philosophy'. But Locke throws in, for contrast, the remark that 'figure'—that is, shape—'never produce[s] the idea of a square by one hand [and] of a globe by another'. Though literally correct, this is unfortunate because it has led careless readers from Berkeley onwards to think that Locke is founding the primary/secondary distinction on the claim that secondary

---

[18] II. viii. 20.   [19] II. viii. 21.

qualities are subject to sensory illusion while primary qualities are not. It is then easy for Berkeley to reply that illusions also occur with respect to primary qualities like shape, size, and motion, and hence that there can be no distinction between the two groups of qualities; and then, adding the further misinterpretation (noted above) that secondary qualities exist only in the mind, to conclude that Locke himself would be required, for consistency, to admit that the primary qualities also exist only in the mind. But of course Locke's argument does not rest on any such claim that illusions affect only the secondary qualities; he himself records illusions that affect primary qualities like size and number;[20] it is rather that the corpuscular theory is confirmed as a scientific hypothesis by its success in explaining various illusions in detail. The explanations which it gives of illusions about secondary qualities make use of the assignment, to the powers to produce the corresponding ideas, of bases which do not resemble those ideas; but the same is not true of the explanations which it would give of illusions about primary qualities. The latter explanations still involve the assignment to material objects of qualities of just the same category as those that occur within our experiential content.

The arguments that Locke explicitly offers, then, add up to something of a case for the primary/secondary distinction, but not to a very strong one. Its best support comes from the success of a certain programme of physical explanation, success which indeed has come mainly after Locke's time. But even in Locke's time it had had some successes, though he does not consider it any part of his task to report them, and it had a fair degree of initial plausibility. Science, including popular science, has, I think, constantly adhered to something like the Boyle–Locke distinction; but philosophers have, in the main, been hostile to it, believing that there are powerful, perhaps even overwhelming, arguments on the other side, in particular those first put forward by Berkeley.[21] What are these objections, and are they really so forceful?

[20] e.g. he notes how distance affects apparent size, and how differently we should see things if we had microscopic eyes (II. xxi. 63; II. xxiii. 12), and he mentions 'that seeming odd experiment of seeing only the two outward ones of three bits of paper stuck up against a wall . . .' ('An Examination of P. Malebranche's Opinion of Seeing All Things in God', *Works*, vol. 9, p. 216).
[21] Especially in the First Dialogue.

3. *Arguments against the distinction*

Berkeley develops at great length the argument that illusions occur equally in our perception of primary qualities. But this, as we have seen, is simply beside the point, since the distinction does not rest at all upon the mere fact that illusions occur with the secondary qualities. A second argument runs thus: '. . . if you will trust your senses, is it not plain all sensible qualities co-exist, or to them appear as being in the same place? Do they ever represent a motion, or figure, as being divested of all other visible and tangible qualities?' The answer is, of course that they do not, but that it is an *ignoratio elenchi* to appeal to 'the senses' and how they 'represent' things, that is, to what we find in the content of sensory or perceptual experience, against a theory whose whole point is that things are in many respects not as they are sensorily perceived. A third argument takes the issue further: 'it is impossible even for the mind to disunite the ideas of extension and motion from all other sensible qualities'—that is, we cannot even conceive an extended moving thing without giving it some colour or some other secondary quality. In so far as this is just an appeal to what we can or cannot imagine, it is hardly relevant. If, as the second argument has stressed, we always experience extended things as having either colours-as-we-see-them or tactile surface qualities as we feel them, it is not surprising if our imaginings are similarly restricted. But behind this there is a more serious conceptual problem. Nearly all the primary qualities which Locke lists are, in a broad sense, geometrical ones. Shape, size, texture, motion-or-rest, and number are all only aspects of the spatio-temporal patterning or distribution or arrangement of some stuff (or stuffs). Each of these, and even all of them together, are essentially incomplete: there must be something that occupies some spatio-temporal regions and not others. It would be useless to draw the boundary of a certain shape if there were no difference between what was on one side of the boundary and what was on the other. But have we not forgotten about solidity? This is not a purely geometrical feature; could it not be the item of which each specific extension is the extension? Locke says 'This is the idea [that is, quality] belongs to body, whereby we conceive it to fill space.'[22] As Hume very forcibly pointed out, if solidity is just

[22] II. iv. 2.

impenetrability, the power to exclude other things of the same sort, it cannot do this job. If two things are to keep each other out of the regions they occupy, each must be not only something other than just a specific region, but also something other than the ability to keep others out of that region.[23] But, as we have seen, Locke's view is that solidity is not just impenetrability, not just a power but the ground of this power. However, this creates a difficulty for Locke's claim that solidity is a primary quality in the sense that the quality itself resembles the idea we have of it. If solidity is the space-filling feature which makes the difference between body and empty space and enables each body to keep other bodies out, then we do not have a simple, adequate idea of it, but only the indirect and relative notion of it as the supposed or inferred ground of a power which is itself learned from its manifestations.

In the Boyle–Locke theory primary qualities are meant to play two roles: they are meant to be objective features which resemble the ideas to which they give rise in us, and to be the features that a viable physical theory will use as starting-points of explanation. What our argument shows is that a complete list of items that play the former role is not a complete list of the items that are needed to play the latter. But it does not show that the qualities Locke has listed as primary ones, other than solidity, cannot play both roles. Nor does it show (as Hume thought) that any of the present secondary qualities has to be taken over and transferred to the 'primary' list for the second purpose. Rather, the additional basic physical feature will be something that should not be, and perhaps is not, on either the primary or the secondary list because it does not appear in our ordinary experiential content at all. And of course there may be more than one such feature. Locke's solidity should not have been on either list: it is an inferred physical property. Modern physics will not indeed use this; but electric charge is one feature which has come into physical theory to play a corresponding part, and mass (rest mass) is perhaps another. Neither of these is an immediate object of any of our senses, so neither can be called a primary quality in the sense of an intrinsic feature of material things which is also a 'resemblance' of some ordinary pre-scientific idea.

Developed in this way, then, this Berkeley–Hume objection

[23] *Treatise*, Bk. I, Pt. IV, Sect. 4 (hereafter I. iv. 4).

does indeed point to a revision needed in Locke's account of primary qualities, especially the distinction of their two roles and the recognition of some items which play the second role but not the first. But this objection does not show any need to break down the distinction between primary and secondary qualities. But, it may be said, this is the wrong way to develop the objection. Whether or not physical theory needs further space-occupying properties, which may well be initially quite unknown to us, we need, for a coherent account of what we perceive and can imagine, some *known* space-filling property or properties to make the difference between body and empty space *for us*. And since this cannot be one of Locke's primary qualities (solidity having been removed from the list) and cannot be unknown or unperceived, it must be one (or more) of the secondary qualities. But this need not be conceded. Visually, indeed, it is as coloured that we are able to pick out space-occupying material things. Tactually, it is as having certain felt surface qualities. But what if I feel over the surface of a rigid body, say the top, edge, and the underside of a table-top, not directly with my fingers but with some instrument, such as a pencil? Can I not thus detect a shape without being aware of any quality that fills that shape other than the power, impenetrability? Although this was not an adequate candidate for the space-occupying role from the point of view of physical theory, it is adequate in relation to this other, experiential, way of developing the difficulty. Impenetrability could conceivably be all that made the difference *for us* between body and empty space. But even if this were not so, how would it matter? We should merely be brought back by another route to Berkeley's thesis that neither our senses nor our imaginations ever represent to us collections of primary qualities alone without secondary qualities, and this would be irrelevant as an argument against Locke's view, the whole point of which is that things are not as they are sensorily perceived, that we need to revise and correct the picture of the world which we initially acquire by the use of our senses.

Berkeley's other arguments against the distinction amount to little more than ingenious satire and rhetoric—for example, the way in which Philonous traps Hylas into saying (in attempting to defend Locke's view) that real sounds are never heard, but may—since they are wave motions—possibly be seen or felt. The

Lockean view is at variance with initial common-sense opinions, and it is not easy to express it naturally and coherently in the ordinary language whose primary function is to make statements within the framework of those common-sense opinions. The term 'sound' is thus initially employed both to denote a feature that forms part of the content of our experience—or at least that is of the same category as features that do so—and to denote a supposed independently existing entity. But Locke's account of secondary qualities is precisely that with them nothing plays both these roles; someone who adopts that account must then either say that there are no sounds or else use the word to denote one or other of the items that (in his opinion) do exist but violate its linguistic connection with the other. It will be awkward for him to express his view; but this is no good argument against that view, but rather a glaring example of an invalid way of appealing to ordinary language to settle a philosophical issue.

None of these arguments of Berkeley's, then, tells at all forcibly against Locke's distinction. But in examining them we have shown up an assumption which Locke makes but which is implausible from the start. His primary qualities have to do two jobs: they have to be the constituents of the physical world (and hence the starting-points of explanations in the best possible physical theory), but they also have to be features of which some of our ideas are 'resemblances', that is, they have to be of categories which are fairly correctly depicted in the way in which we sensorily perceive the physical world. But there is little reason to suppose that every real constituent, even basic constituent, of physical things will be recorded in our perceptions, and we have found an argument which shows that physical theory must postulate at least one constituent feature (to be the extension-occupier) of which no pre-scientific idea that we have is a resemblance. It is interesting to note that Locke at least once explicitly left room for such a development, remarking that our ideas of secondary qualities depend 'upon the primary qualities of their minute and insensible parts or, if not upon them, upon something yet more remote from our comprehension'.[24]

But there is still a major difficulty for the distinction as Locke drew it. It is formulated within the framework of a representative theory of perception which distinguishes sharply between ideas in

[24] IV. iii. 11.

our minds and any externally real things, while postulating that our ideas are causally produced by those external things acting upon our sense-organs and through them on our brains, and yet assumes that we can speak intelligibly about resemblances between some of our ideas and those external realities. It is in terms of this theory that primary qualities are distinguished in status from secondary ones, that though we have ideas of both sorts, the corresponding realities in the one case resemble the ideas, but not in the other, that the primary qualities really are *qualities*, and are themselves the ground or basis of the powers to produce the corresponding ideas, whereas the secondary qualities are mere powers, whose ground or basis is the primary qualities of minute parts. But the representative theory has been severely criticized and is widely believed to be completely untenable; if so, this must be fatal for any distinction between primary and secondary qualities that is developed within its framework.

This is the most serious difficulty for Locke's distinction; but I shall postpone discussion of it until the next chapter. In the remainder of the present chapter I shall consider two distinctions which are related to Locke's distinction between primary and secondary qualities, but which do not require any sort of representative theory and which could therefore survive criticisms which might be fatal to the distinction as Locke drew it.

4. *Aristotle's distinction and Molyneux's problem—common and special sensibles*

First, there is a distinction which goes back at least to Aristotle between objects of perception which are perceived by more than one sense—perhaps by all, but at least both by sight and by touch—and those which are perceived by one sense only.[25] This distinction coincides fairly closely with Locke's: Aristotle mentions as 'common sensibles' motion, rest, shape, size, number, and unity, while colour, sound, and flavour are examples of the 'special sensibles'. There is no doubt that there is a distinction which can be drawn in these terms quite innocently, without commitment to any further theory about the objective status of these various items. On the other hand, this difference might be taken as a piece of evidence supporting Locke's distinction, as a

[25] Aristotle, *De Anima*, 418ᵃ. 9–24; 425 . 14–21.

datum of experience for which Locke's account provides an explanation. If material things themselves literally have shape, size, and so on, it is not surprising that we can become aware of their shapes, sizes, and so on, more or less accurately, by way of more than one sensory channel; and if, for example, shapes as we see them and shapes as we feel them both resemble shapes as material things actually have them, intrinsically, they will naturally resemble one another. But if our idea of some secondary quality is merely a causal product of the interaction of something external with some sense-organ and some part of the central nervous system and does not resemble anything external, then it is on the whole to be expected that it will be peculiar to that particular sense.

This suggestion, however, faces some exceptions and problems. Some qualities seem to be common to the senses of taste and smell —there can be a sour smell as well as a sour taste. Are these, then to count as common sensibles? If so, our argument from Aristotle's distinction to Locke's would suggest that sourness is to be a primary quality, whereas it is obviously a secondary one for Locke. But this is easily explained away. The mechanisms of the senses of taste and smell are so similar and so closely related that the same ground in the material object—presumably in minute particles floating in the air as well as in the food—can give rise to similar ideas by way of the two mechanisms.

A more serious question is whether the primary qualities really are common sensibles to sight and touch, for example whether visual and tactual ideas of shape really resemble one another. Locke himself discusses Molyneux's problem, whether a man born blind, who has learned to distinguish by touch a cube and a sphere of the same metal and of about the same size, and who then acquires the sense of sight, would be able to tell which was which of a cube and a sphere by sight alone, before he had touched them.[26] Locke agrees with Molyneux that the man would not be able to do this. Berkeley also agreed, and developed this answer by maintaining that the visual ideas of the two shapes are quite different from the tactual ideas of them, and that it is only experience that enables us to correlate visual with tactual ideas, and so to expect a certain tactual impression where we have had the correlated (but intrinsically quite different) visual one. On Berkeley's

[26] II. ix. 8.

view there is, at least primitively, no one common sensible
shape (or size, and so on: though Berkeley is evasive about number,
attempting to brush it aside as 'entirely the creature of the mind'):[27]
the name of any particular shape, say 'square', stands for a pair of
correlated ideas, one visual and one tactual, and what Aristotle
takes as the perceiving of some one object through two senses is
really the separate perceiving, by each of the two senses, of an idea
special to that sense, accompanied by an inference to or expectation
of the correlated idea which is peculiar to the other sense.[28]

Did Locke, then, in giving the same answer to Molyneux's
problem as Berkeley gave later, commit himself to the denial that
shape, for example, is a common sensible? I think not, for if we
pay attention to the context in which he refers to the problem we
can see that his reason for the negative answer to Molyneux's
question is quite different from Berkeley's. Locke uses it to illustrate the thesis that 'the ideas we receive by sensation are often in
grown people altered by the judgment, without our taking notice
of it'; in other words, perception is modified by unconscious
automatic interpretation, and we owe this to experience. For
example, where all that we see (in one sense) is 'a plane variously
coloured' we get the impression of a convex surface; 'the judgment . . . frames to itself the perception of a convex figure . . .'
We can infer that Locke's reason for saying that Molyneux's man
would not be able, before touching the objects he was now seeing
for the first time, to say which was the sphere and which the cube
is that this man would not have acquired automatic interpretations of various patterns of shading as indicators of three-
dimensional shapes such as spherical convexity or the corner of a
cube projecting towards the viewer. As Locke says, quoting
Molyneux himself, 'he has not yet attained the experience that
what affects his touch so or so must affect his sight so or so; or
that a protuberant angle in the cube, that pressed his hand un-
equally, shall appear to his eye as it does in the cube'. But this
would leave open the possibility that two-dimensional shape
should be a common sensible for sight and touch.

In fact, Molyneux's question is confusing, because it raises
more than one issue. The issues would be discriminated if we
were to ask two separate questions: first, whether Molyneux's

---

[27] *A New Theory of Vision*, §§ 47–9, 96–105, 110–11, 132–6, etc.
[28] Op. cit., § 109.

man would be able to say which was which of two flat plates, one square and one circular, placed with their flat surfaces at right angles to his line of sight, and secondly, whether he would be able to say which was which of a flat circular plate (still so placed) and a sphere. Berkeley would, of course, answer 'No' to both questions. But it would be more plausible to say 'Yes' to the first question and 'No' to the second. This affirmative answer to the first question would rest on the assumption that (two-dimensional) squareness and circularity can each be detected both by sight and by touch, or again that a circle as seen and a circle as felt share the genuinely common feature of being the same all round, whereas a square, whether seen or felt, has the contrasting feature that its four corners are different from its four sides. But the negative answer to the second question would rest on the view that there is no feature genuinely common to convexity as felt and to the shading by which an artist represents convexity—something like the latter being all that Molyneux's man could see when he looked at the sphere for the first time.

In fact there is some (admittedly inconclusive) experimental evidence in favour of an affirmative answer to our first question.[29] R. L. Gregory reports the case of a man who was not indeed totally blind, but with no useful vision, not from birth but from the age of ten months, and whose sight was restored by corneal grafts. It appears that he could recognize ordinary objects by sight, could tell the time by a seen clockface, having previously learned to tell the time by touching the hands of a large watch with no glass, and could recognize capital letters which he had learned by touch. Provided that we can discount his experiences up to the age of ten months and such vision as he had between that age and the operation, this man's performance disproves Berkeley's thesis that the objects of sight have, initially, nothing in common with the objects of touch—of course 'touch' must here be taken to include kinaesthesis. But it says nothing against Locke's thesis that only an experienced correlation enables us to interpret shading as relief. Gregory's report does not include any direct answer to our second question, but it does say that the man had no impression of depth from the Necker cube and

[29] R. L. Gregory, *Concepts and Mechanisms of Perception*, pp. 65–129 (reprint of monograph by R. L. Gregory and Jean Wallace, *Recovery from Early Blindness: a Case Study* (1963)).

similar line-drawings. This indirectly supports a negative answer to our second question, since it shows that the man did not respond to a remotely analogous visual indication of depth. There is, then, some evidence in favour of Locke's negative answer to the precise question with which he was concerned. If a man like Molyneux's could, contrary to what Locke thought, also distinguish a sphere from a flat circular plate, it could only be by some innate or instinctive faculty of interpreting shading as relief. This is not impossible, but it would be much more surprising than the reported achievements which show only an ability visually to recognize two-dimensional shapes and patterns previously learned by touch.

I conclude that Locke could, consistently with his negative answer to Molyneux's question in the context in which he discussed it, hold that we get the same idea of shape from both sight and touch, provided that this is confined to two-dimensional shape. This view is intrinsically plausible, and such empirical evidence as there is supports it against Berkeley's thesis. If there are thus common sensibles for sight and touch, we can take Aristotle's distinction innocently in its own right. But we can also take it, more interestingly, as evidence that supports Locke's more speculative distinction between primary and secondary qualities.

This discussion does, however, force us to qualify Locke's claim that our ideas of shapes resemble the intrinsic qualities of objects which causally produce those ideas. This will hold for both visually and tactually acquired ideas of two-dimensional shape, and perhaps for some tactually acquired ideas of three-dimensional shape. It may hold also for visually acquired ideas of three-dimensional shape, but only in so far as these ideas are the product of unconscious interpretation based on experience, 'a settled habit . . . performed so constantly and so quick, that we take that for the perception of our sensation which is an idea formed by our judgment'. Something similar would apply, I believe, to most tactual perception of three-dimensional shape. We have had to learn both to see and to feel things as making up a three-dimensional Euclidean world. Only by an unconsciously sophisticated performance do we form those ideas of three-dimensional shapes which resemble the intrinsic shape-qualities of the things that give rise to them.

5. Bennett's distinction

Another way of distinguishing primary from secondary qualities has been introduced and defended by Jonathan Bennett.[30] Primary qualities such as size have far more complex connections with our experiences, with the ways in which things interact, than do secondary qualities. Consequently someone can be colour-blind without its being brought home to him by any ordinary conjunction of other experiences that there is anything wrong, whereas to suppose that someone could be size-blind without its showing up almost at once we should have to suppose a fantastically complicated systematic distortion of his perceptions as compared with those of other people. It is therefore a contingent matter that we agree as well as we do about what tastes bitter or what looks green. Bennett mentions phenol-thio-urea as a substance that tastes intensely bitter to three people out of four but which is tasteless to the rest; consequently selective breeding or mass surgery could bring it about that everyone found it bitter or again that no one did. Describable and easily understandable procedures could bring it about that this stuff was, or was not, bitter in just as unambiguous a way as lemons are now sour or sugar sweet. Bennett admits that secondary qualities have some causal connections with other aspects of our experience: red apples are more squashable than green ones, different colours reflect light of different wavelengths, and so on; but these are relatively few and unimportant, and are no obstacle to our basing colour descriptions simply on how things look, and flavour descriptions simply on how they taste.

There is no doubt a difference between qualities in such a degree of causal connectedness, but a primary/secondary distinction based simply on this would be very different from Locke's. Bennett's distinction is one of degree only, not of kind or status. It would lead to the conclusion that the primary qualities are of special importance for a description of the natural world, and particularly for a science or technology that is interested in causation, in bringing things about; but it would not lead to the conclusion that material things as they are in themselves can be

---

[30] 'Substance, Reality, and Primary Qualities'. Bennett also discusses the issue in *Locke, Berkeley, Hume: Central Themes* pp. 88–111.

completely described in terms of primary qualities—including those of their minute parts—alone.

At least in his original article Bennett thinks that this difference is to the advantage of his distinction as against Locke's: 'Locke is *wrong*', he says, 'in that part of each claim which Berkeley *accepts*', that is, in suggesting that 'secondary qualities . . . sit looser to the world than is usually thought', for example that 'things do not really have temperatures'.[31] But this last is a misleading way of putting Locke's thesis: of course things really differ in ways which our feelings of them as hot or cold roughly indicate, and which our measurements with thermometers discriminate better, but Locke may still be right if what he means is that heat as we feel heat and coldness as we feel coldness are not present in the things themselves in the same way as their shape (or, we might now add, their mass).

In his article, Bennett emphasizes only this difference of degree of interconnectedness. Later, in his book, he distinguishes what he calls Locke's *analytic thesis* from his *causal thesis*.[32] The analytic thesis is that a statement attributing a secondary quality to a thing is equivalent to a counterfactual conditional, of the form: 'If x stood in relation R to a normal human, the human would have a sensory idea of such and such a kind'. That is, the analytic thesis equates secondary quality statements with attributions of powers to things. The causal thesis is that 'in a perfected and completed science, all our secondary-quality perceptions would be causally explained in terms of the primary qualities of the things we perceive'.

Whatever else the analytic thesis is, it is not analytically true. This is obviously not what ordinary secondary-quality statements as naïvely used *mean*. It is, however, what Locke is proposing that they should mean. But what supports this recommendation? Why should we give this sort of meaning to secondary-quality statements but not give a similar powers meaning to primary-quality statements? Bennett strangely seems to suggest that it is his distinction between degrees of interconnectedness that would justify this discrimination. But I see no reason why it should, if there is no difference in status between the two sets of qualities. At most, what it would justify is the use of a more complicated

---

[31] *Locke and Berkeley*, p. 109.
[32] *Locke, Berkeley, Hume: Central Themes*, pp. 94-5, 102-6.

sort of powers meaning for primary-quality statements: a primary
quality would be a many-track or multiply-manifested disposition
whereas a secondary quality would be a single-track or singly-
manifested one.[33] But to justify the more extreme difference of
giving a powers meaning to secondary-quality statements but not
to primary-quality ones at all we need rather something like the
causal thesis. For if the causal thesis were true, then the literal
attribution of colours as we see them (and so on) to things would
serve no explanatory purpose; it would therefore be unjustified;
and only by limiting secondary-quality statements to a powers
meaning could we keep them strictly true, whereas primary-
quality statements could still be strictly true with a non-disposi-
tional meaning. So although the analytic and the causal thesis
can be distinguished, they go together very naturally in Locke's
thought: it is the latter that supports the former, and supports it
far better than Bennett's distinction of degree would. These two
theses together, then, with the naturally associated view about
what is and what is not really there, constitute the most important
and interesting, but admittedly speculative and controversial,
distinction between primary and secondary qualities. Bennett's
distinction, like Aristotle's, points to a real and not very controversial difference: but it gains in significance when it is seen as a
preliminary step towards the Boyle–Locke distinction—or some
modernized variant of this.

The phenol argument, indeed, would support Locke's distinction
rather than Bennett's. If one (genetically or surgically producible)
physiological condition makes people classify phenol-thio-urea
along with gall, aloes, quinine, and other paradigmatically
bitter-tasting things, whereas another physiological condition
makes people classify it away from these and along with water,
pure alcohol, fish fingers, the flesh of battery chickens, and other
paradigmatically tasteless things, then it is less plausible to suppose
that flavours as we taste them are ever actually in the things. A
similar powerful argument about colours is given by J. J. C.
Smart.[34] Even for people with normal vision, there is no simple
correlation between seen colour and wavelength of light: the
colour-sensation produced by pure light of a certain single

---

[33] For this distinction, see G. Ryle, *The Concept of Mind*, pp. 44–5, also my *Truth,
Probability, and Paradox*, pp. 122, 145–8.

[34] *Philosophy and Scientific Realism*, pp. 66–75.

wavelength can also be produced by various appropriate mixtures of light of quite different wavelengths, and it is therefore most improbable that there is any single quality, an objective 'resemblance' of, say, my sensation of a particular shade of green, in all the things, or all the light-rays, that give me this sensation; and if it is unlikely that such an objective *quale* is in all of them, it is also unlikely—because quite gratuitous to postulate—that it is in any of them.

There is, then, in the end a strong case for a distinction between primary and secondary qualities which is essentially that of Boyle and Locke, backed up by further arguments from physics of the same general sort as those which they used, but revised by the relegation of solidity to the status of a power and by the recognition of objectively real and physically important properties which are not resemblances of any of our ordinary ideas The question remains whether this account is undermined by objections to the representative theory of perception within whose framework it is formulated.

REPRESENTATIVE THEORIES
OF PERCEPTION

DID Locke hold a representative theory of perception? Can any such theory, whether held by Locke or not, be defended? In any case, what are we to take as a representative theory? Can we distinguish a crude picture-theory from more sophisticated kinds of representationalism? And if Locke did hold any such theory, how important was it for him—was the rest of his thought built on or around it? All these questions have been raised and call for discussion. In Chapter 1, indeed, I have said that Locke's form of the distinction between primary and secondary qualities presupposes a representative theory, but since it has been argued that he could not have held such a theory, at least in the usual sense, my interpretation still needs to be defended.

The questions just listed include substantive philosophical issues and questions of interpretation. But these are closely connected. For if we find that some representative theory is defensible, this will make it easier to believe that Locke adopted it. On the other hand, it is Bennett's belief that what he calls the veil-of-perception doctrine is a serious error, and hence that any primary/secondary distinction drawn within its framework would be equally indefensible, that leads him to think that what Locke was trying to express was Bennett's own less speculative distinction between primary and secondary qualities.

1. *Did Locke hold a representative theory?*

Woozley, while admitting that Locke held '*some kind* of representationalism', denies that he held a 'picture-original theory of sense-perception'. Locke, he says, never talked of seeing ideas of tables, and he quotes Locke's own criticism of Malebranche as proof that he was well aware of what is commonly taken to be the fatal objection to a representative theory (construed as a picture-original theory): '. . . how can I know that the picture of anything is like that thing, when I never see that which it represents?'[1] Woozley comments, 'It is scarcely credible both that Locke should be able to see and to state so clearly the fundamental objection to the picture-original theory of sense-perception, and that he should have held that theory himself. If his own theory of perception were so obviously open to precisely the same objection, how could he have failed to realise it?' However, as we shall see, he did realize it, but thought that he could reply to the objection.

Locke may never have spoken of seeing ideas, but he certainly spoke of perceiving them. When he is making explicit the narrow sense of 'idea' in which ideas are distinguished from qualities, he says 'Whatsoever the mind perceives in itself, or is the immediate object of perception, thought, or understanding, that I call *idea*.'[2] Later, indeed, he says that the mind 'perceives nothing but its own *ideas*', and again these are ideas in the narrow sense, since Locke is here raising, for his own view, the same difficulty that he raised for that of Malebranche, 'How shall the mind, when it perceives nothing but its own *ideas*, know that they agree with things themselves?'[3]

Nor does his criticism of Malebranche show that Locke could not himself have held a picture-original theory. What he is discussing in the work from which Woozley's quotation is taken is Malebranche's strange thesis that 'we see all things in God', and in particular that 'bodies are not visible by themselves, they cannot act on our minds or represent themselves to them'.[4] That is, what Locke criticizes in Malebranche is a non-causal theory of perception. What he says is not that the problem 'How can I know that the picture of anything is like that thing, when I never see that which it represents?' would be intrinsically insoluble, but that it is insoluble *on Malebranche's principles*, that is, on the assumption that bodies do not cause our ideas of them. The specific claim of Malebranche on which Locke is commenting here is that 'the ideas of things are unchangeable, and eternal truths and laws are necessary.'[5] Locke concedes that 'the same idea will always be the

---

[1] A. D. Woozley (ed.), Locke's *Essay concerning the Human Understanding* (Fontana), introduction pp. 27–8, referring to 'An Examination of P. Malebranche's Opinion of Seeing All Things in God', in Locke's *Works* (12th edn. 1812), vol. 9, p. 250.
[2] II. viii. 8.   [3] IV. iv. 3.
[4] N. Malebranche, *De la recherche de la vérité*, vol. iii, p. 74.
[5] Op. cit., p. 76.

same idea', but insists that 'whether the one or the other be the true representation of any thing that exists, that, *upon his principles*, neither our author nor any body else can know' (my italics). That is, Locke is objecting to the claim that we can know necessary truths *a priori* about things which play no part in the production of that knowledge. This is a quite different theory from any version of representationalism that has ever been ascribed to Locke.[6]

In any case, Locke's awareness of the picture-original problem for Malebranche cannot stand as proof that he himself would not have adopted a theory which involved the same problem, in the face of his own explicit admission that his view did involve this problem. After raising this question 'How shall the mind, when it perceives nothing but its own *ideas*, know that they agree with things themselves?' he goes on to admit that 'it seems not to want difficulty'. But he thinks that the difficulty for his account can be solved, and his solution is an appeal to the very causal relationship whose denial was the distinctive feature of Malebranche's view:

I think, there be two sorts of *ideas* that we may be assured agree with things . . . The first are simple *ideas*, which since the mind, as has been shown, can by no means make to itself, must necessarily be the product of things operating on the mind . . . *simple* ideas *are not fictions* of our fancies, but the natural and regular productions of things without us, really operating upon us, and so carry with them all the conformity which is intended or which our state requires.[7]

---

[6] 'Examination of Malebranche', *Works*, vol. 9, pp. 211–55, esp. p. 250. Locke did not publish his 'Examination of Malebranche', thinking that Malebranche's view was so bizarre that, left alone, it would disappear of its own accord: 'he looked upon it to be an opinion that would not spread, but was like to die of itself, or at least to do no great harm' (editor's note in Locke's *Works*, vol. 9, p. 210). How right he was!

[7] IV. iv. 4. 'Intended' here means 'intended by our Maker', and therefore creates no difficulty for the interpretation given in Chapter 1 of Locke's account of secondary qualities as an error theory. However, in II. xxxi. 1–2 Locke says that all our simple ideas, including those of secondary qualities, are 'adequate', that is, they 'perfectly represent those archetypes which the mind supposes them taken from', and this would seem to tell against my interpretation. Locke explains that these simple ideas are adequate because they 'ought only to answer' the power to produce them, and do so answer: that is, he seems to say that each such idea is supposed *by our minds* simply to stand for the corresponding power. Yet immediately afterwards he reiterates the error theory: 'the things producing in us these simple ideas are but few of them denominated by us as if they were only the causes of them, but as if those ideas were real beings in them.' Fire is 'denominated also "light" and "hot", as if light and heat were really something in the fire more than a power to excite those

Critics may well find this reply evasive, since all that Locke thus derives from his causal account is a 'conformity' between ideas and reality, an example of which would be the relation between our idea of bitterness and whatever texture of particles is the ground of the power to produce it. This does not answer the question how, without being able to compare the ideas with reality, the pictures with the originals, we can say that among ideas which all equally 'conform' to reality, some but not others *resemble* that to which they conform. Whether Locke can be defended on this issue I shall consider later; for the moment all I am concerned to show is that we cannot take his criticism of Malebranche as evidence against an interpretation that would expose his own view to a similar question.

Similarly Locke says:

. . . the having the *idea* of anything in our mind no more proves the existence of that thing, than the picture of a man evidences his being in the world . . . It is . . . the actual receiving of *ideas* from without that gives us notice of the *existence* of other things and makes us know that something doth exist at that time without us which causes that *idea* in us . . .[8]

Here Locke himself compares 'the having the idea' with a picture and openly admits holding a view for which the problem arises whether there is something external answering to our ideas, as it would not have arisen if he had been a direct realist (or even if he had held what Jackson calls a 'mixed view', and had been a direct realist about primary qualities only). His criticism of Malebranche, like his remarks in Book IV of the *Essay*, shows only that he was aware of a difficulty; but he thought the difficulty fatal only for one who, by denying any causal process of perception, cut ideas off completely from things. He thought that he could *solve* the difficulty, not that he had to *avoid* it by denying the dualism of qualities and ideas from the start. And if he had been offered, say, direct realism and phenomenalism as alternatives to representa-

[8] IV. xi. 1–2.

---

ideas in us; and therefore are called qualities in or of the fire'. The nearest that we can get to a consistent reading of this passage is to take it that Locke is saying that when his conceptual reform has been accepted, and the 'vulgar notions' have been corrected, the ideas of secondary qualities will be taken to stand only for the corresponding powers, and will then be adequate, though as they are now commonly intended by most people they are not adequate.

tionalism, he would undoubtedly have seen objections to each of these that were so overwhelming that he would have felt bound to hope that the admitted difficulty for representationalism could somehow be overcome.

2. *Picture-original theory: (i) physically real intermediates*

However, we must determine more exactly what is to count as a representative theory, or perhaps how we should distinguish between a 'crudely representative' theory and some more sophisticated and defensible kind of representationalism. Woozley equates the crude view with a 'picture-original thesis', the suggestion that the ideas which are the mind's only objects are literally pictures of inaccessible originals, that we are permanently shut up in a private picture-gallery, and again with the view that we see (and presumably also feel, hear, taste, and smell) ideas. Similarly, Ryle describes the untenable theory as the use of the term 'ideas' to denote certain supposed entities which are 'in the mind', but not as states or operations of the mind, nor yet merely in the way in which the battle of the Marne is 'in my mind' when I am thinking about it, since these (unlike the battle) are 'supposed to be dependent on minds for their existence'; also, this theory holds that minds attend to and think about these mind-dependent entities only.[9]

If this last thesis is essential to the crude theory, then of course it is not tenable for a moment: the very formulation of it would be self-refuting. In saying that ideas represent things, or in formulating his primary/secondary quality distinction, Locke himself is necessarily thinking about and attending to things and qualities as well as his own ideas. At the very least, this last thesis must be softened to the claim that it is only ideas that we attend to and think about *immediately*, that we deal with other things by having ideas of them.

This seems to be what Locke is saying at the very beginning of Book IV. Yet there is no doubt that he is at least embarrassed by his own formulations, and feels that it is hard to explain how, in contemplating only our ideas, we can yet have knowledge or even

[9] Woozley, op. cit. pp. 26, 31; G. Ryle, 'John Locke on the Human Understanding', pp. 19–20.

beliefs about other things. Without following closely Locke's own attempts to overcome this difficulty, let us consider whether, within the limits of what can be called a picture-original thesis, we can give any coherent account of mediate perception, of dealing with other things by way of ideas.

From the start we must distinguish two possibilities. Are the pictures supposed to be physically real pictures somewhere inside one's head, or are they supposed to be strictly *mind*-dependent in the sense that they exist in and by one's awareness of them, that they are purely intentional objects? Let us consider these possibilities in turn.

If ideas were physically real pictures, they ought to be discoverable by physiological examination. Well, perhaps they are. Would images on the retina fill the bill? Would the vibrations of the basilar membrane in the inner ear count as ideas of sounds? There is no doubt that with some of the senses there are intermediates of this sort which play an important part in perception: it is in a clear sense *by way of* these items that we see and hear outside things. (With other senses, notably touch, the only intermediates at all analogous to these will be patterns of stimulations of nerve cells.) Moreover, at least for short-term changes, how we see and hear things will be more closely correlated with these intermediates than with the external things: anything that changes the retinal image will in the short term change 'what we see' in the sense of 'how it looks to us'. But not necessarily in the long term. A new pair of glasses may make one see rectangular sheets of paper as trapezoids, but in a day or so they will look rectangular again, and even inverting spectacles, worn continuously, in time lose their effect, and the wearer again sees things the right way up. In other words, seeing is a complex process whose normal function is to inform us about external things, not about retinal images, and compensations enter automatically in ways that help it to perform this function.

The existence of these physical intermediates and at least the broad outlines of the part they play in perception are, I take it, uncontroversial. What is controversial is whether they should be described as the direct or immediate objects of perception, and whether they can be identified with Locke's ideas-in-the-narrow-sense. It is easy to insist, with an appeal to common sense or to ordinary language, that we do not see our own retinal images or hear the vibrations of our basilar membranes. It is not so easy to tell what is gained by this insistence, or even exactly what it means. Of course we do not see retinal images in the way in which we see tables, but this would not rule out the suggestion that we see them differently, more directly. What is more to the point is that we do not normally make judgements (verbal or non-verbal) about what retinal images etc. we have and thence infer, by some explicit process of reasoning, what the outside world is like. Our naïve judgements are already about external things, and, I imagine, were so already before we learned to speak. We can sum up the truth of this matter by saying that our perceptions of material things are causally mediated but judgementally direct.

But is this enough to dispose of the view that we are shut up in a private picture-gallery, and that external things are inaccessible? The trouble is that these are metaphors whose exact significance, whose literal translation, is unclear. If they mean 'We can never know about external things at all', then of course this is a thesis which neither Locke nor any representationalist has asserted. If they mean 'We know about external things only by inference', then this is still ambiguous; it is false, for reasons just given, if it means explicit inference. But if it means that how we see outside things, and in general have (correct or incorrect) perceptual awareness of them, is the result of a complex process in which information (in the communication engineer's sense) is fed into the central nervous system and unconsciously interpreted and arranged, then this is true.

I suspect that the direct realist's insistence that it is tables that we see, not ideas, and that we are not shut up in a private picture-gallery, is meant to carry the implication that perception is un-problematic. In the sense of 'see' on which he insists, I can see a table only if the table is there, and he may conclude from this that seeing is a self-guaranteeing mode of awareness, something which, when we do it, leaves no room for sceptical doubts, not even for selective scepticism about the outside existence of, say, colours-as-we-see-them. But of course this argument would be unsound. Since 'see', thus used, is an achievement word, a mode of aware-ness will not count as seeing unless it is successful in this way. But then it will be at least in principle problematic whether some-thing that we are inclined to call seeing a table *is* seeing a table. We must not, merely because there is this way of speaking, jump to the conclusion that there is something which we can immediately recognize as seeing in this sense and whose success is therefore beyond question. Nor does judgemental directness ensure correctness. It leaves room at least for selective scepticism, and causal mediateness introduces real possibilities of systematic differences between appearance and reality. Total scepticism is another matter. It seems difficult, at first sight anyway, to reconcile the claim that our perceptual judgements are about external things with the possibility that they should be completely erroneous, that there might be no external things for them to be about. But we shall consider this further when we turn to the other, intentional-object, variant of the picture-theory.

We can throw more light on the first, physical-intermediate, version of this theory by trying to construct a situation about which it would be literally and unquestionably true. What if someone ever since birth had had a large box attached in front of his eyes, on the inside of which, for him to see, fairly faithful pictures of outside, surrounding things were somehow produced? Apart from the sheer cumbrousness of the apparatus, this person would be no worse off than we are. Moving around, picking things up, conveying food to his mouth, and so on he would surely take himself to be visually directly aware of the very things he stepped on and picked up. Unconscious corrections would have grown up for any systematic distortions in the pictures on the inside of his box. If he lived for, say, twenty years without touching the box, without seeing himself in a mirror, and without anyone else's being so tactless as to comment on his non-standard appearance, it would presumably be a surprise to him if after that time he learned that he had been so visually enclosed. But when he learned this, he (and the rest of us who would have known about the box all the time) would surely say that he was seeing things only indirectly, that he was shut up in a private picture-gallery. But if he could be like this, and not know about it, and practically speaking be no worse off than we are, it follows that we may be a bit like this all the time: we may be related to our retinal images in very much the same way that he would be related to the pictures on the inside of his box. In the face of this example, I think the only coherent move for the direct realist to make is the heroic one of saying that even the man in the box is seeing outside things directly, that I have merely described an imaginary human being with a peculiarly reduplicated retina. But if he says that, then this shows how little content he is putting into the phrase 'see directly', and how little he can therefore get out of it.

But, it may be objected, we have constructed a picture-gallery only for the sense of sight: we have left the man able to walk about, to touch things, and to eat things and presumably taste them in passing. It would be different if all his sense-perceptions were similarly indirect.

It is much harder to meet this challenge, to tell a similar story that will carry even a minimum of conviction about all the senses at once. But let us suppose that the person has no senses other than sight and touch, and that the latter sense is confined to his hands, that visually he is equipped as in the last example, and that he never actually touches the outside things which he (indirectly) sees, but that his hands constantly move over scale models of those things. If there were sufficient resemblances and correlations between the shapes and arrangements to be seen on the inside of the box and those felt in the scale models with the hands, this person would—though no doubt more slowly than a normal infant—automatically develop a view of a world of objects that could be both seen and felt, and that had not only the features that were common to both the pictures and the models, but also those that were special to each of the two, say colour and temperature; he would also come automatically to correct for any systematic distortions in the picturing and the modelling which produced not too large mismatchings between the two with respect to the common sensibles (the primary qualities about which there was a fair measure of agreement).

In other words, I maintain that even if a person were literally shut up in a private gallery with respect to all the sense-modalities he possessed, he could and would still arrive at essentially the same view that we have of a material world, and would take his perceptions to be direct perceptions of it in just the sense that we so take ours. His perceptions too would be judgementally direct though (as we could see) causally mediated.

This man would be substantially right in his view of the world, though we should be inclined to say that he was wrong in supposing himself to be perceiving it directly. A certain kind of representationalist might then press the analogy between this man's pictures and models and the various intermediates—retinal images, basilar membrane vibrations, patterns of stimulation of nerve cells, and so on—which undoubtedly play an important part in normal sense-perception, and say that we too are in a sense shut up in a private gallery, and are mistaken when we take ourselves to be perceiving material things directly though we are substantially right in the view of the world that we thus acquire. Admittedly a common-sense realist might resist the analogy, insisting that ordinary language requires us to say that we normal people see and feel tables and so on directly, but that our picture-and-model man sees and feels them indirectly; but this is now a purely verbal, conventional point with no philosophical significance whatever. Ordinary language calls perception direct if it is of objects which we touch with our hands, see by means of rays of light that come straight to our eyes, and so on, but indirect if the rays of light are reflected from a mirror or if a television camera and screen are inserted into the visual path, and so on. But what is so important about eyes and hands, as opposed to all the other actual or possible stages in the process? Why should directness, thus construed, matter? Rather, the correct move for a direct realist to make, if he wants to avoid inconsistency and arbitrariness, would again be the heroic one of accepting the analogy and saying that the picture-and-model man sees and feels things directly, as we do. But it will now be plain in what sense this claim is defensible: this man's perceptions, like ours, are judgementally direct though causally mediated; they are substantially correct; and (though this is a point that I shall discuss again later) they are reasonable: the resemblances and correlations between his pictures and his models constitute some good reason for his taking the features that they have (approximately, despite some distortions) in common as constituents of a single world, both visually and tactually accessible. We can explain this by pointing out that if we take the pictures, with their features, as one set of objects, and the models, with their features, as another set, the coincidences of feature are such as to be more readily explained on the supposition that they have a common source which they both resemble than without this supposition. Of course, the man himself cannot (in his original condition, before he learns of his peculiarities) put the reasoning in this form: but it is because someone else could reason along these lines that his corresponding automatic interpretation is a reasonable one. Nevertheless, the picture-and-model man's perception of things is not unproblematic. There is a question whether things are as he sees and feels them which calls for an answer, and which it would be a mistake to try to preclude just by making the heroic direct realist comment that this man still directly sees and feels outside things—outside the box, other than the models. And analogously any sense in which we can accept a similar direct realist comment on our normal, causally mediated perceptions will not be one which precludes the question whether outside things are as we perceive them to be.

It may be said, however, that none of this has much to do with Locke or with any widely held forms of representative theory. Locke's ideas cannot be retinal images, for instance, since when I am seeing something with my two eyes properly focused I presumably have just one Lockean idea of it but two retinal images. Again Locke speaks of the idea of green, and again of blue being an idea,[10] but not of blue or green ideas; but there are blue and green retinal images, while blue cannot *be* a retinal image. Also, if I see something as square (with straight sides) while the retinal images I have at the time have slightly curved sides, Locke would surely want to say that my idea was of a square. A great advantage of the 'new way of ideas' is that it seems that I need not be in any doubt about what ideas I have: ideas are supposed to be immediately accessible from the inside, from the point of view of the person who has them, and intermediates like retinal images and patterns of nerve-cell stimulations would not be so.

The objection, then, to taking the pictures in the picture-original theory to be physically real intermediates in the causal chain of perception is not that such items do not exist, nor, as we have seen, that they could not be used in something like a representative theory, but merely that they are not what Locke or, I think, any other representationalist is mainly concerned with.

3. *Picture-original theory: (ii) intentional objects*

The view which we need to examine, therefore, is that which treats ideas as intentional objects. There is a construction with such verbs as 'see' such that in 'I see a horse' the phrase 'a horse'

[10] e.g. II. xxxii. 9, 16.

is somewhat like an internal accusative; what in terms of this construction I see is necessarily exactly as I see it, but the statement does not entail that what I see should be there, independently of my seeing it. With this construction I can see winged horses, though there are none, I can hear a loud hammering, though the cause is merely my watch ticking softly under my pillow, and I can feel the ground rocking not only when there is an earthquake but also when I have just landed after spending some weeks on a small ship in not too calm a sea. These intentional objects satisfy many of the requirements for Locke's ideas-in-the-narrow-sense, and fit in even better with Berkeley's use of the term 'idea'. They are just as we perceive them. They are mind-dependent: they exist only in and by being perceived, that is, as contents of states of perceptual awareness. To say that there is an intentional object of a certain sort is only to say, in what could be a misleading style, that that is how things look (or feel, or sound, and so on) to the person in question. It is they that together make up what in Chapter 1 I called the experiential content. The word 'content' must not be allowed to suggest that on this view the mind is literally a container, that perception is being reduced to some other, supposedly more familiar, relationship of items that do, or could, exist on their own being held in something like a basket. In the present account, perception is not being explained at all, let alone reduced to anything else: our seeing (hearing, feeling, etc.) things in various ways is being taken as a starting-point, and the terms 'content', 'idea', 'percept', and 'intentional object' are being introduced merely in order to have some general way of referring to what is a perfectly familiar aspect of any perception.[11]

It cannot, I think, be denied that there are intentional objects thus understood. We do not need any 'argument from illusion' to justify our talking about them. Even if there were no illusions, no perceptual errors, there would still be a difference between the

[11] In my British Academy lecture, 'What's Really Wrong with Phenomenalism?' I spoke of 'sense-data' in these terms, and I think that this word has often been used in this way. But this was not how Moore, in introducing the word, intended to use it; rather he intended it to denote whatever was the immediate object of sensation, leaving its ontological status an open question to be settled by further investigation. In fact what best satisfy Moore's requirements for sense-data are these percepts or intentional objects, but this does not hold by definition. Cf. D. Locke, *Perception and our Knowledge of the External World*, pp. 21–3.

table's being square and my seeing it as square: how I see it would be distinct from how it is, even if they were exactly alike, even if I always saw it exactly as it is. This distinctness is established by the mere logical possibility of perceptual errors and distortions, but it is made doubly secure by their actual occurrence.

It is true that there are some complexities concealed in the apparently simple phrase 'how things look'. The same thing may be said to look in more than one way at a time, according to the amount of interpretation that we allow into the look. A penny seen obliquely still looks circular to any normal adult in that he will take the object before him to be a circular coin; but it also looks elliptical in that we can deliberately hold back from this interpretation and attend just to the immediate visual presentation. But this sort of complication does not entail that we have to abandon the concept 'how it looks', but rather that we must recognize a multiplicity of kinds of looking; and there is no reason why we should not do so.[12]

Moreover, if we interpret Locke's ideas-in-the-narrow-sense in this way we shall have no difficulty in giving a straightforward meaning to his talk about resemblances (and the lack of them) as used in distinguishing primary from secondary qualities.[13] To say that an objective quality resembles the idea of that quality is simply to say that in this respect things are just as they look in a strictly sensory sense of 'look' (with the proviso that we may still say that ideas resemble qualities if how things look is a bit distorted from how they are, but within the same category or determinable); to say that there is nothing in the things like an idea of

[12] Cf. G. A. Paul, 'Is there a Problem about Sense-Data?', *Aristotelian Society Supplementary Volume*, 15 (1936), reprinted in *Logic and Language* (First Series), ed. A. G. N. Flew, pp. 101–16, and G. E. M. Anscombe, 'The Intentionality of Sensation: a Grammatical Feature', in *Analytical Philosophy* (Second Series), ed. R. J. Butler.

[13] Of which Bennett, for example, makes unnecessarily heavy weather: 'Since ideas cannot resemble either bodies or qualities of bodies, this [i.e. II. viii. 15] must be either discarded or transformed. The only plausible transformation is into something like the following: in causally explaining ideas of primary qualities, one uses the same words in describing the causes as in describing the effects (shape-ideas etc. are caused by shapes etc.); whereas in causally explaining ideas of secondary qualities one must describe the causes in one vocabulary and the effects in another (colour-ideas etc. are caused by shapes etc.). If this is not what Locke's "resemblance" formulations of the primary/secondary contrast mean, then I can find no meaning in them.' *Locke, Berkeley, Hume: Central Themes*, p. 106.

a certain class is to say that things are not at all as they sensorily appear in this respect.

However, this account may provoke an objection of a very different sort. Far from being a crude representationalism, it is not a picture-original analysis of perception at all: to interpret Locke thus is precisely to agree with those who have protested against the ascription to him of the sort of representative theory that the first-year student finds it so easy to refute.

Yet it seems to me that this is still a representative theory in the sense that has provoked some of the stock objections. That things *look* thus and so—in the immediate visual presentation sense—is one thing, that they *are* thus and so is another. These are distinct occurrences, whether the thing looks just as it is or whether how it looks and how it is are qualitatively different, either slightly or radically. The same holds for how a thing feels, smells, tastes, or sounds. Then that a thing looks, feels, and so on thus is in a clear enough sense a representation of its being thus. Once this distinction has been drawn, it leaves room for sceptical doubts, more or less extreme. Perhaps things differ widely from how they look and feel and so on to all of us, or perhaps there are no things that correspond at all systematically to our experiential content as a whole. Of course these doubts cannot be naturally expressed in language as it is ordinarily used: it is not made for that purpose. But we must not let linguistic awkwardness obstruct the consideration of doubts that are in themselves perfectly coherent. Again, that things look, feel, sound, taste, and smell to us as they do is, according to our ordinary view of the matter, a causal product of some features of how things are, interacting in rather complex ways with our sense-organs and our central nervous system, the contributions of the latter including corrections which involve a sort of feedback from the results of earlier interactions of the same general sort. But if so, do not our sophisticated, scientifically informed continued acceptance of the broad outlines of the ordinary man's view of the world and our scientifically backed amendments to that view rely on causal inference from that product to one of its causes, and is this inference not then exposed to the stock objections against an argument from an effect to a supposed cause of a type which is never directly observed? However difficult it may be to reject talk about these intentional objects altogether, then, an analysis of perception that takes full account of them will still need to be defended against well-known objections and difficulties.

4. *The veil-of-perception problem, and a Berkeleian argument*

Bennett's treatment may help to pin down the problems. He is not happy with the term 'representative theory of perception' because, he says, 'it does not express what is wrong with the theory'. There is, he thinks, 'nothing wrong in saying that when I see a tree my visual field "represents" a real thing with which I am acquainted', or that without the sense-data I should not see the tree, and he finds obscure and unhelpful (as we have seen, with some justification) disputes as to whether the seeing of the tree is direct or indirect. But what he identifies as 'the essential error in Locke's theory of reality' is 'his setting the entire range of facts about sensory states over against the entire range of facts about the objective realm and then looking for empirical links between them'. It is the *blanket* question 'Do sensory states ever represent the objective realm?' that is, in Bennett's view, a bad one. Such a general sceptical question, he thinks, calls not for an affirmative answer based on empirical arguments but for a criticism of the question itself in the light of inquiry into the meaning of such expressions as 'real things without us'. 'In short, whether we say that ideas represent or are caused by real things, there is serious error only if the thesis is expressed in an all-at-once way, purporting to relate sensory states *en bloc* to objective states of affairs *en bloc*.' It is to this error that Bennett gives the name 'the veil-of-perception doctrine'.[14]

In thinking that this is an error, Bennett is relying on the widely accepted dogma that we can come to know that *A* causes *B* only if we are at some time directly acquainted with *A*. 'To know that there was [such a causal connexion as Locke postulates] we should need independent access to empirical facts about the objective realm'.[15] Given this assumption, it follows that the cause in any causal account must be some item within the content of experience, so that any supposed causal explanation of that content as a whole must be viciously circular.

However, the contrast between an 'all-at-once' and, say, a

---

[14] Op. cit., pp. 68–70.
[15] Op. cit., p. 70; also J. Bennett, *Kant's Analytic*, p. 21.

piecemeal version of the representative theory could be misleading. If separate, piecemeal statements of the form 'This fully objective material thing causes and is represented by this idea' were admitted, it would be impossible to refuse the mere summation or integration of these to yield the all-at-once thesis. What Bennett is saying is rather that piecemeal representation statements must be construed in such a way that the integration of them will not yield this, indeed such a way that they simply cannot be all summed up or integrated. We can say 'This real tree causes and is represented by this idea', but the phrase 'this real tree' still introduces some part of the experiential content—in effect, another 'idea'. The reason why we can never get the whole of experience on the Y-side of the formula 'X causes and is represented by Y' is that we need part of it to play the role of X. Bennett, in fact, is rejecting the very concept of a fully objective reality: he is quite prepared to say that 'reality is a logical construction out of appearances'[16]—and a logical construction out of appearances is very different from something whose existence is logically independent of experiences and which is merely inferred from them.

Bennett's phenomenalism is one conclusion that may be drawn from the dogma about causal knowledge; another is the kind of direct realism which simply refuses to deal with percepts, how things look, and so on, at all. If you either reduce reality to appearances, or forget about appearances and speak only about reality, you can happily accept the dogma; it is troublesome only for someone who, like Locke, wants to retain a full-blooded contrast between reality and appearances and yet to rely on causal inference from one to the other.

We shall, then, have to consider whether this dogma has any authority: but there is one muddle that may need to be removed first. Someone might argue that in any statement of the form 'X causes and is represented by Y', whatever is introduced by 'X' must be part of the experiential content simply because the maker of the statement is speaking and presumably thinking about it: more generally, we can never draw a full-blooded contrast between reality and appearance because the 'reality' must be appearance in virtue of being thought of at all.

This is merely a variant of an argument invented by Berkeley,

[16] *Locke, Berkeley, Hume: Central Themes*, p. 68.

which pleased him so much that he was prepared to rest his whole case upon it: 'When we do our utmost to conceive the existence of external bodies, we are all the while contemplating our own ideas . . . A little attention will discover to any one the truth and evidence of what is here said, and make it unnecessary to insist on any other proofs against the existence of material substance.'[17] And again:

> *Hylas*: What more easy than to conceive a tree or house existing by itself, independent of, and unperceived by any mind whatsoever. I do at this present time conceive them existing after that manner . . . *Philonous*: The tree or house . . . which you think of is conceived by you . . . And what is conceived is in the mind . . . You acknowledge then that you cannot possibly conceive how any one corporeal sensible thing should exist otherwise than in a mind . . . And yet you will earnestly contend for the truth of that which you cannot so much as conceive.[18]

It is evident that this argument, if sound, would prove too much—too much, that is, for Berkeley and for anyone except a solipsistic phenomenalist. Since the choice of *material* things, trees and houses, as what Hylas tries to conceive existing unconceived plays no special part in the argument, it would, if sound, show equally that no one can coherently postulate the independent existence, out of his own mind, of other human minds or of God. But, fortunately, it is unsound. Although if *there is a tree about which I suppose that it exists unconceived*, my supposition is self-refuting, since I, in supposing this, am conceiving the tree, it does not follow that there is anything wrong if *I suppose that there is a tree which exists unconceived*. The latter does not entail the former, and the latter is not self-refuting: the existential quantifier is a barrier to my supposing's giving of the status 'conceived' to any tree so introduced. Berkeley in effect confused the two kinds of formula (with the existential quantifier and the 'suppose that' operator in different orders), and, seeing that one would be self-refuting, wrongly took the other to be self-refuting too. There is also another fault in his application of this argument. Even if he had thus established that if one supposes that there exist trees and houses, one must, for coherence, suppose that they are also

[17] *Principles of Human Knowledge*, §23.
[18] *Three Dialogues between Hylas and Philonous*, the First Dialogue.

conceived, he would not have shown that one must suppose that they exist in and by being conceived, which is the conclusion that he really wants.[19]

All this can be applied to the issue about reality and appearance. What Locke or any other representational realist is supposing is that *there is* something of such and such a character which causes and is represented by the content of his experience, and once again the presence of the quantifier blocks the argument that this *something* must be part of the content of his experience merely because he is supposing this.

But this is only a preliminary muddle: the real strength of the dogma about causal knowledge lies elsewhere. When it is argued that if we start within the circle of our own ideas we can never break out of that circle, or when Bennett says that in order to know that there was such a causal connection as Locke asserts between things and ideas 'we should need independent access to empirical facts about the objective realm', two problems are being run together, a problem of meaning and a problem of justification.

---

[19] The fallacy in Berkeley's argument can be shown more clearly in a symbolic formulation. In the Polish notation, in which 'Np' stands for 'not p', 'Kpq' for 'p and q', and 'Cpq' for 'if p then q, and 'Σx' and 'Πx' are the existential and universal quantifiers respectively, let us put 'Ty' for 'y is thought of' or 'y is conceived', 'Ixy' for 'x imagines or supposes that y', and '$I'xy$' for 'x imagines or supposes truly that y'. Then for any ϕ, '$Ix\phi y$' entails 'Ty'. Consequently '$IxNTy$' entails 'Ty'. Now anyone (x) who asserts 'NTy' is committed to asserting that he himself supposes that NTy, that is that $IxNTy$, and hence that Ty. 'NTy' is thus what I have called *operationally self-refuting*: it cannot be coherently put forward: no one can ever coherently assert that a certain thing y exists unconceived. This is Berkeley's quite correct starting-point. But from here on Berkeley goes astray in one or other of two ways. He sometimes seems to write as if 'NTy' were not merely operationally self-refuting but self-contradictory, and therefore something that could not hold for any (unthinking) thing y at all. Alternatively, it is easy to show formally that $NI'xNTy$, that is, x does not suppose truly that y is not thought of, from which a valid universal generalization gives '$\Pi x \, \Pi y \, NI'xNTy$', and hence its equivalent '$N\Sigma x\Sigma yI'xNTy$', that is, 'It is not the case that there is a person and a thing such that the person truly supposes that that thing is not thought of.' But what Berkeley requires is not this, but rather '$N\Sigma xI'x\Sigma yNTy$', that is, 'No one truly supposes that there is something which is not thought of'. The latter is not equivalent to or entailed by the previous formula, and indeed is not provable at all. Berkeley in effect thinks that he has proved it because he fails to distinguish the two statements in which, when they are properly formulated, 'Σy' and '$I'x$' occur in different orders. Berkeley's fallacy is examined formally in this way by A. N. Prior in *Theoria*, vol. xxi (1955), pp. 117–122, and in my 'Self-Refutation—a Formal Analysis' in *Philosophical Quarterly*, vol. xiv (1964), pp. 193–203, where I compare it with other philosophical errors that involve the mixing-up of different kinds of self-refutation and contradiction.

The problem of meaning is this: if all that we are directly acquainted with is ideas (or experiential content, or percepts, etc.) how can we meaningfully assert or even speculate that there is a further reality which they represent: how can we give meaning to the terms that will express this speculation? The problem of justification is this: if all that we are directly acquainted with is ideas (etc.), how can they give us any good reason to believe that there is a further reality which they represent, or that such a further reality helps to cause our having of them, or that some of them resemble aspects of that reality while others do not. What we can call the veil-of-perception problem, what convinces Bennett, for example, that the veil-of-perception doctrine is a fundamental error, is an amalgam of these two problems. The two are, of course, related. The second question presupposes an affirmative answer to the first. We can ask whether we have good reason to believe something only if we can give some meaning to the sentences which express what we believe. So it is suggested (by Bennett among others) that the scepticism which results from pressing the second question can be countered by pressing the first: if we cannot give meaning to the assertion or speculation that there is a further reality, we equally cannot give meaning to the question whether there is such a further reality, and the problem of justifying any views about it does not arise. But there is also another connection between the two problems. Anyone who adopts a verificationist or confirmationist theory of meaning will assimilate the first to the second, thinking that the only way of giving meaning to statements about such a further reality would be to show what would count as evidence for or against it and for or against specific descriptions of its components.

When the two problems are thus assimilated, they become insoluble and force into phenomenalism anyone who accepts the thesis that all that we are directly acquainted with is ideas. For on this view the verification or confirmation of any statement would rest ultimately on someone's having certain ideas or experiences, and consequently its meaning would have to be something to do with such ideas or experiences.

5. *Verification and constructive theories of meaning*

I see no plausibility, however, in a verificationist or confirmationist theory of meaning. From the start it seems to involve a confusion of categories, in that what has (or lacks) meaning will be a sentence or some such linguistic entity, while what can be true or false, verified or falsified, confirmed or disconfirmed, is a statement, something which a meaningful sentence may be used to express or convey. The question of meaning must have been answered satisfactorily before any question of truth or verification or confirmation can arise. Nevertheless, there is an element of truth in the theory. A meaningless sentence will fail to make any verifiable statement. Also, the meaning of an indicative sentence will in general be closely related to the truth-conditions of the statement that, with this meaning, it can be used to make. (These cannot quite be identified, since two sentences might have the same truth-conditions but differ in meaning in that in certain other conditions one of them would be false while the question of the truth or falsity of the other did not arise; and again, two sentences which differ in structure might have, as a result of their different structures, exactly the same truth-conditions (and perhaps also falsity-conditions and question-doesn't-arise conditions), but they could reasonably be said to differ in meaning just because their structures were different.) Also, an idiomatic, unitary meaning can be given to a sentence taken as a whole by stipulating that it is to have such-and-such truth- and falsity-conditions, and the meaning of a sentence-form taken as having internal structure can be given by stating how the truth-conditions of any sentence of that form will be a function of, or depend upon, the truth- (or satisfaction-) conditions of its constituents.[20] And one way of indicating the truth- and falsity-conditions of a statement will be to show what observations would verify or falsify it. So, showing how the statement it is standardly used to make could be verified or falsified is one way of giving the meaning of (or of giving meaning to) a sentence. Indeed, it is plausible to suppose that when a language is first being learned by an infant meaning is

---

[20] This truth-definition approach to meaning is familiar from the work in particular of A. Tarski and D. Davidson. I have discussed it more fully in my *Truth, Probability, and Paradox*, pp. 30–44.

initially given to sentences as units by its being shown in what recognizable circumstances their use is appropriate or inappropriate, and for indicative sentences these will be circumstances in which the corresponding statements can be verified or falsified by the learner. But where the verification theory goes wrong is in supposing that this is the only way in which meaning can be given to linguistic expressions. I shall not stress the well-known difficulties of finding any precise formulation of a verification principle or confirmation principle that will allow factual, descriptive meaning to all those items which empiricists commonly want to admit as meaningful (such as statements about the past, including the unrecorded past, and the general hypotheses and theories of science) while denying factual, descriptive meaning to such undesired items as metaphysical and theological statements.[21] Rather I would stress the sheer initial implausibility of any such proposal. It is clear that we recognize many sentences as meaningful simply in and by seeing how they are built up out of meaningful components, before we even consider how the statement which the sentence as a whole makes can be verified or confirmed. The obvious requirements for meaningfulness are, first, that either sentences or phrases or words should have been given senses or references or both, and, second, that if what have been given sense and/or reference are only parts of a sentence, the form in which those parts are put together should also have been given a structural meaning, that is, it should have been determined how the sense and/or truth value of any sentence of that form would depend on the senses and/or references of its parts. It is because the requirements for linguistic meaning are thus constructive that, as linguists like Chomsky have emphasized, any competent speaker of a language can construct *new* meaningful sentences himself and can understand new sentences used by other speakers. By contrast, a verification or confirmation theory, while it could allow a certain amount of constructiveness (in that it could allow rules for the verifying of a linguistic complex to be derivable from rules for the verifying of its components or of other sentences that use these components) would insist that every

---

[21] See e.g. C. G. Hempel, 'Problems and Changes in the Empiricist Criterion of Meaning', *Revue internationale de philosophie*, vol. iv (1950), reprinted e.g. in *Classics of Analytic Philosophy*, ed. Robert R. Ammerman; also A. J. Ayer, *Language, Truth, and Logic*, introduction to the Second Edition.

meaningful sentence is one which someone *could* learn as an idiom, ignoring its internal structure, and paying attention only to the way in which the sentence as a whole could be verified. But there is no good reason for asserting this possibly-idiomatic character of every meaningful sentence; this view is at variance with our actual understanding of, and ability to use, language. We can concede, as I have done, that some sentences are initially learned as idioms, and that these include the bits of language that an infant first learns: but then, by implicit comparisons and contrasts, sentence-components—subjects and predicates and the subject-predicate form, and so on—are distinguished within what were originally learned as idioms, and new combinations of them understood, so that in effect sense and/or reference have been given to these distinguishable sentence-components.

The only objection to such a natural constructive theory of meaning is that it seems to be too liberal: it seems to allow meaningfulness to any grammatical sentence built up out of meaningful words, but some of these appear to lack meaning. It seems meaningless to say that a chair is thinking, that someone slept furiously (though it is meaningful to say that someone marched furiously into the room), that honesty weighs ten pounds, that a certain particle is travelling backwards through time, and so on. Such grammatical but apparently meaningless combinations of meaningful words and phrases suggest that we need to add to any theory of grammar a theory of categories imposing additional restrictions on what can go with what. But in fact this line of thought has not been fruitful: the allocation of words to categories seems merely to follow and not to explain in any systematic way our intuitive judgements about what sentences are meaningful. Consequently we seem to be driven back from a constructive theory of meaningfulness to something like a verification principle which will decide whether whole sentences are or are not meaningful even if they appear, linguistically, to be properly put together.

But this is not necessary. Many sentences which philosophers have been inclined to call meaningless are quite meaningful but make statements which are either very plainly false or so implausible and unsupported as not to be worth taking seriously. Since to march furiously into a room is to walk into the room in a way that reveals and expresses extreme annoyance, to sleep furiously would be to sleep in a way that does this: but there is no such way. So any sentence of the form 'X slept furiously' is meaningful but makes a statement that is simply false. How we handle 'That chair is thinking' will depend on how we interpret 'Peter is thinking' where 'Peter' is the name of a person. If we are physicalists about persons and identify their thinkings with some neurophysiological processes that go on in them, we can say that 'That chair is thinking' is false because no comparable neurophysiological processes are going on in it. Alternatively 'Peter is thinking' could be said to involve presuppositions about Peter such that if they are unfulfilled the question whether Peter is thinking does not arise; then, since the corresponding presuppositions about the chair are presumably unfulfilled, we may prefer to say that 'That chair is thinking' is not false, but rather that the issue of its truth or falsity does not arise. But there is no need on that account either to call the sentence meaningless or to appeal to any criterion of significance for whole sentences: on this view it will again have been shown what has gone wrong in the construction of the sentence. The trouble with 'Honesty weighs ten pounds' is different. The ordinary sense of abstract nouns like 'honesty' is given by transformations from more concrete expressions: for example, 'Tom displayed honesty in returning the wallet' is a transformation of 'Tom returned the wallet; doing so was honest' or perhaps 'that was what an honest man would do'. Again, 'Honesty is the best policy' is a transformation of 'The best policy for anyone is for him to be honest'. Talk about honesty is given meaning only in circumstances where it is equivalent to something about honest actions or honest people. Since no plausible transformation leads correspondingly to 'Honesty weighs ten pounds', the word 'honesty' has not been given a meaning *for this sort of construction*. (It could, implausibly, be a transformation of 'Any person who is honest weighs ten pounds more than he would weigh if he were not honest', and then, of course, the sentence would be meaningful but would make a false statement.) 'Travels backwards through time' is prima facie obscure because even 'travels (forwards) through time' is so: it seems to presuppose, falsely, another time dimension; but if the latter means simply 'persists through time', it leaves, so to speak, no place for the adverb 'backwards' to occupy: 'backwards' has been given meaning only for movements, facings, and the like. Thus no meaning for 'travels backwards through time' emerges automatically from the meanings standardly given to its components, though of course it could acquire meaning as a metaphor or as an idiom.

Initially puzzling cases, therefore, of sentences which lack meaning as a whole, though their constituents (including their phrase-forms or sentence-forms) have meaning, can be dealt with in these ways: they may indeed lack meaning because some of their constituents have been given meaning only for constructions of some sort other than these, they may be meaningful but involve unfulfilled presuppositions so that they fail to make true or false statements, or, most commonly, they may be meaningful but make statements that are trivially false. But they constitute no obstacle to a constructive theory of meaning, and give no grounds for reintroducing the implausible thesis that meaning is to be tied to the procedures for verifying or confirming sentences as a whole.

6. *Solution of the problem of meaning*

What follows if we combine such a constructive theory of meaning with Locke's claim that 'the mind perceives nothing but its own ideas', or, as we may prefer to put it, that for those sentences to which meaning is initially given by the verification of the statements they are thus shown to make, all that we can use in this verifying is some content of experience? Clearly what follows is that everything that we can meaningfully say about the world must be built up out of features which are found somewhere within the contents of our experiences. This is the traditional empiricist doctrine, expressed for example in Russell's dictum, *Every proposition which we can understand must be composed wholly of constituents with which we are acquainted.*[22] But it does not follow that what we meaningfully say must be about actual or possible experiences, that our statements must really mean only that such-and-such kinds of experiences do or will or may occur. To reach this conclusion on the basis of a constructive theory of meaning we

[22] B. Russell, *The Problems of Philosophy*, p. 58. (This formulation is not ideal, since it invites trouble about 'acquaintance', and there is more to be said about how 'propositions' are 'composed'. But it makes a correct and important point in allowing the composition of new wholes provided that all their components are respectable.)

should need to add two further premisses: the first, that it is part of every content of experience *that it is perceived,* the second, Berkeley's rule that it is impossible to abstract the remainder of this content from its being perceived. The first of these is plainly false. In fact it is necessarily false, since if it were true there would be an infinite regress of perceivings. (If being perceived were part of something which is perceived and which, being an intentional object, is just as we perceive it, then what we perceive must include also that we perceive that we perceive that something; and so *ad infinitum.*) The second premiss is also false, and quite without support, since, for example, Berkeley's attack in the Introduction to the *Principles* on abstract general ideas has no connection with this sort of abstracting, and since his specific argument in Section 23 is, as we have seen, fallacious.

This can be put in another way. Bennett thinks that Locke should have worried about the meaning of such expressions as 'real things without us'. But what we seem to see, feel, hear, and so on, the contents of our experience, *are seen as real things without us*—that is, outside us. We just see things as being simply there, of such-and-such sorts, in such-and-such relations—though we might be wrong, though our seeing them so is logically distinct from their being so—and this phrase 'real things without us' is only a general expression intended to cover any such things as we seem to see. 'Real' and 'outside us' are not positive terms, introducing some further features that need special explanation; they only deny the downgrading from simply being there to being merely how things look. It is difficult to make this point in words without getting into a tangle, but a moment's consideration should make it clear. What are in their own nature intentional objects or appearances—explicable as how things look—present whatever they depict not *as* appearances but as realities: there is therefore no problem about the building-up on this foundation of sentences that meaningfully assert—or question—real existences. What we perceive, as an intentional object, is mind-dependent; but mind-dependence is not part, let alone a non-detachable part, of what we perceive. Mind-dependence, therefore, will not be carried over by a constructive theory of meaning into the meaning of everything we say. It would do no harm to say that, though not reality itself, yet everything we can assert, believe, speculate, or even question about reality is a logical construction out of the *contents* of our experiences; but this will carry no phenomenalist implications. Thus once we have got rid of verificationism, the meaning part of the veil-of-perception problem can be solved.

7. *The problem of justification*

The very disposal of the problem of meaning, however, makes acute the problem of justification: it allows us to give meaning to the questions that express sceptical doubts. There is a logical gap between ideas and reality, or between how we see things and how they are, and synthetic judgements are required to bridge that gap. Take, for example, the sceptical question, 'Is it all a dream?' Once we have given meaning, in a thoroughly familiar way, to the contrast between something's being dreamed and the going-on of something of the same sort in what we take to be the reality of waking life, we can use that contrast over again in asking whether what we take to be the reality of waking life has itself only the status of being dreamed in comparison with some further (unknown) reality.

Locke, of course, relies on causal inference to bridge this gap: his thesis about reality has, in effect, the form 'There is something of such-and-such a sort which causes and is represented by things looking etc. the way they do to us'. But granted that we can give meaning to the descriptions summed up here by 'There is something of such-and-such a sort', our problem is to say how we are justified in postulating this as a *cause* (or rather, a set of causes) of things looking the way they do. Causal laws are not merely not analytic, logical truths, they are not known or knowable *a priori* in any other way either. There is no method by which, from the mere inspection of an effect on its own, we can say from what sort of cause it must have arisen. So to justify an inference from an effect to a cause, we need a synthetic, *a posteriori*, causal law. This must be independently established; but how can it be established except by our observing on at least some occasions the occurrence of the cause being followed by the occurrence of the effect?[23]

Our reliance on this argument may be somewhat shaken by the

[23] It is, of course, a Humean view of causation that underlies this criticism. I have discussed this view in Chapter 1 of my *The Cement of the Universe—A Study of Causation*, and have argued for certain revisions of the Humean view in later chapters of that book. But these revisions do not in themselves undermine the sort of argument summed up here.

consideration that modern physics seems systematically to violate its principles. Various aspects of the behaviour of large-scale things are explained as being caused by the doings of atomic and sub-atomic particles, but the latter are never directly observed, being rather inferred from the observation of those large-scale performances which they are supposed to cause and hence to explain. Are not the physicists guilty of using causal inferences in terms of laws which cannot have been independently established by the direct observation of the causes in question being followed by their supposed effects?

One could reply by rejecting realism about 'scientific entities', by interpreting in some non-literal positivist or pragmatist way statements about sub-atomic particles. But there is some case for saying that this is one instance in which it is defensible to introduce both the causes and the causal laws that connect them with the observed effects as parts of a system of explanatory hypotheses. If we think of just one cause–effect pair, such a procedure seems arbitrary: if we can introduce the joint hypothesis that X occurs and that X causes Y to explain Y, we could introduce with equal plausibility any joint hypothesis of the form that Z occurs and that Z causes Y: the 'X' in the first explanation is freely replaceable. But if we are considering not just a single cause–effect pair but a systematic explanation of a whole body of effects, there may not in practice be anything like the same degree of freedom with regard to the various Xs that we can postulate even if the laws connecting Xs with Ys are also to be postulated, and are not independently established.

However, another possible reply is that in this case the laws, or some of them, *are* independently established. Laws relating electric charge, mass, motion, and so on are discovered and confirmed first for large-scale bodies which are (in an ordinary sense) directly observed, and these laws are used again as part of the system of laws governing the behaviour of atoms and sub-atomic particles and are among those that connect the latter with what is directly observed. This is true of some of the laws in question, which puts a further constraint on the small-scale, not directly observable, causes that can be postulated: they are to be in some respects of the same kinds as things that are large enough to be directly observed and hence they must conform to some of the same, independently established, laws.

Returning, with these analogues in mind, to the justification part of the veil-of-perception problem, we might hope to solve it in either of two ways—or perhaps in both ways together. One way would be to argue that the real existence of material things outside us is a well-confirmed outline hypothesis, that it explains the experiences we have better than any alternative hypothesis would, in particular better than the minimal hypothesis that there are just these experiences and nothing else. I call it an outline hypothesis to allow for revisions within it. One form of realist hypothesis that would, I consider, be well confirmed as against the minimal phenomenalistic one would be what we can call *common-sense realism*.[24] This view distinguishes appearances from reality, allows for errors and differences of perception between people, including those between the colour-blind and people with normal colour vision, and yet draws no distinction between primary and secondary qualities—in effect treating colours and the like as primary qualities, allowing colours-as-we-see-them to be resemblances of qualities actually in the things. Another, revised, form of realism is the Lockean view with its distinction between primary and secondary qualities. But both of these fall within what I have called the outline hypothesis of (representative) realism, and I am initially concerned with the confirmation of this outline hypothesis rather than with either special form of it. What is essential in this outline hypothesis is that it fills in gaps in things as they appear, so producing continuously existing things and gradual changes where the appearances are discontinuous. Its resulting merit is a special sort of simplicity, the resolving of what would, on the rival, phenomenalist, view, be quite unexplained coincidences: what we now regard as successive observations of the same thing at intervals would be the repeated springing into existence of complex groups of appearances remarkably like other groups which had passed out of existence before. This argument from simplicity is, I believe, a powerful one: I shall have more to say about it below.

The other approach to a solution is to argue that we can find, within appearances, confirming instances of the very causal laws that we need to carry us from appearances to reality—much as we can find, among large-scale things, illustrations of some of the

---

[24] Not 'naïve realism', because this phrase has been used to name a more extreme philosophical thesis than is, I think, ordinarily held by unsophisticated people.

causal laws that we use in going beyond these to not directly observable small-scale entities. There is, on the face of it, no difficulty in checking that things cause our sensations, and no obstacle in principle to a detailed physical and physiological and psychological investigation of how they do so. This seems to be an obvious truth, and yet it would be said that it encounters logical difficulties. Is not my reasoning viciously circular if I rely on my seeing of an object, say a cup, to support the judgement that it is the cup's coming to be there that has caused this new visual sensation in me? But I can use a different sense, say touch, to ascertain that a certain solid object has just come to be before me at the time when I begin to have these visual sensations, and so on. However, Bennett could reply that this shows merely that there is no difficulty in establishing piecemeal causal and representative relations, but that these hold only within appearances, and that there is no justification for extending these to hold between a supposed reality and appearances as a whole. But on the kind of representative view that we are now examining, appearances are not a special kind of entity: to speak of appearances is just to speak generally of such matters as how-it-looks or how-it-feels. So what I seem to be presented with is just that when a feelable cup-shaped object comes to be before my eyes, I begin to have a certain visual sensation, and when the object is removed I cease to have it, the whole set of observations being repeatable in just the ways needed to confirm a causal relationship: I seem to be getting evidence of a real solid object causing sensations. Still, there is a vicious circularity in appealing to causal relationships thus established against a radical scepticism, against a doubt whether there is any reality at all of which our percepts are appearances. The radical sceptic will not allow any authority to the interpretation, however tentative, of my experience as being of a real solid object causing sensations. That may be how it looks to me, he will say, but how it looks may be completely wrong.

Consequently we cannot use such confirmations of object-sensation causal laws within appearances to make the first inroads on scepticism: these must be made rather by the argument from simplicity for realism considered as an outline hypothesis. But once these first inroads have been made, once the realist view has been given some initial plausibility, we can further strengthen it, as well as filling in the more detailed accounts it requires of the specific causal processes in perception, by detecting such object-sensation causal laws within appearances. The vicious circle, once broken, changes into a virtuous spiral. But it is important, for this purpose, that we should take the correct view of appearances on which I have repeatedly insisted. If appearances were real objects, but distinct from 'real things outside us', then causal relations between them would be very poor evidence for any like causal relations (and they could not be very like) between real things and appearances. But if to speak of an appearance is just to speak of how-it-looks, then what we are calling a causal relation between appearances can be its looking as if there were a causal relation between a real thing and, say, my having a certain sensation, and once any credence has been given to such claims, they can build up into powerful support for the kind of representative view we are considering.

The details of a causal theory will thus look after themselves, but it is worth reconsidering the argument from simplicity which has to provide the first step in solving the problem of justification. Simplicity of various sorts has been seen as a merit in scientific theories and hypotheses, but the special kind with which we are here concerned is very dramatically illustrated by the contrast between Copernican and Ptolemaic theories. The key difference between them is not, say, over the mere number of cycles and epicycles used. Rather it is this. In a Ptolemaic account of the motions of the planet Jupiter, for example, there will occur somewhere a cycle or epicycle with a period of 365 days. Similarly in the account of the motions of the planet Mars there will occur, quite separately and independently, a 365 days' cycle or epicycle. And similarly with each of the planets, as well as for the sun. But since these are all independent, the recurrence of the same period, 365 days, in different places is a sheer unexplained coincidence. On the Copernican hypothesis, however, these separate epicycles disappear into the single revolution of the earth about the sun: there is no longer any coincidence to be explained. It is this, I believe, that constitutes the real initial superiority of the Copernican hypothesis over the Ptolemaic, as distinct from its subsequent confirmation by the way in which it led on to the more complete astronomical theories of Kepler and Newton. It is simplicity of this sort that I would call *the elimination of unexplained coincidence*; and this sort of simplicity is of the greatest importance as a guide to the choice between alternative scientific hypotheses. And while the existence of material things is not itself what we would ordinarily call a scientific hypothesis, being rather a framework within which the particular hypotheses that we so describe are formulated, it can, when the question of its justification is raised, be seen to be like a scientific hypothesis and to have in its favour this same sort of simplicity, this same elimination of unexplained coincidence.

This argument from simplicity is what Hume describes as the manner in which the 'constancy' and 'coherence' of certain impressions 'give[s] rise to the opinion of the continu'd existence of body'.[25] But whereas Hume thought that he was tracing only the irrational behaviour of our imaginations, pointing out the bad though plausible reasons that we have for certain beliefs, I think that they are quite good reasons, and they are certainly closely analogous to what we recognize as good reasons for preferring one scientific theory to another. This view was taken, for example, by Russell, and has also been adopted by Ayer, who while acknowledging his debt to Hume says that whereas Hume 'found in the relations of "constancy" and "coherence" . . . a means of explaining how we are deceived into treating [our "perceptions"] as persistent objects, I have represented these relations not as accounting for a deception but as justifying an acceptable theory'.[26]

8. Is naïvety indispensable?

Both in Hume and in Ayer, however, there is a curious twist to the argument. Hume insists that we cannot get directly to the sophisticated sort of realism which distinguishes 'objects' from 'perceptions' (that is, external reality from the experiential content) and further distinguishes primary from secondary qualities. We can reach this only by way of a very naïve realism which asserts just the continued unobserved existence of our perceptions themselves.[27] In a similar spirit Ayer argues that the causal analysis

[25] *Treatise*, I. iv. 2.
[26] B. Russell, op. cit., Chapter 2; A. J. Ayer, *The Central Questions of Philosophy*, Chapter 5, esp. p. 106.
[27] Loc. cit.: 'There are no principles either of the understanding or fancy, which lead us directly to embrace this opinion of the double existence of perceptions and objects, nor can we arrive at it but by passing thro' the common hypothesis of the

of perception can be brought in only after 'we have already established our claim to have some knowledge of the physical world'.
Accepting the dogma which I have questioned, that causal statements can be made only if the objects taken as causes are 'independently identified', Ayer thinks that we must first be naïve realists
in order to identify the objects that we subsequently treat as
causing our perceptions. The observer is not initially permitted
to 'conceive of the data with which he works as private to himself',
that is, *as* percepts. This is 'eventually possible, but only when the
theory has been developed and is allowed to transform its own
origins'.[28] But is either Hume or Ayer right about this?

First, it is true that historically, in the thought of each of us,
there is a phase of something like naïve realism, a stage in which
we do not distinguish between objects and percepts. It is also true
that between this and the stage where some of us adopt a Lockean
view there is a phase of what I have called common-sense realism,
with a distinction between objects and percepts but without one
between primary and secondary qualities. It is through these
stages and by patterns of reasoning that belong to them that any
of us comes in the first place to consider anything like the Lockean
view, and even when we are trying to consider it, our language
and our natural ways of thinking keep pulling us back to one or
other of these more primitive views. But both Hume and Ayer,
in their different ways and with their different purposes, are
making something much stronger than this contingent historical
claim; they are suggesting that it is somehow logically necessary
for us to pass through the first stage.

I have argued, secondly, that it is vital for the solution of the
problem of meaning—even after we have a constructive rather
than a verificationist theory—that the contents of our experience
are not undetachably labelled as such: mind-dependence is not a
part of what we perceive, and certainly not a part from which it
would be impossible to abstract, for constructive use elsewhere,

---

[28] Op. cit., pp. 87, 98, 106.

identity and continuance of our interrupted perceptions. Were we not first per-
swaded, that our perceptions are our only objects, and continue to exist even when
they no longer make their appearance to the senses, we should never be led to
think, that our perceptions and objects are different, and that our objects alone
preserve a continu'd existence. "The latter hypothesis has no primary recommendation either to reason or the imagination, but acquires all its influence on the
imagination from the former".'

other parts of that experiential content. That this should be so is a logical requirement for the development, in meaningful language, of a representational view. But what is thus logically required is not the actual passing through a naïve realist stage, but merely that the contents of experience should be such as not, in themselves, to preclude naïve realism.

Thirdly, I have conceded that if we try to set up the Lockean view by causal inference, relying on causal laws which are themselves initially established within appearances, the reasoning would be viciously circular unless there were some initial plausibility in some kind of realist view: we cannot begin at this point an effective argument against an obstinate sceptic. But what moral is to be drawn from this? If this were our only line of argument, and if, as this point suggests, it could get started only by our making what would have initially to be a naïvely realistic assumption, then surely it would be Hume's conclusion rather than Ayer's that would be vindicated. The line of thought that leads to a Lockean view would not really be defensible: there would have to be some support for the conclusion before there was any genuine support for the premiss, and this vicious circularity would reduce the whole case for realism to a performance that might be psychologically explained but could not be defended. What allows us to escape from Hume's conclusion is the other line of thought, in which the object-sensation causal laws do not have to be independently established before we rely on them for an inference from appearance to reality, but we can rather see both the reality and the laws that connect it with appearances as joint parts of a systematic explanatory hypothesis. (But in calling it an hypothesis we are referring to the order of the justification of beliefs, not to the order of their acquisition. It has been conceded that in the order of acquisition of beliefs naïve realism comes first, followed by common-sense realism: we do not first introduce the external world as an hypothesis. But when the question of justification is raised, we can then speak of a complex hypothesis, which is confirmed just by its explanatory success). Since he also uses this line of thought, Ayer need not, and shuold not, accept Hume's view that naïve realism is, in this third way, a (logically) necessary stage in our thinking.

9. *Conclusions*

It seems, then, that there is a kind of representative theory, dealing with 'ideas' as intentional objects, which while it is prima facie open to the objections that are commonly thought fatal to any representative view, can in the end be defended against them. To put it simply, it is just not true that if in this sense we start within the circle of ideas we cannot break out. Equally, we found that there is another variant of representationalism, dealing with 'ideas' as physical intermediates, which could also be so defended, though it is of less interest and less historical importance. But a close historical study would probably show that the representative theories that have been discussed have often been mixtures, and perhaps incoherent mixtures, of these two separately defensible views. We can conclude that in order to avoid being forced into phenomenalism, and to arrive at some sort of realism, we do not need to regard perception as a mode of awareness that is so direct as to be self-guaranteeing and unproblematic, as simply *giving* us real external objects. It is just as well that we do not need this, since we could not obtain it. In particular, as we have seen, we cannot derive this conclusion either from the undeniable judgemental directness of ordinary perception or from the ways in which in everyday speech we talk about seeing and feeling things. I think also that the intentional object variant which I have defended is fairly close to what Locke was trying to state. If this position is defensible, we can the more readily accept something like this as an interpretation of Locke, knowing that we are not thereby pushing him into a position which any first-year student can refute. We can see that at least in principle Locke was right not to be disturbed by what he admitted to be initial difficulties for this sort of view. However, there is at least one problem outstanding: how is Locke, or a Lockean, to defend the view that some ideas, but not others, resemble the corresponding qualities of external things, if we have no 'direct access' to the things in order to compare our ideas with them? But this is only the problem of the distinction between primary and secondary qualities over again, and that, as we saw in Chapter 1, could be defended against other objections: the only remaining difficulty for it was that (in Locke's form) it required a representative theory for its formulation. Now that such a theory has been vindicated, we can argue in favour of the primary/secondary distinction on essentially scientific grounds, that it is involved in the best detailed explanation of perceptual processes: it is thus, and not by direct comparisons, that we can decide which ideas are, and which are not, matched by objective qualities that resemble them, which of them literally depict reality and which merely 'represent' it and 'conform' to it.

Reading the *Essay* as a whole, one certainly does not get the impression that the representative theory had anything like the importance for Locke himself that it has had for his critics from Berkeley onwards. It was something that he took pretty much for granted, rather than something that he was specially concerned to put forward, develop, and defend. Yet it could not simply be excised from the *Essay*: if it were abandoned, much else would at least need to be put very differently. We need not apologize for taking so much more trouble over this question than Locke himself did: however inadvertently, he introduced into philosophical discussion a topic that his successors have in general not been able either to cope with adequately or to leave alone, and one about which some of the most widely and firmly held philosophical opinions are, I believe, very much open to dispute.

3

SUBSTANCE AND ESSENCE

1. *Berkeley's criticism of 'material substance'*

LOCKE's view of substance, and particularly of material substance, has been thought very much open to criticism. Berkeley attacked it with vigour:

It is said *extension* is a *mode* or accident *of matter*, and that matter is the *substratum* that supports it. Now I desire that you would explain what is meant by matter's *supporting* extension: say you, I have no idea of matter, and therefore cannot explain it. I answer, though you have no positive, yet if you have any meaning at all, you must at least have a relative idea of matter; though you know not what it is, yet you must be supposed to know what relation it bears to accidents, and what is meant by its supporting them. It is evident *support* cannot here be taken in its usual or literal sense, as when we say that pillars support a building: in what sense therefore must it be taken? . . . If we inquire into what the most accurate philosophers declare themselves to mean by *material substance*, we shall find them acknowledge, they have no other meaning annexed to those sounds, but the idea of *being in general*, together *with the relative notion of its supporting accidents*. The general idea of being appeareth to me the most abstract and incomprehensible of all other; and as for its supporting accidents, this, as we have just now observed, cannot be understood in the common sense of those words; it must therefore be taken in some other sense, but what that is they do not explain.[1]

That is, Locke can offer no account of substance itself, and only an unexplained metaphor for its relation to qualities. If what Berkeley is here criticizing is indeed Locke's theory, it is in considerable difficulties. Moreover, Berkeley thought that Locke needed this substance or substratum, unsatisfactory though it is, to provide an anchor for qualities outside the mind: he thought that if Locke gave up material substance, he would have to let the primary qualities slide into the mind and survive only as ideas, just as, Berkeley wrongly thought, Locke had already allowed the secondary qualities to do.[2]

[1] *Principles*, §§ 16–17.
[2] Cf. *Three Dialogues*, Second Dialogue: '*Hylas*: The reality of things cannot be

2. *Locke's account of substance*

What Locke actually says in the *Essay*, however, should make us hesitate about ascribing to him the view that Berkeley criticizes. In the key passage he is not putting forward what he 'declares himself to mean' by *material substance*, but explaining the ideas that people ordinarily have of substance in general and of particular substances.

> The mind . . . takes notice . . . that a certain number of these simple *ideas* [that is, qualities] go constantly together; which being presumed to belong to one thing . . . are called, so united in one subject, by one name; which, by inadvertency, we are apt afterward to talk of and consider as one simple *idea* [that is, thing] . . . because . . . not imagining how these simple *ideas* [that is, qualities] can subsist by themselves, we accustom ourselves to suppose some *substratum* wherein they do subsist, and from which they do result; which therefore we call *substance*.[3]

We find, in other words, a number of features regularly going around together—for example, the shape, size, colour, habitual movements, noises, etc. of a cat: we use the one word 'cat' to refer to this collection of features: we then suppose that there is some one thing for which the word 'cat' (or the phrase 'the cat') stands, and that there is some one central core which both produces and holds together all these cat-features, and it is to this supposed item, and all corresponding items, that we give the

---

[3] II. xxiii. 1. This is one of many passages where Locke, as he himself admits (II. viii. 8) uses the word 'idea' carelessly, in a very broad sense, where if he were writing more accurately he would have said 'thing' or 'quality': I have indicated in square brackets the amendments which he invites us to make.

maintained without supposing the existence of matter.' But it must be admitted that Berkeley usually puts the argument the other way round: the denial of matter is a conclusion that follows from, rather than supports, the transfer of all 'sensible qualities' into the mind—e.g. Second Dialogue: '*Philonous*: . . . at first, from a belief in material substance you would have it that the immediate objects existed without the mind; then that their archetypes; then causes; next instruments; then occasions: lastly, *something in general*, which being interpreted proves *nothing*. So matter comes to nothing.' And again *Principles* § 17: 'But why shou'd we trouble ourselves any further, in discussing this material *substratum* or support of figure and motion, and other sensible qualities? does not it suppose they have an existence without the mind? and is not this a direct repugnancy, and altogether inconceivable?' For Berkeley, with his theological concerns, matter rather than external existence is the real villain, so he uses the denial of the non-mental existence of qualities as a step towards the denial of matter.

general name 'substance': 'So that if anyone will examine himself concerning his *notion of pure substance in general*, he will find he has no other *idea* of it at all, but a supposition of he knows not what support of such qualities which are capable of producing simple *ideas* in us . . .'[4] And Locke adds '. . . here, as in all other cases where we use words without having clear and distinct ideas, we talk like children . . .'

Locke explains further that once we have this 'obscure and relative idea of substance in general', we get the ideas of particular sorts of substances by taking combinations of ideas representing qualities that are found going around together, which 'are therefore supposed to flow from the particular internal constitution or unknown essence of that substance': our ideas of a man, a horse, gold, water, and so on are thus collections of simple ideas along with 'the confused *idea* of *something* . . . in which they [or rather, the corresponding qualities] subsist'.[5]

Since Locke had to defend himself against Stillingfleet's criticism that he makes 'the general idea of substance to be framed, not by abstracting and enlarging simple ideas, but by a complication of many simple ideas together', it would be as well to retrace carefully the rather complicated procedure he describes. First, we notice, say, the collection of instantiated cat-features going around together, and we frame what we might call a purely phenomenal idea of *this cat*: this *is* a 'complication of many simple ideas together'. Secondly, we suppose an unknown central core to be what those features subsist in and result from: we now have the idea of this particular substance, that is, this concrete existing thing, this cat: this is the combination of the phenomenal idea with the idea of an unknown core. Thirdly, from this and many like cases we abstract the general notion of the unknown central core of a thing, which is the idea of pure substance in general. Fourthly, from the particular phenomenal ideas of this cat, that cat, the other cat, and so on we abstract a general idea of a collection of general cat-features, combine this with the idea of pure substance in general, and so get the general idea of a particular sort of substance, namely *a cat*.

It is plain from these passages themselves that Locke is primarily describing what he takes to be our ordinary way of thinking, and is not necessarily endorsing it himself. He is certainly not

---

[4] II. xxiii. 2.   [5] II. xxiii. 3.

constructing here anything that we could call his own theory of substance; rather we find him here, as in several other places,[6] disapproving of some parts of this ordinary way of thinking, as an example of what he later calls 'the first and most palpable abuse [of words] . . . the using of words without clear and distinct *ideas*.'[7] This comes out still more plainly in his satirical comments on those who try to make a positive use of the notion of substance, as a ground for criticizing the physical theory that there can be empty space:

If it be demanded (as usually it is) whether this *space*, void of *body*, be *substance* or *accident*, I shall readily answer I know not, nor shall be ashamed to own my ignorance, till they that ask show me a clear distinct *idea* of *substance* . . . And I desire those who lay so much stress on the sound of these two syllables, *substance*, to consider whether applying it as they do to the infinite incomprehensible GOD, to finite spirit, and to body, it be in the same sense; and whether it stands for the same *idea*, when each of those three so different beings are called *substances*?[8]

Locke does not think that his opponents will dare to say that three such different things all have some common nature that is called substance, while if they recognize these as three quite different sorts of substance, he sees no reason why they should not recognize space as a fourth. The doctrine of substance, then, is not something that Locke is himself constructing, using, and relying upon; rather it is something he found already in use, of which he was both critical and suspicious, anxious that it should not be allowed to restrict scientific inquiry.

On the other hand, Locke does not go so far as explicitly to reject this notion of substance, either proposing a different notion or rejecting the term 'substance' altogether. Indeed he remarks in Book I that if nature had been going to give us any innate ideas, a clear idea of substance is one that it would have been handy to have as innate, since we cannot get any such clear idea in the ordinary way, by sensation and reflection.[9] Unless this section is ironical, Locke is here expressing the belief that there is such a

---

[6] See particularly III. x. 17–20, which (with related passages) is discussed in Section 7 below as including an anticipation of a thesis recently advanced by Saul Kripke.

[7] Compare II. xxiii. 2 with III. x. 2.   [8] II. xiii. 17–18.

[9] I. iv. 19.

thing as substance, over and above the collections of qualities of which we can have what I have called phenomenal ideas, and yet admitting that neither he nor anyone else can get nearer to it than in the unsatisfactory way described above.

3. *Substance and real essence*

In considering how far Locke is committed to the notion of substance which he himself finds unsatisfactory we shall have to sort out several things which he misleadingly runs together. In what I called above the second stage of the complicated procedure, Locke suggests that it is because we use, for convenience, the single word 'cat' for the collection of instantiated cat-features that we suppose that there is some further thing for which this word stands. But this verbal argument need not be the whole of the story. The readily perceivable cat-features have no observable connection with one another—the fur does not produce the miaow—and especially since, as Locke says, our ideas of particular substances are made up largely of ideas of powers, it is reasonable and natural to suppose that there are occurrent grounds for these powers, and hence that there is some not immediately detectable internal structure to which all the readily perceivable features and powers are related, and which would causally explain the co-occurrence of observable features. It is in this sense reasonable to postulate a thing which has all these properties and to use the phrase 'this cat' to stand for this postulated thing, or for the combination of the postulated central core, the perceivable features, and the powers found to be associated with them. It need not be, as Locke sometimes suggests, that such a phrase as 'this cat' stands initially, and ought only to stand, for the collection of readily perceivable features (and perhaps the associated powers)— that is, for that of which we have what I called a phenomenal idea. If the core is reasonably postulated, we are not necessarily being fooled by the use of the one word 'cat' into supposing that there must be a unitary referent for it. But what sort of entity would be thus reasonably postulated? Surely some combination of further instantiated properties, including arrangements and motions of minute parts, which are too small to be perceived, as well as macroscopic structures and processes which are not readily perceivable merely because they are inside the animal. This internal and partly minute structure will, however, on Locke's view be made up of primary qualities, and even if we supplement these in the way I suggested in Chapter 1, it will still be made up of properties of some sort: it will not be a 'substratum' underlying all properties.

On the other hand, philosophers have often toyed with a logico-linguistic argument which seems to introduce such a substratum. We say that the thing here, the cat, *has* each of the properties, not only the readily perceivable features but also the powers, the internal, not immediately detectable features, and even those properties of the minute parts which may remain forever unknown. So it seems that the thing itself must be distinct from each of its properties, and therefore from all its properties together: it must be something other than the properties, something in which they all inhere, and to which they all belong; and it is by belonging to this one underlying something that they are all held together and go to make one complete thing. We cannot conceive how qualities could subsist alone: they need something to subsist in. Also, qualities in themselves are general, they are universals; they need to be instantiated or individuated by being attached to something whose very nature it is to be particular. What we thus need to supplement all the properties is the substratum, which must therefore be something which considered purely in itself has no properties and is not constituted by any combination of properties.

It is plain that this argument for a substratum is different from the argument for what I called a central core, the latter being close to what Locke calls a real essence. It is the latter of which he is speaking when he says that the qualities 'are supposed to flow from the particular internal constitution or unknown essence of that substance'. When Locke speaks of 'some substratum wherein [the qualities] do subsist, and from which they do result' he is in effect identifying the substratum with the real essence.[10] But the argument just sketched would lead us to distinguish the two notions. The real essence is the *particular* internal constitution. The real essence of gold will be the way in which gold is built up out of some minute fundamental particles; water will have a different real essence, being built up in some different way, either

[10] II. xxiii. 3; II. xxiii. 1.

from different fundamental particles or from the same ones differently combined and arranged. But a substratum which in itself was devoid of all properties, all distinctions, would presumably be the same in gold and in water. Again, though Locke says many times that real essences are unknown, this is only contingently so. It is conceivable that we should have senses 'acute enough to discern the minute particles of bodies and the real constitution on which their sensible qualities depend',[11] and angels may well be able to provide themselves with organs of sensation adapted to whatever scale of observation they prefer.[12] But a substratum underlying *all* properties would be unperceivable in principle: having no features of its own it could not be detected in itself by any conceivable form of perception. Since we can equate Locke's real essences with what we should now call the molecular and atomic structure of things, we may say that many real essences that were unknown in Locke's day are now pretty thoroughly known by chemists and physicists; but any substratum that underlies all properties, and fulfils merely the logical functions of the individuation of general features and of holding features together by being that in which they all inhere, must still be as remote as ever from our view.

Moreover, the logico-linguistic argument for a substratum is not cogent. Of course, what we encounter is instantiated qualities: but this combination of particularity with universality is the unavoidable starting-point of any explanation. It is both unnecessary and the source of insoluble puzzles to split it up into purely universal qualities and some purely particular complement of them which have then to be somehow reunited.[13] Instantiated properties, at least of all the kinds with which we are at present concerned, are spatio-temporally located. As we saw, Locke needs, in addition to his primary qualities—unless solidity can play this role—at least one space-occupying feature, perhaps something like rest mass or electric charge. The other, geometrical, primary qualities could not, indeed, subsist alone; but they need nothing more to subsist in than such an objective space-occupying feature. And while we can speak of a thing as distinct from each of its properties, including this one, so that we can say that the thing *has* this or that property, it does not follow that we must regard the thing as

[11] II. xxiii. 11; cf. IV. iii. 25.　　　[12] II. xxiii. 13.
[13] More of these puzzles will be examined in Chapter 4.

distinct from all its instantiated properties at once. If our ordinary style of speaking did commit us to this conclusion, we could only say, so much the worse for our ordinary style of speaking: there is no need to let it be authoritative in leading to so unacceptable a result. But in any case our ordinary style of speaking does not so commit us. It can be interpreted harmlessly in either of two ways. When we say that this cat, for example, has property X, whatever X may be, we can take the subject-term, 'this cat', as referring to the whole collection of properties, including X, and then to say that it has X will be to say that it has X as a constituent, as a member of the collection; alternatively we can take the subject-term, 'this cat', as referring to some sub-set of the collection which excludes X, and then to say that it has X is to say that X co-occurs with it.

This argument for a substratum, then, should be rejected. No doubt it has convinced some philosophers, including some scholastically trained thinkers against whom Locke was reacting. But he was surely wrong if he thought that we all, in our ordinary thought, introduce for some such reason as this the notion of pure substance in general and use it as a component in our complex ideas of particular sorts of substance. There is no reason to suppose that anyone except a few philosophers has had this notion and used it in this way. But is Locke himself one of those few?

On this topic of substance, Locke has been attacked from both sides. After his death Berkeley rubbed in the difficulties—foreshadowed by Locke's own words—about an unknowable substance. Other critics too found his thesis that real essences are unknown a threat to established religious doctrines.[14] But during his lifetime the strongest criticism was that of Stillingfleet from the opposite side: he accused Locke of doing away with substance, or at least making its existence doubtful. In reply Locke insists first that he of course recognizes particular substances, such as a man, for instance himself, but secondly that he accepts the same argument as Stillingfleet does, that 'we cannot conceive how modes or accidents can subsist by themselves', and hence we suppose that they exist in and are supported by some common subject. Locke is here quoting what he gave in II. xxiii. 4 as the

[14] Cf. J. W. Yolton, *John Locke and the Way of Ideas*, pp. 126–48.

source of our ordinary idea of substance in general, but he now adds 'Which I think is a true reason'.[15] That is, he now explicitly endorses what we might have written off merely as a report (even if not a correct one) of our ordinary way of thinking: thus Locke seems to accept, under pressure from Stillingfleet, the weak logico-linguistic argument outlined above. He admits that he can introduce in this way only an obscure, confused, imperfect, inadequate idea of substance; but, he points out, neither Stillingfleet nor anyone else can produce a better one.

Yolton has argued that Locke's account of substance is an attempt to reconcile two incompatible views, a 'phenomenalistic' one which identifies substance with a collection of qualities, and a 'non-phenomenalistic' one which introduces a real essence hidden away in an 'unknowable but necessary substratum'.[16] There are, however, at least four possible views here. A strictly phenomenalistic (or Berkeleian) one would equate a substance with a collection of ideas or appearances: but Locke shows no tendency to do this. A second view would equate it with a collection of readily observable qualities, both such large-scale primary qualities as the over-all shape and size of objects big enough for us to see as having some particular shape and the powers with which Locke identifies secondary qualities, and therefore approximately with what Locke calls nominal essence. A third view would equate substance with real essence, an unknown micro-structure of instantiated primary qualities. The fourth view would equate substance with a sub-stratum underlying all the properties, even those that constitute this micro-structure.

When Locke is discussing the names of substances, he tends to say that they can be coherently used only to stand for nominal essences, and this might pull him in the direction of the second view of substance. Yet when he is discussing substance itself, both in the text of the *Essay* and in his reply to Stillingfleet in the First Letter, he explicitly rejects this view and admits a substance of which we have only a relative idea, which is inferred as that in which modes and accidents inhere, in which even the (observable) primary qualities exist, by which they are supported, to which they belong, and from which all these sensible qualities result. He

---

[15] Reply to Stillingfleet, printed in many editions of the *Essay* (but not in Everyman) at the end of II. xxiii.

[16] Op. cit., pp. 126, 134–5, 139.

endorses the view of substance as something we know not what in which even solidity and extension inhere.

But does this mean that he accepted the third view, or the fourth, or some confused mixture of the two? Was he endorsing the reasonable argument for a real essence, or the weak logico-linguistic argument for a substratum underlying all properties, or both, and failing to distinguish them?

Michael Ayers has argued that Locke coherently adopts what I have called the third view.[17] Although Locke distinguishes 'pure substance in general' from specific real essences, the former is just an unknown determinable something of which each real essence is a determination or 'modification'. It is usually the 'modes and accidents' or 'sensible qualities' that Locke says need something to subsist in. Also, as we have seen, he at least sometimes equates the substratum with the real essence. Ayers's interpretation would therefore give him a more consistent view than any other. Also, Locke does not need to postulate a substratum underlying all (general) properties as the principle of individuation and identity since (as we shall see in Chapter 5) he has a quite different account of these matters. When he speaks about substance and substratum, he is concerned not with the conjunction of properties in an individual subject, but with sorts of substances and the regular clustering of properties in a natural kind.

However, to maintain this interpretation we must take it that when Locke says that while colour and weight inhere in the solid extended parts, extension and solidity themselves inhere in substance,[18] this applies not to extension and solidity in general, in particular not to the extension and solidity of minute parts (for these constitute the real essence, and therefore on this interpretation the substance, and cannot inhere in it) but only to large-scale, observable extension and solidity. If this is what Locke meant, then it is a pity that he did not say so more explicitly, and indeed that he did not reject the whole language of inherence and confine himself to saying that the substance or real essence is that of which the sensible qualities are further properties, to which they in some sense belong and from which they result.

I am not, therefore, convinced that Locke did confine himself

[17] M. R. Ayers, 'The Ideas of Power and Substance in Locke's Philosophy', *Philosophical Quarterly*, vol. 25 (1975), 1–27.
[18] II. xxiii. 2.

strictly to what I have called the third view, without any admix-
ture of the fourth and without any endorsement of the logico-
linguistic argument. But there is no doubt that this is what he
should have done. We can, then, sum up what he should have
said about substance, though it may not be quite what he does
say.

There are particular substances, such as a horse, gold (or a piece
of gold), and so on, each of which is constituted not only by a
combination of easily detectable instantiated properties that go
around together but also by many accompanying powers, and
also by an internal constitution which holds these properties
together and is their source and the basis of those powers. This
internal constitution is mostly unknown, but is reasonably postulated. We have only a relative idea of it, but still a defensible one.
It may be regrettable that we do not have a clearer and more
adequate idea of it, but that is how things stand: no other philosophy can improve on this account. It is also reasonable to assume
that the internal constitutions of different tokens of the same type
are alike—for example, different horses, different pieces of gold—
so that we can speak of the real essence of a natural kind. Still,
things that we group together as having the same nominal essence
may in fact have different real essences. (Whether we can also
speak of real essences of individuals will be considered later, in
Chapter 5.) So far we have introduced particular substances and
real essences; we can also speak of substance in general, but
merely as the determinable of which each real essence is a particular determination. Some philosophers have also introduced
the notion of a substratum underlying all properties, which would
be in principle unknown, unknowable, and indescribable. These
philosophers arrive at this notion by thinking of all the properties
of something as being only properties that belong to that thing
(or substance), and hence of the thing as distinct from all its
properties at once, and as something that they all together need
to subsist in. The notion that we could thus get of such a substratum is even more obscure and relative than the idea of a real
essence: it would be something we know not what related to the
properties some of which we know and some of which we merely
infer to be present by a relation which in turn we could describe
only vaguely by using the metaphors of inherence and support,
and these metaphors could not now be explained in the way that

they could be explained if applied to the relation between the real essence and the observable features. We have, therefore, no good reason for postulating such a substratum underlying all properties; it will not even supplement the primary qualities in the way that is required if they are to provide an adequate set of data for physical explanation; nor, as we shall see, is it needed to account for identity, diversity, and individuation.

4. *Material substance and reality*

It should be clear that the rejection of such a substratum has no tendency to undermine the objective existence of particular substances with their properties and powers and real essences. In this context, Bennett accuses Berkeley of having confused and conflated two quite different doctrines, the substratum doctrine which is a 'theory about what it is for a property to be instantiated' and the veil-of-perception doctrine about the relation between appearances and reality. Quoting parts of the passage I have quoted at the beginning of this chapter,[19] Bennett comments:

Berkeley wants to make a point about substratum-substance. Not only does he distractingly call it 'matter', but he also drags 'extension' into the limelight . . . With the phrase 'existence without the mind' as his pivot, he modulates into an attack on the veil-of-perception doctrine! A complaint against a wrong analysis of subject-concepts is thus jumbled with a complaint against Locke's insufficiently idealist analysis of the concept of reality.[20]

However, I see no conflation here. Berkeley is not writing a series of separate essays in analytical philosophy, but making out a case against a certain body of doctrine, in particular what he would have identified as materialism and saw as the ground of scepticism and atheism. 'Matter' is not what substratum-substance is distractingly called, it is what the argument is primarily about. As Berkeley saw it, the case for matter involved two main steps: the step from the ideas of which we are immediately aware to qualities and collections of qualities existing outside and independently of the mind, and the step from these to matter as their substratum and support. He makes the point about the obscurity of the support relation as a criticism of the second step in this argument. This

[19] p.72 and note 2, quoting from *Principles*, §§ 16–17.
[20] Bennett, *Locke, Berkeley, Hume: Central Themes*, pp. 70–4.

could be a general criticism of the substratum analysis of subject-concepts, but that is not what Berkeley here wants it for. He wants it to undermine this part of the case for *matter*, and extension is used because it is the most obvious and generally recognized mode or quality of matter. Berkeley goes on to the objections to what Bennett calls the veil-of-perception doctrine because it is thus that he can attack what I have called the first step in the case for matter: if the materialist cannot establish the non-mental existence of qualities the question of a substratum for them, such as matter, will not even arise. If there is a conflation, it is not of the two doctrines Bennett mentions but of the substratum and real essence concepts in the notion of matter, and that, as we have seen, may already be there in Locke's discussion. On the other hand, Bennett is right in ascribing a conflation of the substratum and veil-of-perception issues to a number of later writers, including C. R. Morris and Warnock and Ayer.[21] But it seems that what were two distinct steps in Berkeley's argument, criticizing two corresponding steps in the case for matter, have been run together by some of his successors. If we keep the two steps apart, we can agree with Berkeley's criticism of the move from objective qualities to a substratum underlying all properties without agreeing with his criticisms of the move from ideas to objective qualities. We can also resist any objections to the move from the readily observable features to the things or particular types of substance which have these features but are constituted not only of them but also of unobserved but reasonably postulated internal properties.

Far more faintly suggested in Berkeley's discussion than the two steps mentioned is the argument in the opposite direction, that if we reject the substratum the qualities will on that account slide back into the mind as mere ideas. This thought, it is interesting to note, involves another use of the very principle that led Locke (and Stillingfleet) to postulate a substratum, namely that modes and accidents cannot subsist by themselves. It is by holding on to this principle while rejecting the substratum that Berkeley concludes that modes and accidents must subsist in a different sort of substance, namely a mind, and must therefore be ideas. But since, as we have seen, Locke could reject a substratum that was supplied to underlie all properties while retaining a material

[21] Bennett, op. cit., pp. 81–3.

substance identifiable with real essence, this argument has no force against his main position.

5. *Real essence and nominal essence*

Locke discusses the distinction between real essence and nominal essence at considerable length and in several places; he was obviously greatly concerned about it.[22] Yet at first sight it seems straightforward and unproblematic. Locke's favourite example is gold. The nominal essence of gold, he suggests, is a certain complex abstract idea which we associate with—or, as he puts it, 'to which we have annexed'—the name 'gold'. This is the idea of a yellow, shining colour, great weight in proportion to size, malleability, fusibility, and so on—that is, the idea of something that has all the characteristics by the joint possession of which we recognize an object as being a piece of gold. Locke usually says that the nominal essence is such a complex abstract *idea*, and sometimes that it is an idea in our minds; but the narrow sense of 'idea' which confines it to mental entities is of little importance here, and in so far as it makes a difference it is unfortunate.

Locke's main purpose would have been better served if he had identified the nominal essence rather with the set of characteristics of which the complex idea in question is the idea, saying that the nominal essence of, for example, gold is the set of defining characteristics of gold, the set of features such that recognizing that a thing has them all is both necessary and sufficient for classifying that thing as a piece of gold. This way of putting it still secures the point behind Locke's talk about an idea, namely that these characteristics count as the nominal essence because we know them and use them as criteria of recognition, we associate the name 'gold' with the conjunction of them: it is a human mental operation that groups these characteristics and no others together and uses them in classification. By contrast the real essence of gold is the real internal constitution which all pieces of gold have, and on which all these defining characteristics in fact depend, but which we may well know little or nothing about, though we surmise that there is something of the sort. As I said, the distinction seems straightforward; but why was it important for Locke to insist upon it?

[22] III. iii; III. vi; III. x; IV. vi. 4–9; IV. xii. 9.

He was, clearly, reacting against a scholastic (and ultimately Aristotelian or even Platonic) view of essences which he thought was not merely erroneous but seriously misleading, which had for centuries led thinkers to pursue wrong and fruitless methods of investigation and had made them 'pretenders to a knowledge they had not'.[23] This view, he thought, resulted from a failure to draw this distinction, a failure to see that for the most part it is nominal essences only that are known and that the knowledge of them yields (about substances) only trifling propositions. This scholastic view is the doctrine of *substantial forms*. Locke's opponents thought that there was 'a certain'—that is fixed, determinate— 'number of . . . essences, according to which all natural things are made and wherein they do exactly every one of them partake, and so become of this or that *species*'. They thought of these essences as 'forms or moulds wherein all natural things that exist are cast', each essence being fixed and unchangeable. They were, Locke says, 'using the word *essence* for they know not what', but they believed that in defining things and classifying them into genera and species they were, merely by processes of ratiocination and verbal disputation, arriving at knowledge of the true essential natures of things. But these procedures not only failed to lead to any knowledge, they were bulwarks of ignorance. 'For if, according to the useless imagination of the Schools, anyone supposes the term *gold* to stand for a species of things set out by nature by a real essence belonging to it, it is evident he knows not what particular substances are of that species, and so cannot with certainty affirm anything universally of *gold*.'[24] Locke contrasts this worthless method with the more rational opinion of 'those who look on all natural things to have a real, but unknown, constitution of their insensible parts, from which flow those sensible qualities which serve us to distinguish them one from another'—that is, corpuscularian scientists like Boyle. Making Locke's criticism of the scholastic view more explicit than he himself made it, we could say that the scholastic essences combined features that in fact belong separately to (Boylean) real essences and to nominal essences. The scholastic essences were like real essences in that they were supposed to be what make things to be as they are, what determine their readily detectable features and modes of operation and powers; but they were like

[23] III. viii. 2.   [24] IV. vi. 8; cf III. iii. 17.

nominal essences in that they formed a finite set of fixed, unchanging natures, all clearly marked off from one another, and discoverable merely by thinking—for since we make our nominal essences by abstracting and combining ideas, we can by reflection discover what we are taking to be the nominal essence of, say, gold; we can ask ourselves, 'Would we call something gold if it had such and such properties but lacked such and such others?'; we shall have only a finite number of such sortal terms, and shall presumably have made them so that each is kept apart from every other by having different and incompatible defining characteristics; and our complex abstract idea, or the corresponding set of characteristics, can of course remain fixed no matter how much physical things change. In Locke's opinion, the failure to draw the distinction between real and nominal essence gives rise to two main errors, a belief that genuine, non-trifling, knowledge of the nature and necessary characteristics of things can be reached by scholastic procedures, and a belief that things naturally sort themselves out into separate species or natural kinds. The first of these is undoubtedly an error, but the second is more controversial. Surely there really are natural kinds, for example chemical elements and compounds (as opposed to mixtures) such as gold, water, and common salt, and the various species of plants and animals. There are natural kinds because properties are not randomly and independently distributed among things, but tend to cluster. We can say roughly that wherever we find some set of properties— those that could be used as a defining set for, say, cats—we also find many other properties common to the class of objects picked out by the first set, including a number of other sets of properties each of which would serve as an alternative defining set for that class, being distinctive of, as well as common to, cats. Admittedly this is only rough, because not all cats have all the properties that are in general typical of cats; but each natural kind is constituted by a clustering of properties which approximates to the description given. Whether there are natural kinds in this sense is an empirical question: all that Locke could argue on logical grounds is that it would be a fallacy to infer from our handling of terms and their nominal essences that there must be natural kinds. But he goes further, arguing that species are not as clear cut as we commonly suppose, that intermediate forms can and do arise (sometimes, but not only, by crosses between species, of which he reports some improbable stories).[25] He also points out that super-ficial likenesses have led to materials being classed as belonging to one species which have later been found to have very different properties: 'chemists especially are often, by sad experience, con-vinced of [this], when they, sometimes in vain, seek for the same qualities in one parcel of sulphur, antimony, or vitriol which they have found in others'. But he should have noted that when they encounter this sort of difficulty chemists go on to classify separa-tely the materials that they had initially taken to be of the same kind—perhaps what they had taken to be pure sulphur was a mixture of sulphur and something else. Locke sometimes goes too far in his denial of natural kinds, and other considerations force him to recognize them.[26] Indeed, as we shall see, the doctrine of real essences that do not coincide with nominal essences is im-plicitly a doctrine of natural kinds. His valid objection to the scholastic view is to its pretence to *a priori* knowledge.

6. *Essences of non-substances*

Locke distinguishes modes and relations from substances, and all of these from simple ideas.[27] Modes 'contain not in them the supposition of subsisting by themselves, but are considered as dependences on or affections of substances'. A shape, such as a triangle, is a 'simple mode of space'; a duration, say a day, is a 'simple mode of time'; such words as 'slide', 'roll', 'tumble', 'creep', and 'skip' stand for simple modes of motion; sensation, remembrance, reverie, and so on are simple modes of thinking; hope, anger, envy and the like are simple modes of pleasure and pain. Of great importance are mixed modes, 'consisting of several combinations of simple ideas [that is, qualities] of different kinds', such as gratitude, a murder, a reprieve, an ostracism, or a triumph. Ideas of relations arise from 'the considering of one

[25] e.g. III. vi. 12 mentions flying fish, cold-blooded aquatic birds, amphibians, seals and porpoises, mermaids, and intelligent beasts; III. vi. 23 says that women have conceived by drills (i.e. baboons), mares not only by asses but also by bulls, and that 'I once saw a creature that was the issue of a cat and a rat'. Locke was relying on the notion of 'the great chain of being'. He was not anticipating Darwin: it was not in the interests of an evolutionary theory that he denied the fixity and separateness of species.

[26] III. vi. 8; cf. III. x. 20. In III. iii. 13 and III. vi. 36–7 Locke admits that there are natural kinds.

[27] II. xii, xiii, xiv, xviii, xix, xx, xxii.

thing with another which is extrinsical to it', which can be done in indefinitely many ways.

As all these have already been differentiated, it is natural for Locke, when he later distinguishes real and nominal essences, to ask whether this last distinction can be applied to things other than substances, to simple ideas, to modes, and, in particular, to mixed modes. His view is that though the distinction can be applied to all these, it is there of little importance, since in all these cases the real essence and the nominal essence coincide. The simple idea of whiteness is the nominal essence of whiteness—it is that to which the word 'whiteness' is annexed—but it is also the real essence of whiteness: there is nothing in this idea beyond what we are aware of and thus associate with the name. Equally a simple mode like *triangle* or *circle*, being only a slightly complex idea of extension, consists precisely of those features by which we recognize something as a triangle or a circle, and it is from these fully known features that its further geometrical properties flow: being a plane closed figure with three straight sides is therefore the real as well as the nominal essence of a triangle. Again, a mixed mode, that is a complex abstract idea built up out of simple ideas of different sorts, such as the idea of murder, or incest, or of a procession, likewise consists of ideas of just those characteristics that we have arbitrarily put together in framing this complex idea:

. . . these abstract *ideas* being the workmanship of the mind and not referred to the real existence of things, there is no supposition of anything more signified by that name, but barely that complex *idea* the mind itself has formed . . . and [this] is that on which all the properties of the *species* depend, and from which alone they all flow; and so in these the *real* and *nominal essence* is the same . . .[28]

This difference between substances on the one hand and simple ideas and modes on the other has, Locke thinks, an important bearing on 'the certain knowledge of general truth'. Demonstrative knowledge is possible (and has actually been achieved) in mathematics, including geometry, because the mathematician needs to consider only those constitutive properties of a circle or a rectangle which are included in his ideas of these figures: his resulting propositions are indeed true of real, objective things, but only in so far as these things agree with those archetypes in

[28] III. v. 14.

his mind.[29] And moral knowledge can similarly be achieved by demonstrations with regard to various mixed modes. 'For the *ideas* that ethics are conversant about being all real essences, and such as I imagine have a discoverable connexion and agreement one with another: so far as we can find their habitudes and relations, so far we shall be possessed of certain, real, and general truths . . .'[30] But with substances '. . . we are to take a quite contrary course, the want of *ideas* of their real *essences* sends us from our own thoughts to the things themselves as they exist. *Experience here must teach me* what reason cannot . . .' In other words, we simply have to observe what qualities and powers go along with what others.

There is much here that can be disputed. Admittedly if we stick to the ideas in each case, there is no room for a real essence separate from the nominal essence. But the word 'whiteness', by Locke's own account, refers to a power which has as its basis some arrangement and motion of the minute parts of the white surface: why should we not say that the real essence of whiteness is this basis, while the nominal essence, that to which we annex the word, is the power to produce in us the sensation of whiteness-as-we-see-it?[31] Following this train of thought, we should say that it is only with the primary qualities that real essence and nominal essence coincide. Again, the word 'suicide', though clearly the name of a mixed mode, is used to refer not merely to the complex *idea* of someone's killing of himself, or even to that combination of characteristics alone, but also to suicide as a concrete performance, a kind of behaviour, a socio-psychological phenomenon which may well have much more to it than is known automatically to everyone who uses the word correctly. Books are written about suicide, and they do not contain only analytic statements. Contrary to what Locke says, this idea is 'referred to the real existence of things', and there is the supposition of something more signified by the name—something more than the complex idea. Locke could no doubt reply that if we thus separate real and nominal essences in the case of simple ideas of secondary qualities and mixed modes, we are in effect treating these as sub-

[29] IV. iv. 6.

[30] IV. xii. 8. Cf. IV. iii. 18–20; IV. iv. 7–10, etc.

[31] Contrast III. viii. 1, where the 'essence of whiteness' (presumably both nominal and real) is said to be 'a power to produce the *idea* of whiteness in one whose eyes can discover ordinary objects'.

stances, and so we are if the term 'substance' is used in a broad sense, to cover any (objective) reality with a nature of its own which is not exhausted by the features used in our method of recognizing it. But to say this would be to make analytic the thesis that in substances, and only in substances, are real and nominal essences separate: to be a substance in the broad sense proposed is just to have a real essence that is other than or goes beyond the nominal essence. And the words used to refer to substances in this sense would include not only what Locke would ordinarily count as names of substances but also (in some uses) words and phrases that he would count as names of secondary qualities and mixed modes.

However, a distinction could still be drawn between the two groups of terms. Suppose that we treated suicide, for example, as such a quasi-substance, a socio-psychological entity with more to it than we ordinarily know, and suppose further that we succeeded in finding a real essence for it, that is, that we had framed and confirmed some fairly unitary theory of how and why suicides occur—always, perhaps, as the reaction of a certain sort of temperament to a certain kind of social pressure. If we then raised what we should then regard as the counterfactual possibility that someone might kill himself in different circumstances and for different reasons, we should not say 'But that wouldn't be suicide'. We should speak about the possibility of there being further kinds and causes of suicide, not about the possibility of there being a sort of self-killing that was not suicide. But with genuine substance-terms the case is different. If we have framed and confirmed a theory about the atomic structure of what we now recognize as gold, and then consider (regarding it still as counterfactual) the possibility that some material with a different atomic structure should mimic all the readily detectable properties and powers of gold, we are most likely to refer to this not as the possibility that there should be an additional kind of gold, but rather as the possibility that something which is not gold should be very like gold. In this respect there is a real difference between our handling of substance-terms and of the names of mixed modes even when they are treated as quasi-substances. Having extended not merely the distinction but also the separation, the non-coincidence, of real and nominal essences to such modes, we find that it is still to the nominal essence of a mixed mode like suicide that the name is firmly and unshakably annexed, even when we are considering counterfactual possibilities. But with substances the name is intended to be annexed not to the nominal but to the real essence. Hence when we consider a counterfactual possibility that splits the two apart, we let the name remain annexed to the real essence and be detached from the nominal essence.

Locke emphasizes the difference between the way in which we use the names of substances and that in which we use those of mixed modes with an amusing story of how Adam might have invented the Hebrew words *kinneah* (jealousy), *niouph* (adultery), and *zahab* (gold).[32] Adam thinks, wrongly as it turns out, that Lamech is troubled by suspicion of his wife's adultery, and invents the words *kinneah* and *niouph* with which to discuss the problem. Though in fact there was no adultery, nor even any suspicion of it (Lamech had quite a different worry), these words remain annexed to the complex ideas which Adam thus arbitrarily put together. But when one of Adam's children brings home a lump of gold and Adam names this substance *zahab*, he 'acts quite differently from what he did before in forming those *ideas* of mixed modes . . . For there he put *ideas* together only by his own imagination, not taken from the existence of anything . . . the standard there was of his own making. But . . . here he has a standard made by nature . . . He takes care that his *idea* be conformable to this *archetype*, and intends the name should stand for an *idea* so conformable.' So when he finds out more about this stuff, he adds the newly discovered qualities to the former idea, making them also part of the essence that the word *zahab* stands for. But this would commit him to saying that whatever qualities are ever in the future found in samples of the same stuff as this archetype must also form part of the essence of *zahab*, and hence that the idea of *zahab* that we have at any time (the nominal essence) will always be inadequate. It will also follow that different speakers will associate the word *zahab* with different nominal essences: 'the *names of substances* would not only have (as in truth they have) but would also be supposed to *have different significations as used by different men*'. Locke thinks that it is in a vain attempt to avoid this that men have supposed a real essence for every species, from which all its properties flow and 'would have their name of the species stand for that'.

[32] III. vi. 44–51.

This story is illuminating, but also a bit misleading. The key difference is not that with *zahab* Adam had a standard made by nature, but not with *kinneah* and *niouph*. He might have had standards for these too made by nature: adultery and jealousy are not always imaginary. What matters is that for the meaning and use of *kinneah* and *niouph* it makes no difference whether Adam had an objective standard or not, because with these on the one hand and *zahab* on the other his intentions were different. He intended *zahab* to stand for *that stuff, whatever properties and constitution it may turn out to have*; but he did not intend *kinneah* to stand for *the sort of trouble, whatever it may turn out to be, from which Lamech is suffering,* nor *niouph* for *whatever Adah has been up to lately*. But of course Adam's intentions about *zahab* would have been to some extent frustrated if his children had brought him samples of several different metals and he, failing to distinguish them, had given the name *zahab* to them all. The successful use of a substance-name rests on the contingent fact that either such mistakes have not occurred (or have been progressively corrected) or the differences of constitution are not too great; we can tolerate different isotopes of the same element.

7. *Locke's anticipation of Kripke*

That we handle the names of substances in this way is rather embarrassing for Locke. He recognizes this tendency, but deplores it. He admits that we intend that such names should stand for real essences, but thinks that we cannot really achieve this, and that we ought to be content to let them stand only for nominal essences. In dealing with this problem Locke made, but set aside, a discovery about an ordinary use of language which has only recently (and independently) been made again by Saul Kripke.[33]

Locke thinks that we can annex words only to features with which we are acquainted, so that the word 'gold', for example, can be associated only with the nominal essence, the set of characteristics which enable us to recognize as gold anything which possesses them. He sees, however, that the nominal essence of gold, and, in consequence, the meaning of 'gold', will differ from one speaker to another, and for the same speaker at different

---

[33] Saul Kripke, 'Naming and Necessity', in *Semantics of Natural Language*, ed. D. Davidson and G. Harman, pp. 253-355, esp. pp. 315-16 and 319-21.

times. Children may recognize gold simply by the shining yellow colour, and then this will be all that the word 'gold' signifies to them, so that in their language they rightly call parts of a peacock's tail gold.[34] Others may include weight, malleability, fusibility; some will and some will not include solubility in *aqua regia*, and so on. But then, it seems, different speakers talking to one another and all using this same word 'gold' will be talking at cross purposes. Locke half sees the solution to this problem, but repeatedly draws back from it. He admits that *'nature makes many particular things, which do agree* one with another in many sensible qualities, and probably too in their internal frame and constitution' —that is, there are natural kinds. But, he hastens to add '. . . it is not this real essence that distinguishes them into *species*: it is *men* who . . . *range them into sorts* . . . according to their conformity to this or that abstract *idea* . . .'[35] 'But', he says, 'though these *nominal essences of substances* are made by the mind, they are *not* yet *made so arbitrarily as those of mixed modes* . . . the mind, in making its complex *ideas* of substances, only follows nature and puts none together which are not supposed to have a union in nature.' And this is necessary for communication: '. . . if they will be understood when they speak of things really existing, men must in some degree conform their *ideas* to the things they would speak of; or else men's language will be like that of *Babel* and every man's words, being intelligible only to himself, would no longer serve to conversation and the ordinary affairs of life . . .'[36] That is, for communication men need a public language and must avoid talking at cross purposes, and the existence of natural kinds gives them the means to achieve this. Since there is a great cluster of properties that go together in gold, different speakers using different criteria of recognition may still pick out very largely the same things. A fairly well-marked-off denotation for the term 'gold' makes up for the differences in connotation, and specimens from this denotation are what we rely upon in the teaching and learning of the use of the word. It does not matter that different speakers have different nominal essences so long as they are led by them to recognize as gold much the same set of parcels of material.

But since this is how language flourishes, it is not surprising

[34] III. vi. 31; III. ix. 17.   [35] III. vi. 36.
[36] III. vi. 28.

that people should intend their words to belong to the real essences rather than to the nominal essences which may well vary from speaker to speaker. Locke stresses this intention in two chapters which deal with the 'imperfection' and the 'abuse' of words.[37]

... when a man says *gold is malleable*, he means and would insinuate something more than this, that *what I call gold is malleable* (though truly it amounts to no more), but would have this understood, viz. that *gold*, i.e. *what has the real essence of gold, is malleable* ... It is true, the names of substances would be much more useful . . . were the real essences of substances the *ideas* in our minds which those words signified . . . therefore the mind, to remove that imperfection as much as it can, makes them, by a secret supposition, to stand for a thing having that real essence . . . there is scarce any body in the use of these words but often supposes each of those names to stand for a thing having the real essence . . . Which is so far from diminishing the imperfection of our words that by a plain abuse it adds to it, when we would make them stand for something which, not being in our complex *idea*, the name we use can no ways be the sign of . . . though in that called *gold*, one puts into his complex *idea* what another leaves out . . . yet men do not usually think that therefore the species is changed, because they secretly in their minds refer that name and suppose it annexed to a real immutable essence . . . But . . . by this tacit reference to the real essence the word *gold* (which, by standing for a more or less perfect collection of simple *ideas*, serves to design that sort of body well enough in civil discourse) comes to have no signification at all, being put for somewhat whereof we have no *idea* at all, and so can signify nothing at all when the body itself is away . . . it will be found a quite different thing to argue about *gold* in name and about a parcel of the body itself, v.g. a piece of *leaf-gold* laid before us . . .[38]

If, as Locke here admits, speakers commonly intend substance-names to refer to the real essences or internal constitutions, it will follow, as he also notes, that those using different criteria of recognition for some stuff will not be talking at cross purposes: the species is not thereby changed. But it is also a consequence of

[37] III. ix and x. These two fascinating chapters are omitted altogether from the abridgement of the *Essay* by A. S. Pringle-Pattison, 'as containing nothing of philosophical importance that does not occur elsewhere in the *Essay*', and the key passages for the present topic are very inadequately represented in other widely used abridgements. Similar but less explicit remarks do occur in II. xxxi. 6 and, as noted above, in III. vi. 44–51. But III. x. 17–20 are particularly well worth reading in full and with close attention.

[38] III. x. 17–19.

our using the word 'gold' with this intention that if we contemplate the counterfactual possibility that something with this same internal constitution was (through some change in other things or in the laws of nature) not shining yellow in colour, not malleable, not fusible, not soluble in *aqua regia*, and so on, and contemplate it *as counterfactual*, we would express this by saying that *gold* might not be yellow, etc., whereas if we contemplate the counterfactual possibility that something with a different internal constitution had all these features, we would say not that (some) gold might have a different internal constitution, but only that something else might look and behave like gold. Kripke has argued just this, that if gold does in fact have atomic number 79, it is not possible that *gold* should have a different atomic number, though it is possible that gold should lack the features by which we now recognize it, and that some other substance should have them.[39] The kind of possibility Kripke is speaking of is sharply distinguished from epistemic possibility. It is of course epistemically possible that gold does not have atomic number 79: the physical chemists may be wrong. But our way of using substance-names like 'gold' is such that if we assume that gold in fact has atomic number 79—that is, the atomic structure indicated by that number—we shall describe the above-mentioned possibilities, considering them as counterfactual, in the ways described. Locke does not really give any evidence that we use substance-names in this way: he just asserts, rightly, that we do. Kripke has supplied a test which confirms that we do have the intention that Locke says we have, namely seeing how we handle these terms in relation to neutrally described possibilities while we consider them as counterfactual. If in these we keep the word 'gold' attached to the internal constitution and let it be separated from the present criteria of recognition, this is evidence that our intention even in ordinary circumstances is to 'annex' this word to that internal constitution. What we can call in Kripke's theory the necessities of constitution are not epistemic, not a matter of *a priori* knowledge, and not analytic; they do not arise from our having included 'having atomic number 79' in the meaning of the term 'gold'; yet they are in a remoter way based on the use of language. They arise from and reflect our intention of using a substance-name, say 'gold', to refer to the stuff with the internal constitution,

[39] Op. cit.

whatever it may be, of which what we recognize (using our various ordinary criteria) as pieces of gold are samples.

Though Locke correctly reports this way of using substance-names, he disapproves of it. He thinks that though it would be advantageous to use such terms to refer to real essences if we knew them, if we had clear and adequate ideas of them in our minds, it is a mistake, an abuse of words, to try to do this when we lack these ideas: we cannot 'remove that imperfection' by merely intending to refer to an unknown real essence. Yet he sees that it has some point, in that it makes it possible for different speakers not to be at cross purposes even though they have different nominal essences in mind. Again, he thinks that this way of speaking is all right if we have a piece of gold actually in front of us to refer to: we can then meaningfully say 'that stuff'. What he fails to see is that we can still do this meaningfully when we have no gold in front of us: we can introduce the stuff by way of the criteria of recognition, and yet annex the word by way of them to that stuff and not to those criteria.

No doubt we could, alternatively, do what Locke thinks we ought to do, namely annex the word 'gold' to some nominal essence, that is, make 'is gold' simply *mean*, say, 'is shining yellow, heavy, malleable, fusible, and soluble in *aqua regia*'. Why don't we? What are the relative merits of the alternative linguistic policies? Locke sees that our ordinary practice rests on the belief that there are natural kinds, that nature works regularly. But he fails to see that the complexities, the apparent failures, of this regularity give extra point to our ordinary practice. What a nuisance it would be if a discoloured piece of gold could not be called gold, or if a sufficiently convincing counterfeit diamond had to be called a diamond. Sorts of substance do have internal constitutions, the causal relationships between these and the more immediately detectable features and operations are complex, so that those we have been relying on can be upset, but in the end and for most purposes, practical and even commercial as well as scientific, it is the internal constitutions that matter far more than whatever we have so far used as criteria for recognition. We can hope to explain the complicated behaviour of things in changing circum-stances by reference to a constant internal constitution: the general concept of stuffs whose identity is given by that constitution is justified by its usefulness as a framework for detailed explanations.

Admittedly such justification in detail has come mainly since Locke's time, by the progress of physics along lines about which Locke, as we shall see, was pessimistic. But even prior to such successes, even merely as a regulative ideal, this concept is useful. Though, as Locke insists, our superficial classifications may cut across initially unknown likenesses and differences of internal constitution, once we have the intention of tying substance-names to real essences we can gradually bring our classifications nearer to this ideal. Though such difficulties may initially 'frustrate the expectation and labour of very wary chemists', the chemists in time become still more wary and are no longer frustrated.[40]

On the other hand, the practice Locke recommends would go naturally with a phenomenalist metaphysics that made the superficial appearances of things ontologically primary. Again, it would go with a view which has been put forward by Popper, that *all* physical properties are dispositional.[41] For this would undermine the distinction between powers or dispositions and the internal constitution from which they arise, and so would leave us no reason for tying substance-names to the latter. It is the realism that rejects these views, and the practical usefulness and fruitfulness of the notion of as yet unknown internal constitutions of things, that together establish the superiority of the practice which Locke recognizes but condemns to that which he recommends. And Kripke's necessities of constitution are a consequence of that superior practice.

In fact Locke is here once again subject to tension of the sort mentioned above.[42] His correct perception of how our language works pulls him in one direction, his belief that we can annex words only to features with which we are acquainted, that they become meaningless if they are not associated with clear and adequate ideas, pulls him in the other. I think there is more merit in the realism associated with Locke's perception of the actual working of our language than in the extreme empiricism that has influenced many of his philosophical successors.

---

[40] III. vi. 8; cf. III. x. 20. Locke hints vaguely at this sort of progress in III. xi. 24: '. . . we are not always to rest in the ordinary complex *idea* commonly received as the signification of that word, but must go a little further and inquire into the nature and properties of the things themselves . . .'

[41] S. Körner (ed.), *Observation and Interpretation in the Philosophy of Physics* p. 70; K. R. Popper, *The Logic of Scientific Discovery* (Second English Edition), p. 425.

[42] Section 3 of this chapter, pp. 80-2

However, the distinction to which Locke rightly, though reluctantly, draws attention does not quite coincide with his division between substances on the one hand and modes and relations on the other. An artefact—for example, a table—is a substance, but the names of artefacts behave more like the names of mixed modes than like those of natural kinds. Artefact-names are typically annexed to the performance of functions, and these are fully determined by conscious human purposes. We *determine* everything that is essential to being a table, just as we determine everything that is essential to being suicide or *kinneah* or *niouph*; we do not *find out*, bit by bit, and perhaps always incompletely, what is essential to being a table as we find out what is essential to being gold. On the other hand, some modes have hidden essential natures which we have to discover. Leibniz pointed out that even a geometrical figure, say a parabola, can be defined by some superficial features but will have initially hidden essential properties[43] (such as being the locus of points equidistant between the focus and the directrix). Still closer in use to the names of natural kinds which are substances are the names of processes like rusting. If our archetypes or typical specimens of rusting are in fact oxidation of iron, then if any process, however superficially like rusting it was, were not the oxidation of iron it would not be rusting; that is, by Kripke's test 'rusting' is intended to be annexed to the real essence of the process, not to any nominal essence. But this does not hold for all names of natural kinds of process. 'Sleep', I think, is annexed rather to its nominal essence: anything that had the symptoms by which we recognize sleep would *be* sleep, whatever its physiological basis, and if what in fact produces those symptoms had not produced them (if the relevant laws of nature had been different) it would not have been sleep. The names of diseases and ailments also seem to fall into two classes: 'malaria' is annexed to its real essence, and probably was so annexed even before its real essence (the precise nature of the infection, the malarial parasite) was known, but 'jaundice' is annexed to a group of symptoms. 'Measles' and 'schizophrenia' are like 'malaria': though these illnesses are identified by sets of symptoms which pick out paradigm cases, these names are intended to refer not to the set of symptoms but to whatever underlying physical or mental condition commonly produces

[43] Leibniz, *New Essays*, commentary on III. x. 19.

those symptoms: this same condition would still be measles (or schizophrenia) even if for some reason it failed, in a particular patient, to produce the usual symptoms. Is it important that there are a measles virus and a malaria parasite, that is, that though these diseases are not substances, each is related to a sort of substance? I think not: there is no schizophrenia microbe. What such examples show is that it is not the difference between substances and non-substances that matters here, in the sense of the distinction between items which are supposed to 'subsist by themselves' and items which are not, but rather the difference between cases where it is useful or fruitful to think and speak preferentially of a possibly unknown or inadequately known 'nature' and cases where it is more appropriate to concentrate attention on a *syndrome*, a collection of symptoms or superficially observable features.

8. *The possibility of explanatory science*

Locke displays a curious mixture of optimism and pessimism about the prospects of an explanatory science centred on real essences. He repeatedly says that real essences are, in his time, unknown; he also sometimes suggests that this ignorance is incurable. But he thinks that, if we did detect the internal constitutions of things, we could then infer *a priori* the properties and powers to which they give rise. Our want of precise ideas of the primary qualities of the insensible corpuscles 'keeps us in an incurable ignorance . . .' But 'if we could discover the figure, size, texture, and motion of the minute constituent parts of any two bodies, we should know without trial several of their operations one upon another, as we do now the properties of a square or a triangle. Did we know the mechanical affections of the particles of *rhubarb*, *hemlock*, *opium*, and a *man* . . . we should be able to tell beforehand that *rhubarb* will purge, *hemlock* kill, and *opium* make a man sleep: as well as a watchmaker can that a little piece of paper laid on the balance will keep the watch from going till it be removed . . . The dissolving of silver in *aqua fortis* and gold in *aqua regia*, and not *vice versa*, would be then perhaps no more difficult to know than it is to a smith to understand why the turning of one key will open a lock and not the turning of another.' As it is, we can find out such operations only by trial, and 'whether they will succeed again another time, we cannot be certain'. *A posteriori* knowledge is plagued by doubts about induction.[44] We may be able to advance 'useful and experimental philosophy in physical things', but, Locke fears, 'scientifical philosophy will still be out of our reach'.[45] That is, we may be able empirically to learn of concomitances of features which will be of practical use; but we shall not achieve an explanatory science providing 'certainty and demonstration'. But this is not because such an explanatory science is in principle impossible, but merely because of our contingent limitations, in particular our lack of ultra-microscopic eyes. However, Locke is inclined to take these limitations as decisive, and therefore although he adopts the corpuscularian theory in principle, he does not see physical science as centred upon it. As Yolton stresses, the kind of physical science in which Locke was most interested and for whose progress he had the strongest hopes was the careful observation and experimental discovery of coexistences of properties, not the detailed working-out of the corpuscular hypothesis.[46]

Looking back after nearly three centuries of scientific advance, we can easily see where Locke was mistaken about these issues. Chemists and physicists have achieved the sort of detailed knowledge of microstructure of which Locke despaired, and they have achieved it not, in the main, by devising more powerful microscopes but by framing and testing detailed hypotheses, a method whose power and value Locke did not realize. In fact his philosophy of science in this respect failed to keep up with the science of his own time, let alone anticipate the future advances of physics: some of the contemporaries whom he knew and respected were beginning to use the hypothetico-deductive method in the sort of way that has been so fruitful, but Locke was still reacting so strongly against the deductive pseudo-science of 'the Schools' that he stressed rather the careful collection of directly observed facts—which of course was also a large part of the work of the scientists of the Royal Society.

Locke's pessimism, then, was unfounded; but was his optimism unfounded too? Was he wrong in his hypothetical claim that *if* we could detect microstructure we could base on it *a priori*, demonstrative, and certain knowledge of how things would interact,

---

[44] IV. iii. 25; IV. vi. 7–9.   [45] IV. iii. 26.

[46] J. W. Yolton, *Locke and the Compass of Human Understanding*, esp. Chapter 2.

with medical as well as chemical applications? The currently orthodox view is, of course, that this is wrong, that the fundamental laws of physical processes and interactions are not only synthetic but empirical, that it is a mistake to look for necessity or *a priori* knowability in the subject-matter of physics. But while I subscribe to this orthodoxy, I think it would be unfair to Locke to leave the issue there. After all, what he most clearly asserts in such passages as those I have quoted is that if we could detect microstructure our knowledge of the operations of materials on one another would be *as a priori, as* certain and demonstrative, as interpreted geometry and applied mechanics are. Now if the micro-operations had been purely mechanical, as the corpuscular hypothesis supposed, this would obviously have been correct. Even if the micro-operations include, for example, electromagnetic interactions, the laws governing them may well be *as* 'intelligible' as those of mechanics: what goes on may be built up largely of persistences, qualitative continuities, and such very simple relations as the cancelling-out of units of positive and negative charge. Locke was in principle right in not drawing a line between interpreted geometry and mechanics on the one hand and what we might call, in recognition of his 'extravagant conjecture',[47] angelic chemistry and medicine on the other—that is, the conceivable but, he thought, to us contingently impossible sciences based on detailed knowledge of microstructure. Where he was wrong was in thinking all of these more intelligible than they are, and this is an error with respect to, say, Euclidean geometry that many of his successors have shared. A geometry can be made deductively watertight, so that its theorems follow by purely logical derivations from its axioms and definitions; but what is then logically true is not its theorems but its theorem-hypotheticals, that is, statements of the form 'If (the conjunction of all the axioms and definitions) then (the theorem)'. But whether the axioms are true of the concrete empirical things that constitute the intended interpretation of the system—for example, straight lines as determined by light-paths in the absence of interfering bodies or by stretched strings or by coincidences of surfaces of rigid but movable bodies—is a purely empirical question, and the derivation of theorems from axioms ensures that theorems are true of the intended interpretation only on condition that the

[47] II. xxiii. 13.

axioms are so.[48] That is, interpreted geometry is at best empirically true, not, as so many thinkers have supposed, *a priori* or intelligible; it is in the same category as mechanics, whose empirical character has been generally recognized. A very charitable reading of IV. iv. 6 would allow us to ascribe the correct view of geometry to Locke himself: 'The mathematician considers the . . . properties belonging to a rectangle or circle only as they are in *idea* in his own mind . . . real things are no further concerned . . . than as things really agree to those archetypes in his mind'. If we take these ideas or archetypes not as spatial images but as abstract sets of features constituted by the axioms of some geometrical system, then what Locke says here gives a correct account of truth in geometry. But with a less charitable and more natural reading Locke's mistake would still not have been, as is commonly thought, in failing to draw a line between geometry on the one hand and mechanics and even angelic chemistry and medicine on the other, but merely in supposing all of them together to be more *a priori* than they are.

Besides, while Locke suggests that it is only contingent limitations that prevent us from achieving rational, demonstrative knowledge of *some* of the operations and interactions of things, he also suggests that there are some areas in which such rational, demonstrative knowledge is (for us) unattainable in principle. One of his rare excursions into speculative physics is an ingenious regress argument to show that we could never rationally explain the cohesion of all material bodies.[49] The communication of motion by impulse, he maintains, is also incomprehensible, and it seems that this would remain an irreducible brute element no matter how much microstructure we could discover.[50] Nor could we ever discover a necessary connection between our ideas of secondary qualities and the primary qualities of invisible material particles that immediately give rise to them: God has 'annexed' these effects to their causes, but there is no connection here that could ever be intelligible to us.[51]

[48] See, for example, E. Nagel, *The Structure of Science*, pp. 219–31 and my 'Proof', *Aristotelian Society Supplementary Volume*, xl (1966), pp. 23–38, esp. pp. 23–5.
[49] II. xxiii. 23–4.   [50] II. xxiii. 28.
[51] IV. iii. 13; cf. II. viii. 13.

9. *The essentiality of essences*

So far we have been using the phrases 'real essence' and 'nominal essence' just as technical terms, as synonyms for 'internal constitution on which a thing's more readily detectable properties and powers depend' and 'set of criteria of recognition'. But is there any point in calling either of them an *essence*? In what sense are the properties thus referred to any more essential to the things than any other properties they happen to possess? Some feature is thought of as being essential if it is supposed to belong to the very being of the thing for which it is essential, without which it would not be that thing. But this is obscure and indeterminate until we have clarified the notion of *being that thing*. Essentiality is relative to identity. Identity divides into generic identity (identity of kind) and numerical identity (identity of an individual). The identity of individuals, and the associated question of what is essential to an individual as such, will be considered in Chapter 5; for the present we can confine ourselves to what is essential to things as being of this or that kind. We should then expect the 'nominal essence' of gold to be that without which a thing would not be *called* gold, while its 'real essence' would be that without which it would not really *be* gold.

This makes it clear in what sense the set of criteria of recognition are the nominal essence. For any one speaker, whatever he uses as this set of criteria for gold will indeed be that the lack of which will prevent him from calling something gold. Yet this is not the whole of the relevant truth. In the public use of the language, we have the notion of things being called gold correctly or incorrectly: our one speaker's criteria may on some occasion have misled him. And to be correctly called gold is not even to be such as to be recognized as gold by the majority of the speakers of the language. In view of the Kripkean point discussed in Section 7, to be correctly called gold is to have whatever internal constitution the ordinary specimens of this stuff have in common: it is part of the meaning of such substance-names that they are intended to be annexed to internal constitutions. So that what Locke calls the real essence of gold in a way deserves the title of 'nominal essence' rather better than does any set of criteria of recognition. These criteria would be strictly the nominal essence only if the name were unshakeably annexed to them, as is the case with the names of mixed modes like suicide.

In what sense is the internal constitution of gold that without which it would not really *be* gold? An internal constitution is not, of course, unchangeable: water can be divided into two gases, and radium will gradually change into lead: real essences have no necessity of continued existence. The most obvious sense of 'it would not really *be* gold' is the one already noted, 'it would not be correctly called gold, in accordance with the notion of correctness embodied in our standard intended use of substance-names'. It is after all a linguistic fact which makes even a 'real essence' essential. But this dictum requires some qualification. Underlying and giving point to this linguistic practice is the non-linguistic fact that there are natural kinds, of which what we recognize as gold is one: there are, as we have noted, clusters of readily detectable properties and powers; and the internal constitution is what causally gives rise to these: it is that without which there would not be this particular cluster of observable features. But the connections between the internal constitution and the observable features are, as we saw in Section 8, not even in principle quite as intelligible as Locke thought.

10. *Conclusion*

It seems, then, that much, though not all, of Locke's view of substance and real essence and nominal essence can be defended. Rejecting the notion of a substratum underlying all properties and the logico-linguistic argument by which it is introduced, we can retain not only the objective reality of particular substances but also the reasonable postulation of internal constitutions and in particular of real essences of natural kinds including some modes as well as many, but not all, substances. These can, moreover, play a bigger part than Locke thought both in the meaning of words and in science. He was too ready to confine physical science to ground-floor empirical observation of sequences and coexistences, and to restrict the meanings of words to sets of criteria of recognition. Science has achieved detailed knowledge of real essences by the use of the hypothetico-deductive method, and there is an important and valuable use of language by which words can be annexed by way of sets of criteria of recognition—

which need not be the same for different speakers—not to those sets of criteria themselves but to the underlying but initially unknown internal constitution. Yet it is to Locke's credit that he recognized this use of language, though he disapproved of it, and that he stated a philosophical theory which left room for scientific advances that he did not himself expect. Whereas later philosophers have often condemned him for not being empirical enough, his main mistakes on these topics resulted from too simple and extreme an empiricism, from tying words and theories too closely to clear and adequate ideas that can be acquired in direct observation, and this can be understood and partly excused as a reaction against the procedures of 'the Schools'.

4

ABSTRACT IDEAS AND UNIVERSALS

1. *Locke's basic account of abstraction*

LOCKE's account of abstract general ideas was, like his account of substance, the target of one of Berkeley's keenest attacks. But the passage which Berkeley used for his 'killing blow' is not that in which Locke gave his positive theory of abstraction: indeed one could never find it by looking through Locke's chapter- and section-headings for references to generality or to abstract ideas.[1] It is buried in a chapter in which Locke is discussing the 'Maxims' which were believed to be innate principles on which our knowledge is based, such tautologies or near tautologies as 'Whatever is, is' and 'It is impossible for the same thing to be and not to be'. It is while arguing, rightly, that these are not the foundation of our knowledge that Locke stresses the extreme abstractness of their terms and the difficulty of the process of abstraction that would lie behind them. He is here, for this purpose, denigrating abstraction, and it is hardly to be expected that this passage would display fairly and adequately his own positive theory of abstraction. It can indeed be interpreted in the light of that theory, but only after we have understood it as it is put forward more explicitly elsewhere.

But one preliminary difficulty must be faced. The over-all subject of Book III, where most of what Locke says about abstraction is to be found, is 'Words', and the general theory of language to which the account of abstract ideas is intended to contribute is that 'The use . . . of words is to be sensible marks of *ideas*, and the *ideas* they stand for are their proper and immediate signification.'[2] This view, that the meanings of words are to be found in ideas, would be almost universally rejected by contemporary philosophers

---

[1] This is pointed out clearly and correctly by Aaron (*John Locke*, pp. 195–207), who also quotes from Berkeley's *Commonplace Book* his decision 'To bring the killing blow at the last e.g. in the matter of abstraction to bring Locke's general triangle at the last'. It will be obvious that my discussion in this chapter owes a lot to Aaron's treatment. Locke's remark is in IV. vii. 9, and is quoted in Berkeley's *Principles*, Introduction, § 13. See note 13 on p. 115 below.

[2] III. ii. 1.

of language,[3] and it might be thought that Locke's basic assumptions have by now been so thoroughly refuted that nothing that he has to say on these topics can deserve much attention. However, the ambiguity of the term 'idea' and the looseness with which Locke uses it are here something of an advantage. The thesis that would really be indefensible is that the meaning of every word or phrase is some mental image with which it is associated, but Locke does not as a rule write as if he believed this. As we saw when we were discussing nominal essences in Chapter 3, although Locke says that the nominal essence to which a substance-name is annexed is our idea of a set of properties, it would serve most of his purposes at least as well if we identified the nominal essence with the set of properties: the point of speaking of the idea here is merely to insist that the properties with which a word is thus associated must be ones of which the speaker is fairly directly aware. We have, indeed, found reason to question the degree of empiricism which makes Locke unwilling to admit that words can be usefully annexed to reasonably postulated real essences, but his important theses have very little to do with any suggestion that words stand for or refer to mental images or that meanings are to be studied by an investigation of the imagery associated with words. Locke's stress on ideas does exert some cramping influence on his discussion, as we shall see, but in general it amounts to little more than a quite appropriate requirement that we should be able to sketch some intelligible account of the thought processes that underlie our use of words of various sorts.

But what problem is the account of abstraction intended to solve? It is meant to explain how we are able to use general words—simple descriptive adjectives like 'white', names of simple modes like 'triangle', of mixed modes like 'manslaughter' or 'procession', substance-names like 'horse' or 'gold' and still more general ones like 'animal' and 'metal', and so on—and how we are able to frame general statements about kinds of things and to reason with regard to them. Talk about abstract ideas and about the operations that produce them and are performed on them is meant to describe the thinking that makes possible the use of words of these kinds. But although 'words' are the over-all subject of Book III, language use is no longer the specific subject

[3] e.g. M. Dummett, *Frege—Philosophy of Language*, pp. 157-9.

of the discussions about abstraction: thought processes are now the specific subject, and the uses of language are only a symptom of that subject. The use of general signs—which need not be words, and are not, for example, in 'men who through some defect in the organs want words'—is evidence that their users have 'universal *ideas*'; it is because non-human animals do not use any general signs that Locke infers that they do not have universal ideas, and lack the faculty of abstracting that would produce them.[4]

The thought processes in question are of several kinds. They include the recognition of things as being of certain sorts, shown in the application of general terms to things when those things are present, and thinking about things, especially when they are absent. They make possible, and enter into, communication between people. But underlying this psychological problem of the capacity to generalize there is the traditional problem of universals: just what place does generality have in the world? This is a topic which I shall take up in the second half of this chapter.

Generality is seen by Locke as a problem because while he recognizes that most words are general, he assumes that 'all things that exist are only particulars': where then can we find 'those general natures they are supposed to stand for'?[5] General ideas are offered as a bridge between particular things and general words, and abstraction is suggested as what makes ideas general.

Locke's basic theory of abstraction and generality is stated thus:[6]

. . . the mind makes the particular *ideas* received from particular objects to become general; which is done by considering them as they are in the mind such appearances, separate from all other existences and the circumstances of real existence, as time, place, or any other concomitant *ideas*. This is called ABSTRACTION, whereby *ideas* taken from particular beings become general representatives of all of the same kind; and their names, general names, applicable to whatever exists conformable to such abstract *ideas*. Such precise, naked appearances in the mind, without considering how, whence, or with what others they came there, the understanding lays up (with names commonly annexed to them) as the standards to rank real existences into sorts, as they agree

[4] II. xi. 10–11.   [5] III. iii. 6.
[6] II. xi. 9. Cf. III. iii. 1–12; II. vi. 32.

with these patterns, and to *denominate* them accordingly. Thus the same colour being observed today in chalk or snow, which the mind yesterday received from milk, it considers that appearance alone, makes it a representative of all of that kind; and having given it the name *whiteness*, it by that sound signifies the same quality wheresoever to be imagined or met with; and thus universals, whether *ideas* or terms, are made.

In other words, I see a white piece of paper at a particular time and place, and notice that it resembles in colour other pieces of paper, cups of milk, fields covered with snow, and so on; I pay attention to the feature in which it resembles these other things and pay no attention to the shape or size of the piece of paper or its surroundings or even to the time at which I see it; I remember this feature and associate the word 'whiteness' with it—and, what is really prior to this, though Locke does not mention it here, I associate the predicate expression 'is white' with the paper's having of this feature—and I am thus ready to use the same word 'whiteness' with respect to that same feature in any other things at any other places and times, and to apply this predicate expression to them. This readiness to use these expressions about other cases can be described by saying that I take the whiteness I am seeing in this piece of paper, with which I initially associate the expressions, as a representative of the whitenesses of all other white things. It is thus that this idea, though it is, like everything else, 'particular in its existence', is 'general in its signification', and similarly the particular word 'whiteness' (or phrase 'is white') is general by being able to be applied to any of the various white things. The general nature of words and ideas is 'nothing but the capacity they are put into, by the understanding, of signifying or representing many particulars . . . the signification they have is nothing but a relation that, by the mind of man, is added to them'.[7]

That is, Locke uses a theory of selective attention, aided by resemblances and comparisons, to explain how we have something in or before our minds with which we can distinctively associate a general expression, such as 'whiteness' or 'is white', and a theory of representation, of the capacity to signify many particulars, to explain in what way both what we have before our minds and the associated expressions are general or universal.

It is curious that Locke does not notice that what is now called

[7] III, iii, 11.

the type/token distinction applies to words and phrases: there are many tokens of the one type 'whiteness' or 'is white'. This would not in itself solve his present problem: the general significance of 'is white' (for example, in 'Anything that is white . . .') is not ensured or explained by there being many tokens of this one type, since there can equally be many tokens of a type-word that refers only to one individual thing. The problem is, how can I reason generally about white things while using one or two tokens of the type-word 'white'? But still the solution can be stated clearly only if this distinction is recognized: what Locke means to say is that a single token of 'is white' may represent or signify many particular white things, and that this signifying or representing consists in the fact that speakers of the language are prepared to apply to any appropriate particulars what they will recognize as other tokens of the same type as this one.

We may well question whether ideas are as essential as Locke supposed for bridging the gap between the particularity of things and the generality of words; for his own account presupposes that things themselves have common—and therefore surely general—features. This issue will be taken up in Sections 6 to 9 below. But whether they are or are not essential in a theory of meaning, there surely are thought processes underlying the use of general words, and as an account of those processes what Locke says seems unobjectionable and indeed at least broadly correct as far as it goes. It may be objected that it does not go far enough, that it takes for granted things that cry out for further analysis and explanation. It simply assumes that things resemble one another in various respects and that we can observe this, even when the two partially alike things are not present at once. But the traditional problem of universals arises when it is asked what it is for two things to resemble one another. This itself splits into two questions. Two things may resemble one another exactly in a certain respect—they may be, say, of just the same shade of red, or both perfectly spherical in shape—but things can also be described by the same adjective or referred to by the same common noun when they are not exactly alike in any respect in which they do not also exactly resemble many other things that are not so described. These two sorts of case constitute respectively what we may call the problem of exact universals and the problem of extended universals: some account is required of each, and presumably different accounts for the two. Again, philosophers have wondered how we remember something, for example the snow we saw yesterday, in order to be able to compare it with the piece of paper we see today. But Locke takes all this for granted. Though he says that '*general* and *universal* belong not to the real existence of things; but *are the inventions* and *creatures of the understanding*', and again that 'the *sorting* of [things] under names *is the workmanship of the understanding*', he states quite clearly that the mind has something real and natural to work from, namely the multitude of objective resemblances between things: the understanding is 'taking occasion, from the similitude it observes among [things]'.[8]

Locke's basic theory of abstraction, then, is that it consists in paying selective attention to one feature in a complex particular object of experience and ignoring the other features which are in fact occurring along with it, and in associating verbal expressions (or other signs) with the selected feature in such a way that one is ready to apply them to other objects that are like this one with respect to this one feature.

However, this basic account applies most naturally to such single-quality terms as 'white' and the ideas that go with them. It requires some development if it is to cope with our use of such words as 'triangle', 'manslaughter', 'horse', 'man', 'animal', 'metal', and to the ideas that go with these terms.

2. *Complex abstract ideas*

Locke says repeatedly that the mind can put together simple ideas in new ways and thus make complex ones: 'In this faculty of repeating and joining together its *ideas*, the mind has great powers in varying and multiplying the objects of its thoughts, infinitely beyond what *sensation* or *reflection* furnished it with'.[9] He constantly speaks about ideas as entities which can be compounded and decompounded, cut up, isolated, repeated, combined, rearranged, and so on, and he seems to regard this way of describing mental operations as unproblematic. For example, '*theft*, which being the concealed change of the possession of anything, without the consent of the proprietor, contains, as is visible, a combination of several *ideas* of several kinds . . .'[10] Thus we are led to

[8] III. iii. 11, 13.   [9] II. xii. 2.   [10] II. xii. 5.

imagine a set of instructions for framing the idea of, say, manslaughter which might run something like this:

Think of a human being—not a particular person, such as Plato or Queen Elizabeth, but a human being in general; you do this by cutting out and retaining your ideas of all those features in which all the human beings you know resemble one another, and throwing away your ideas of all the features in which they differ. Repeat the process, but so that you are now somehow thinking of two human beings, not of the same one twice. Now think of being dead. Now think of causing. Now put all these ideas together so that you are thinking of one human being's causing another human being's being dead. You now have the idea of homicide. Add the following ideas as qualifications . . . Now you have the idea of manslaughter.

It is obvious that no such set of instructions can be followed literally, though Locke, when he is reifying ideas, writes as if he thought they could. But there is a perfectly real and familiar process of which they could count as a metaphorical description, but which could be more literally described somewhat as follows, in terms of selective attention, the acquisition of capacities for recognizing, and the joint use of a number of such capacities:

Having paid attention to the various features in which human beings you have met or learned about resemble one another, and especially to the sub-set of these in which they differ from non-humans, and having associated the term 'human being' with these features (or, through them, with a supposed internal constitution from which they arise) you know what it is for something to be a human being; you can recognize human beings as such pretty well, though perhaps not infallibly. Also, you can distinguish one human being from another, most easily if they are present at the same time in different places: you know what it is for there to be two of them. Somewhat similarly you know what it is for something to be dead, and again what it is for someone to bring something about. Since you could use all these capacities together, you know what it is for one human being to bring about another human being's being dead, and you could check, though perhaps not conclusively, whether some sequence of events which you observe comes under this description. All this constitutes your having the idea of homicide. The addition, in the same general style, of suitable qualifications will give you the idea of man-slaughter.

Of course Locke does not say this explicitly, and what he does say is closer to our previous set of instructions. But this second account is the one which would harmonize better with Locke's basic account of abstraction in II.xi.9, and if we are fairly chari-table, but not absurdly so, we can read what he says about com-bining ideas to make complex abstract ideas as a metaphorical description of what is conveyed by our second account.

Something along these lines is needed to explain the construc-tion of new ideas: but some complex ideas will be based more directly on experience. Wherever we encounter in experience complex objects and processes of the right sorts, we can pre-sumably have complex abstract ideas by employing selective attention (with varying degrees of selectiveness) alone. One degree of selection yields the idea of a human being, a further selection, based on comparisons between men, horses, oysters, and so on yields the idea of an animal. To have the abstract general idea of a triangle is just to pay selective attention, in one observed triangle, to the set of features in which this figure resembles the various other figures that we would also call triangles, to re-member this set, to associate a word, say 'triangle', with it, and so to be ready to apply this word (that is, other tokens of this type-word) to other triangles. But this case differs from that of whiteness not only in that there is a set of features to be attended to, but also in that the relevant features call for checking against something like rules rather than for immediate qualitative recog-nition—they are that the figure has a closed boundary, made up of straight sides, and that there are just three of them. Other complex ideas are based on experience in a more subtle way. We learn the meaning of such terms as 'intelligent' from examples, and surely by some sort of selective attention, but not by learning rules that give necessary and sufficient conditions for intelligence.

Interpreting Locke's abstraction as selective attention would largely disarm Berkeley's criticisms. In fact Berkeley concedes that we may abstract in this sense:

And here it must be acknowledged, that a man may consider a figure merely as triangular, without attending to the particular qualities of the angles, or relations of the sides. So far he may abstract: but this will never prove that he can frame an abstract general inconsistent idea of a triangle. In like manner we may consider Peter so far forth as man, or so far forth as animal, without framing the forementioned abstract idea, either of man or of animal, inasmuch as all that is perceived is not considered.[11]

But what, then, are the abstract ideas that Berkeley is rejecting? It is *inconsistent* ones such as that of a triangle that is 'all and none of these [equilateral, scalene, etc.] at once', or of a man who has some colour but no particular colour, some stature but no particular stature, and so on. But these are not inconsistent as objects of consideration. I can consider a man as having stature without there being any particular stature that I consider him as having, and likewise for colour.[12] But if an idea had to be an image, then indeed this sort of abstractness would be impossible —though even images can have some degree of indeterminacy, as we shall note in Section 5 below. One could hardly have an image of a man with some colour but no particular colour, and one certainly could not have an image of a triangle that covered triangles of all possible proportions at once. Berkeley's valid objection here is to any attempt to combine a theory of abstract general ideas with an interpretation of all ideas as images. But if we think of having an idea as what is indicated by our selective attention account, Berkeley's objections dissolve.

We can now interpret the remark about the abstract idea of a triangle which seemed to give Berkeley his killing blow.[13] But as it is highly compressed, we must take it step by step. Locke means that we start by observing (and in this sense having ideas of) several different particular triangles, some equilateral, some scalene, some isosceles, some right-angled and some not, and so on. These complete particular ideas are inconsistent with one another. We take from these inconsistent ideas the parts in which

---

[11] *Principles*, Introduction, § 16. This remark was added in the Second Edition.

[12] Formally, 'I consider a man and I consider that there is some stature such that the man has that stature' does not entail 'I consider a man and there is some stature such that I consider that the man has that stature.' If Berkeley were arguing from the first to the second of these, he would be committing a fallacy similar to that which underlies *Principles*, § 23. Cf. Chapter 2, pp. 53–4 above.

[13] IV. vii. 9: '. . . the *general idea* of a triangle . . . must be neither oblique nor rectangle, neither equilateral, equicrural, nor scalenon; but all and none of these at once . . . it is something imperfect that cannot exist, an *idea* wherein some parts of several different and inconsistent ideas are put together.'

they all agree and put these parts (which are not inconsistent but merely repetitive) together. Taken literally, this would mean the procedure of cutting up and recombining ideas. But taken metaphorically, it just means selectively considering, and associating verbal expressions with, those features in which our different particular triangles are alike. Now this idea is the idea of something imperfect that cannot exist; nothing can merely have three straight sides without those sides being either equal or unequal. It cannot exist because this is a necessarily incomplete description, but not because it would be inconsistent even as an object of consideration, as it would be if it had to be equilateral *and* isosceles *and* scalene. But then why is it 'all and none of these at once'? Would not just 'none of these' have been more accurate? Yes, it would, and we must set down the 'all ... at once' as an unnecessary mistake: Locke was carried away in a dramatic exaggeration of the difficulties of abstraction. What he requires is merely that the abstract general idea should apply to or represent or signify all of these at once, and this it can do in two ways. By being an incomplete object of selective consideration, a set of features, it could actually apply to each of the mutually inconsistent particulars. And it could be that with which the word 'triangle' is associated in such a way that a speaker is ready to apply that word to any particular triangle.

It is sometimes suggested that Locke had two or more different theories of abstraction and generality. Thus Aaron finds (at least) three 'strands' in his thought which can be summed up by saying that they respectively identify a universal with (i) a particular idea that is made to stand for all other particular ideas of the same sort, (ii) what remains when many qualities have been eliminated from a particular appearance, for example when we have eliminated from the idea of Peter every quality that he has but some other men do not, (iii) a character or group of characters shared by particulars of the same sort.[14] But Aaron admits that he has to go to Berkeley for an explicit statement of the first 'strand', which never appears nakedly in the *Essay*, and even in the early draft which he quotes it is mixed up with what would count as strand (ii). I shall argue in Section 3 below that what Locke says about representation is not really an anticipation of Berkeley's view. Nor are strands (ii) and (iii) really distinguishable: eliminating Peter's

[14] R. I. Aaron, *John Locke*, pp. 197–203.

distinctive characters will leave behind those characters which he shares with other men: the only contrast to be drawn here is between those common characters as such and my idea of them in Peter. There could be a (largely verbal) dispute whether the title 'universal' is to be given to the characters themselves or to the idea of them that I have in and by selectively attending to them in Peter, but any complete theory of what is going on must recognize both the common characters and the selective attention or elimination by which I focus on them and so have something to which to annex the word 'man'.

Similarly Mabbott speaks of a 'Sign Theory' and a 'Resemblance Theory'. In the Sign Theory a general idea is an abstracted particular idea—say, the whiteness of this sheet of paper—made to stand for all other particular white things, while in the Resemblance Theory abstract general ideas 'are the *meanings* of general terms' and each of them is 'the quality or group of qualities common to a class of particulars.'[15] Mabbott admits that Locke is unaware of the difference between the two 'theories' and tends to run them together. But I think that Locke is right, that these are not rival theories but unavoidably complementary aspects of a single account. First, if Locke were writing carefully he could not say that abstract general ideas *are* common qualities, but only that they are the ideas of common qualities. Secondly, any idea that I have of the qualities common to men is either the content of my selective attention in, say, Peter to the features in which he resembles James, John, and so on, or the result of my 'combining' of a number of such abstracted contents. The very passages which Mabbott quotes as presenting the Resemblance Theory insist that in framing a general idea men 'make nothing new, but only leave out of the complex *idea* they had of *Peter* and *James, Mary* and *Jane,* that which is peculiar to each, and retain only what is common to them all'.[16] What is 'retained' is still 'particular in its existence', as the content of a particular experience, so Locke still needs the relation of representing or signifying to explain how this idea (as opposed to the corresponding quality) is general. Thus the Resemblance Theory would be incomplete, as an account of general ideas, without the Sign Theory. But equally the latter cannot even be stated without referring to resemblance, and the passage (from an early draft)

[15] J. D. Mabbott, *John Locke*, pp. 42–50.   [16] III. iii. 7 and 8.

which Mabbott quotes as presenting it mentions as having been received from paper, lilies, and so on 'the selfsame sort of ideas which perfectly agree with that . . . received from milk', and says that one idea 'becomes as it were a representative of all particulars *that agree with it*' (my italics).[17] The sign and resemblance 'theories' are, then, complementary parts of one account: the sign relation explains how an idea which in itself is particular can yet be general, while resemblance both guides our selective attention (or elimination) and determines what other particular ideas one particular idea is taken to represent.

It is true that Locke's account of general ideas is not absolutely unitary, but this is mainly because there are different sorts of general ideas which call for somewhat different treatment—simple ideas like that of whiteness, simple modes like the idea of a triangle, mixed modes like the idea of theft, the varying degrees of generality in the ideas of man and animal, and so on. There is also at least one point of strain, the question how far generality is the work of the mind, which I shall discuss in Section 9 below. Also, while Locke is consistently realist about resemblances, he also speaks sometimes about common qualities, so that there is some uncertainty whether his theory of objective universals is a pure resemblance theory or a mixture of this with an Aristotelian doctrine of real universals in things as common characters. We could discount his references to common qualities as careless use of an ordinary way of speaking, and take it that his intended strict theory is one of resemblances only; but if, as I shall argue in Section 8, Aristotelian realism is a correct account of part of the subject, it will not be surprising if Locke made inadvertent concessions to it. However, any hesitancies that there may be in Locke's theory of objective universals do not undermine the substantial unity of his account of abstract general ideas.

3. Berkeley's theory of generalization

In criticizing Locke on abstraction, Berkeley makes two concessions. One is that we can separate and recombine in thought parts of things which are in fact found already combined, but

---

[17] *Essay*, Draft C, quoted in Aaron, op. cit., p. 65.

which could exist separately; we can consider an eye or a hand separated from the rest of the body, and we can imagine centaurs and men with two heads. The other is that already mentioned, that we can consider a figure merely as triangular, and Peter merely as a man or merely as an animal. This latter concession recognizes the principles of selective attention, but Berkeley does not develop this into anything like the account of complex abstract ideas that I have offered as a reinterpretation of Locke. Berkeley keeps more closely than Locke does to a view of ideas as images, and therefore has a more acute problem of explaining how we can reason generally while using ideas that are purely particular. He solves his problem by making much fuller use of Locke's hint that an idea which is particular in its existence can be general in its signification by being set up as the representative of many particular things or ideas. Berkeley finds an illustration of this in the geometrical procedure (which goes back to Euclid and beyond) of proving a theorem with regard, say, to some particular triangle ABC of which a diagram is drawn, but then taking the theorem to have been proved generally because no use was made in the proof of any of the peculiar features of this particular triangle ABC—the sizes of its angles, the absolute or relative lengths of its sides, and so on were not mentioned in the proof. This procedure is comparable to algebraic proofs using 'x', 'y', etc. as variables which are taken to establish general truths about numbers, and again to the procedures formalized in modern logic under the title of natural deduction. This principle, that a particular idea of, say, a black straight line one inch long is made general by being used in a demonstration as a representative of all straight lines, is credited to Berkeley by Hume, who looks upon it as 'one of the greatest and most valuable discoveries that has been made of late years in the republic of letters'.[18] Hume is right to credit this to Berkeley rather than to Locke, because although the hint is there in Locke, it is used differently by the two philosophers. In Locke, it is the idea of the whiteness, in, say, a particular piece of paper that is used to represent the whiteness of other pieces of paper, of quantities of milk or snow, and so on; that is, something already abstracted (by elimination or selective attention) from a concrete particular represents or signifies other similar items. But in Berkeley it is the whole concrete

[18] *Treatise*, I. i. 7.

particular (idea) that represents other concrete particulars which are in some respect of the same sort as it. The point of Berkeley's treatment is that it shows how reasoning can be general although it has, as objects before the mind, only fully concrete particulars. The same is true of Hume's elaboration of Berkeley's view, in which an idea's being general in its representation is explained in terms of customs and habits by which other equally particular ideas are called up. The Berkeley–Hume theory is a theory of generalization without abstraction. It would have been a real alternative not, indeed, to a resemblance theory (for it too needs the notion of resemblances between particulars) but to the principle of elimination or omission which Aaron takes as the second strand in Locke's thinking.

What Berkeley and Hume thus draw attention to is an important class of reasoning procedures, but it has little to do with the meaningful use of general terms. In using, say, the word 'manslaughter' one does not need to have before one's mind a particular concrete homicide episode and to use this as a representative of other cases of manslaughter, being protected from wrongly ascribing to them whatever features are peculiar to this one by a tendency for other, different episodes to crowd into one's mind if one embarks on such a wrong ascription. For most general terms we need something more like the account which I have offered as a reinterpretation of Locke, centring on the notions of selective attention and capacities for recognition. Similarly Locke is nearer to the truth in saying that the whiteness that I observe and attend to in this sheet of paper represents the whiteness of other things than Berkeley or Hume would be in saying that what does the representing is my whole idea of this particular sheet of paper, with its size, shape, texture and so on thrown in as well as its colour, and that what is represented is all other white things, not merely their whitenesses. In so far as the Berkeley–Hume theory uses the notion of representation to defend an image theory of mental contents and operations, to maintain that the mind works always by having fully concrete particular ideas before it, it is a step in the wrong direction. What is of value in it is the admission of customs, habits, tendencies, and so on with which it is forced to supplement the mere having of images.

Berkeley criticizes a number of different kinds of alleged abstraction. We cannot, he thinks, abstract a thing's colour from its extension, or its motion from the rest of what constitutes a moving thing. Nor can we abstract colour in general from red, blue, white, etc., nor motion in general from specific determinate motions. We cannot frame the idea of a man who has some colour and some stature, but no particular colour or stature, or of an animal that has no particular shape or covering or spontaneous motion. We cannot abstract unity or number from countable things.[19] But though they are all different from one another, all these supposed kinds of abstraction have something in common: they would all conflict with the requirement that what is before the mind must be the idea of a complete concrete particular. But even this requirement, and the denial of all these kinds of abstraction, would not justify the use to which Berkeley puts his criticism of abstraction in §5 of the *Principles*: '. . . can there be a nicer strain of abstraction than to distinguish the existence of sensible objects from their being perceived . . .?' Its being perceived is not part of the idea of any complete concrete particular thing. And even if it were, Berkeley would have to withdraw the concession by which he allows selective attention if he were to make out, on this ground, a coherent case against the very conceivability of the extra-mental existence of sensible things.

4. *Abstract ideas of numbers*

What Locke says about ideas of numbers is best forgotten.[20] But we cannot altogether ignore the topic, since it has seemed not only to Berkeley but also to more recent thinkers a fatal counter-example to Locke's view of abstraction. 'We say one book, one page, one line; all these are equally units, though some contain several of the others.' The moral that Berkeley draws from this is that 'the same thing bears a different denomination of number, as the mind views it with different respects . . . Number is so visibly relative, and dependent on men's understanding, that it is strange to think how any one should give it an absolute existence without the mind.'[21] However, there is no need to drag the mind into it. The object just is one book, and contains three hundred and three pages, and twelve thousand or so lines, whether anyone is

---

[19] *Principles*, Introduction, §§ 8–10, main text, §§ 13, 120.
[20] II. xvi.   [21] *Principles*, § 12.

considering it or not. What matters is that counting requires count-nouns, that an object does not have number as an isolated charac-ter, but only in that there are here so many books, so many pages, so many lines. Number as a feature of an objective situation is essentially tied to some other suitable predicate. We encounter numbers first as exact numerical quantifiers—for example, 'There are four sheep in that field.'[22]

This would be fatal to a view of all abstract general ideas as images. It would make no sense to speak of an image of three-ness, or of three, that is not three of anything—not even three dots or three strokes—and that is not the symbol '3' (or 'III' or 'three') either. But is it equally damaging to a view of abstraction as selective attention? It shows that we could not attend *exclusively* to the feature of being three. We can note this feature only by taking some account also of some sort of thing that there are three of. But, first, this has no tendency to show that the selective attention account is wrong in those many other cases where obstacles of this kind do not arise. Secondly, we can compare cases where there are three men, three books, three coins, and so on, and pick out and attend to what these have in common, namely there being three somethings in each case, and so use it as the feature with which the quantifier 'There are three . . .' is associated. It is true that in the most elementary kind of arithmetical reasoning we shall use determinate somethings, we shall calculate with pebbles or fingers or strokes on paper, but using them, as Berkeley says, as representatives of all other sets of countable things, making no use in our calculations of their peculiar pro-perties as pebbles or fingers or strokes. In any more advanced reasoning, as Berkeley also says, we shall simply use signs in accordance with rules, though this need not make pure mathe-matics quite so 'jejune and trifling' a pursuit as Berkeley thought it.[23] Even in recognizing each of the common features of sets of same-numbered groups, as soon as we get beyond the number four or five, we shall have to use the procedure of counting, that is of correlating objects one-one with the words of some standard

---

[22] Cf. D. Bostock, *Logic and Arithmetic—Natural Numbers* pp. 4–6; G. Frege, review of Husserl's *Philosophie der Arithmetik*, quoted in *Philosophical Writings of Gottlob Frege*, eds. P. Geach and M. Black, pp. 81–2. But Frege's mockery of Huss-erl's use of the notion of selective attention (op. cit., pp. 84–5) does not seem to me to affect what I say below.

[23] *Principles*, §§ 120–2.

sequence of numerals, 'one, two, three . . .' It would be along these lines that we should have to explain in detail the meaning of number words as they are first introduced into language and what we can call our elementary ideas of numbers. This account will show some interesting differences from the accounts appropriate for other kinds of general words. But none of this has any tendency to show that the notion of selective attention is out of place even here, let alone in other cases. This notion does not in itself provide a detailed theory of meaning. But neither does it make us look in the wrong direction for such a theory, as would the suggestion that the meanings of words are to be found in images.

5. *The indeterminacy of images*

However unsatisfactory they are in other ways as possible referents for general terms, images seem to have one point in their favour: they can have the indeterminacy which seems to go along with generality. Locke and Berkeley both seem to have assumed that images are wholly determinate, and Hume insisted that if something 'be absurd in *fact and reality*, it must also be absurd *in idea*'.[24] But this is not so. Even the most immediate, pictorial, content of experience can be, and commonly is, somewhat indeterminate. I can, as Bennett points out, see a face without noticing whether it is smiling or not, and I can correspondingly have an image of a face which is not the image of a smiling face nor yet the image of an unsmiling face.[25] Whereas any real spotted dog will have some precise number of spots, not only can I think of a spotted dog but I can even have a visual image of a spotted dog without giving it any precise number of spots. We are tempted to say that experiential contents generally, including images, escape the law of excluded middle. But strictly speaking (as Bennett says) no thing escapes that law: experiential contents are not things. The truth is just that I can picture to myself a spotted dog without picturing one with fifty-three spots, or with any other precise number.

This sort of indeterminacy is interesting in itself, and it is highly relevant to discussion of the ontological status of ideas and

---

[24] *Treatise*, I. i. 7.

images and intentional objects in general.[26] But it has nothing to do with our ability to use general terms or, consequently, with any important sense in which we can be said to have abstract ideas. Such indeterminacy is quite limited: Bennett (following Michael Tanner) suggests that it is restricted by the principle that one can omit from an image only such details as one could have failed to notice in a perception. But we have the general idea of an animal, which covers giraffes and earthworms and oysters, whereas no one could notice an animal while remaining completely vague about whether it was an oyster or an earthworm or a giraffe. The generality of ideas can be far more extensive than the indeterminacy of images, and it is reasonable to suppose that it arises from a quite different source.

To sum up, then: I have argued that Locke has a fairly unitary positive theory of abstraction and generality which is on the whole defensible and which certainly does not deserve Berkeley's mockery. Its faults are one exaggerated remark, motivated by a special controversial purpose, in a passage that was plainly not designed to contribute to the theory of abstraction, and a habit of using literally expressions about separating and recombining ideas which can be defended only if taken metaphorically, but for which we can find a defensible literal replacement that harmonizes with Locke's basic account. In so far as his theory needs improvement, the corrections will not move it in the direction of the Berkeley–Hume theory of generalization without abstraction, of the representative use of concrete particulars. The latter has a place in the theory of mathematical reasoning and logical proof by natural deduction, in which universal generalization can follow bits of reasoning with respect to specimens; but it does not contribute to the central account of our use of general terms and of the thought processes that underlie it.

There is, however, one major problem outstanding. Locke, as I said in Section 1, assumes that things are particular, whereas most words are general, and he sees general ideas as a bridge between the two. But his account of how ideas can be general could be developed only on the assumption that things themselves contain some generality in the form of resemblances or common characteristics or both: and if things can be general in some such ways

---

[26] Cf. my *What's really wrong with phenomenalism?*, pp. 118–19, and 'Problems of Intentionality' in *Phenomenology and Philosophical Understanding*, ed. E. Pivcevic.

as these, it seems that we shall no longer need general ideas as a bridge between them and the generality of words. Locke's theory, coherently worked out, is in danger of making itself redundant. I want, therefore, to consider the traditional problem of universals, especially objective universals, and, in the light of some conclusions about this, to come back to the question whether generality is in any important respects the work of the mind.

6. *Realism about universals*

The traditional controversy about universals is between the adherents of two kinds of realism, and those of conceptualism, nominalism, and the resemblance theory. It has, no doubt, been fostered partly by mistakes and confusions. For example, it is often assumed that the giving of names to individual persons and things, and the subsequent use of those proper names, are straightforward and immediately intelligible, and therefore that the use of general terms and abstract nouns could be made intelligible if we could find entities to which these are given and of which they are used much like proper names. But a great deal of recent discussion has shown that the use of proper names has its own puzzles and obscurities, and that in analysing it we may well have to take as our starting-point the use of general descriptive terms. If so, the explanation of these as a variety of proper names would be circular. Again, it has sometimes been thought that the very existence of abstract nouns like 'whiteness', 'justice', and 'unity' is evidence that there are entities of some sort of which these are the names, and that the problem of universals is simply the problem of locating and identifying these entities. But it is easy to show that the commonest sorts of sentence which superficially appear to be about, say, justice are only transformations of sentences about just decisions and the like, and when these nominalizing transformations are reversed the appearance of talk about an entity, justice, disappears. Also, in at least some places in Plato's dialogues, the logical or metaphysical question of universals is mixed up with causal questions: his 'Forms' or 'Ideas' are seen as supplying answers to such questions as 'What makes equal things equal?' where this is ambiguous between 'What (causally) brings it about that any two things are equal?' and 'What constitutes the being equal of any two equal things? To what objective reality does our talk about equal things refer?'[27] But it is clear that any answers that the Forms offer to causal questions are spurious: these questions must be investigated in a quite different, scientific way. It is, however, an equal, though contrary, error to suppose that realism in general about universals and Plato's theory in particular arise simply from misunderstandings of the linguistic function of abstract nouns. The Greek language before Plato made little use of abstract nouns: many of them, including that of which 'quality' itself is a latinization, he coined for his own philosophical purposes, and in his earlier discussions the Forms were often introduced by odd circumlocutions.[28] The philosophical theory on the whole precedes the linguistic phenomenon from which it is sometimes believed to have arisen. Realism about universals, then, can neither be established by an appeal to linguistic forms and uses nor be explained away as a misunderstanding of them, but must be considered on its own merits.

The correct answer to the question 'What, if anything, in the objective things underlies and justifies the use of general terms?' may not be unitary. In Section 1 I distinguished the problems of exact and of extended universals, which may well require different solutions. But such distinctions have not usually been drawn, and various attempts have been made to give a unitary answer to our question.

Plato's Theory of Forms (or of 'Ideas', but this name is now misleading, since they are not ideas in any mind) may be interpreted as the thesis that there are self-subsistent universals, separate from and independent of the concrete particular things in space and time which copy them or approximate to them or strive after them or participate in them. The Forms exist in a supersensible realm, and are known directly by minds without the aid or intervention of the senses; our souls, before being imprisoned in our bodies, knew the Forms and can regain a clear knowledge of them by a process of recollection, which may be stimulated by sensory observation of particulars that imitate the Forms in question, but which does not owe its positive content to anything sensory.

---

[27] Plato, *Phaedo*, 96–101.
[28] e.g. αὐτὸ τὸ καλόν (etc.) 'the beautiful (etc.) itself'; τι καλὸν αὐτὸ καθ' αὑτό 'something beautiful itself by itself'.

However, the Theory of Forms is much more than a theory of universals. It is also a theory of rational, particularly mathematical, knowledge, and since the Forms are ideal standards of value, it is the foundation of interrelated ethical, aesthetic, and political theories. The Forms are the homes of eternal truths, the ideal objects of rational science, and the standards of rational choice and artistic endeavour. It is these developments that have lent the theory most of its charm. As a theory of universals, as an explanation of how two or more things can be of the same sort, it is open to well-known and devastating criticisms, some of which were stated by Plato himself in his later dialogues and which were emphasized repeatedly by Aristotle.[29] It is uneconomical to postulate a whole realm of supersensible entities. No coherent account can be given of how they are known or of how the knowledge of them contributes to our ordinary knowledge of things that are perceived by the use of the senses. If the resemblance between two particular things in some respect is reduced to or needs to be explained by some relation that each of them has separately to some common Form, and this relation is itself wholly or partly one of resemblance (as such descriptions of the relation as 'imitating', 'approximating to', and so on suggest), will not this resemblance between particular and Form need, in turn, to be reduced to or explained by some similar relation to a second Form, and so on for ever? How large is the population of the world of Forms?[30] Is there a Form for every general term, as its role as a theory of universals would require, or are there Forms only for values and ideals and perfections? Is there, for every kind of artefact, a Form to guide the artificer? If, as Plato suggests, there is the Form of the Bed, are there also, existing eternally in the Platonic heaven, the Forms of the Egg-beater, the Motor Car, and the Hypodermic Syringe? Conflicts break out between the requirements of the different tasks that the theory is supposed to perform. But the fundamental objection is that as a theory of universals the postulation of separate Forms is gratuitous. Whatever it is, about the ordinary world of things existing in space and time and perceived by the senses, that encourages us to postulate this other world of Forms, must surely be in principle

---

[29] e.g. *Metaphysics*, 990b–992a, 1039a–b, 1078b–1080a.
[30] Plato, *Parmenides*, 130; Aristotle, *Metaphysics*, 990b, 8–17; W. D. Ross, *Plato's Theory of Ideas*, Chapter 11.

intrinsically describable, and this description, whatever it is, will be the simple answer to our question about what underlies and justifies the use of general terms. It would be only if we were looking not for what constitutes, say, equality but for something like a causal explanation of equalities that it would make sense to postulate some related further entity.

In fact, even on the logical side, this theory was first developed not as a theory of universals, not as an attempt to explain predication, but rather as a way of dealing with various difficulties about predication, various kinds of case where common nouns and adjectives do not quite fit. Forms are introduced where there are comparative terms like 'tall' or 'hot', where particulars are inexact or inadequate specimens of what they are said to be—geometrical examples are the most obvious, but moral and aesthetic terms also illustrate this sort of defect—where particulars appear variously—now beautiful, now ugly, right by one moral rule, wrong by another—and where initial evaluations are socially relative. Plato explicitly says this when in the *Republic* he is discussing what studies 'draw the soul towards being'—that is, towards the Forms. The mind is roused to reflection not by perceptions which are 'judged adequately by sense' but by those with regard to which 'sense does nothing sound'. Each finger is quite satisfactorily a finger, so this fact does not excite thought, but the difficulties of deciding whether a finger which is between two others in length is large or small, and of deciding between sense-perceptions of the same thing as hard and as soft, and so on, do excite thought which leads ultimately to the Forms.[31] Similarly in a later dialogue Socrates is made to express serious doubts about there being Forms for those kinds with respect to which 'the things are just as we see them'.[32] Admittedly, the single move of postulating a Form is not the right way of dealing with these various difficulties and complications about predication, but what I want to stress now is that the Theory would be even less plausible as a general account of universals.

Criticism of a Platonic theory of separate Forms—*universalia ante res*—leads naturally to the Aristotelian variant of realism—*universalia in rebus*: universals exist only in particular things. The same character can be common to any number of individuals, but it exists only as a character of individuals. However, this thesis is

[31] *Republic*, 523–5.   [32] *Parmenides*, 130.

ambiguous. It could be taken as an attempt to explain the like-nesses between things in terms of some other, supposedly more intelligible or familiar, kind of relation or situation, taking a common character or quality as an entity of some special sort which (without losing its identity) can be in many places at once, and at different times, and so can be literally in any number of distinct individuals. But no such explanation will work. There is no other, separately familiar sort of sharing or having in common which is sufficiently analogous to the having of characters in common to throw any light on this situation, and the notion of an identical thing being in many places at once is quite obscure unless it is itself elucidated in terms of the very sort of situation that it is here being used to explain. But there is another way of taking the thesis, not as an explanation but simply as a description, merely inviting us to take note of the kind of situation that consists in things having common characters. It will be objected that on this interpretation the thesis is unexplanatory. And so it is. But we can explain why we have to put up with such a lack of explanation. Situations of this sort—things being of certain kinds, in such a way that other things are, or at least could be, of the same kinds—are indispensable in the data of any explanation, they will unavoidably be used as starting-points to explain any-thing at all. Consequently the general fact that there are situations of this sort cannot itself be explained without circularity. We cannot reduce this general pattern of existence to anything else. Another possible objection is that what the thesis presents as an objective sort of situation, things having a character in common, is a mere shadow of the linguistic phenomenon for which we are trying to find an objective basis: 'Each of these things is white' is either just another way of saying that we apply the descriptive predicate 'white' to each of these things, or a fiction produced by mistaking this linguistic form for an element of non-linguistic reality. But this objection, too, can be met. What the Aristotelian thesis claims is that this linguistic form of description is adequate or appropriate, that it mirrors in language fairly satisfactorily the way that things are—more appropriately, for instance, than such roughly equivalent expressions as 'Each of these things partakes of whiteness' or 'Whiteness inheres in each of these things'. Of course, what the Aristotelian thesis claims may be wrong, but we cannot dismiss it either as empty or as an obvious mislocation of a linguistic truth. A third objection, one with which Locke was much concerned, is that the Aristotelian view wrongly suggests that for every general word there is some clear-cut natural feature or cluster of features, that nature supplies the separate moulds in which all things are made, so that there need be no indeterminacies and no arbitrarinesses in classification. This will be considered further in section 9, but we can admit at once that not all general words are attached to common qualities or clusters of common qualities; there are what I have called extended universals. But this admission leaves it possible that the Aristotelian account should hold for some cases, namely for all 'exact' universals, that is, wherever a number of things are exactly alike in some respect.

7. *Conceptualism and nominalism*

A pure conceptualism would be utterly implausible. Whatever account we give of general ideas or concepts, it cannot be that the whole explanation and justification of our applying the same general term to two or more things is that we bring these things into relation to some one concept or idea. To say this would be to say that classification is totally arbitrary, and this would be far more absurd than the extreme contrary view (which, as I have just said, we should also reject) that there need be no arbitrariness in classification at all. Of course there is something about two horses that makes it easier and more natural to classify them together than to relate, say, a grain of sand and a herd of elephants to some one idea. In fact conceptualism is never held in a pure form, but is always associated with some kind of resemblance theory. The particular things objectively resemble one another, perhaps in multifarious criss-crossing ways, and we classify things by concentrating on some of these natural resemblances while neglecting others. Locke's own theory seems to be mainly such a mixture of conceptualism with a resemblance theory.

Conceptualism is initially attractive if we start by assuming that a universal must be a thing of some sort which somehow belongs to each of a set of particulars. Assuming this, but rejecting Platonic Forms as an extravagant speculation and rejecting as incomprehensible a substantial interpretation of Aristotelian universals as things multiply located in ordinary things, we may well feel that a concept is something satisfyingly familiar and yet plainly multiply applicable. But this attraction is due mainly to ambiguities in the term 'concept'. If it refers to some datable mental occurrence, some token-concept, then as Locke says this will be as particular 'in its existence' as anything else. If it refers to the corresponding type of mental occurrence, then while this will be universal it will be so in just the same way as any other type; the universality of the type *concept-of-a-horse* is neither more nor less acceptable and comprehensible than the type *horse*, and there is no way in which the former can be said to explain the latter: nothing is gained by the move from kinds of things to type-concepts. If the term 'concept' refers to what is conceived, what we may call the content of some act of conceiving, then this as a feature or cluster of features may indeed apply to many particulars, but to say this is just to say that the particulars may have characters in common: this is just the Aristotelian view over again, and once more nothing is gained by the introduction of the act of conceiving. Alternatively, if we think of this content not as the set of possibly objective features but as an intentional object, as something that exists only in and by being conceived, then this indeed may be universal in a distinctive way, it may be as Locke says general in its signification in that the conceiver may actually be ascribing a set of features to each of a number of things, or considering the possibility of their belonging to various things. But this sort of performance would be arbitrary and pointless unless there were also objective situations that exemplify the Aristotelian account.

Pure nominalism would be as implausible as pure conceptualism, and for the same reasons. What is called nominalism is therefore nearly always mainly a resemblance theory. Logicians may indeed prefer to work with individuals and sets, taken purely extensionally, as being more reliably concrete and having clearer criteria of identity than any intensional entities like qualities or even resemblances. If two terms have the same intension, and only then, they will have the same extensions in all possible worlds; so for many purposes extensions in possible worlds can be used instead of intensions. Methodological nominalism has some attractions. But such manoeuvres are plainly artificial: resemblances and/or common qualities, predicates and relations taken intensionally are what we obviously encounter in experience and what motivate our descriptive and classificatory procedures, and it is only in terms of general features that we can describe possibilities and possible worlds. Ontological nominalism has no plausibility at all.

There are hints, however, of ontological nominalism in Goodman's discussion of 'entrenched' and 'projectible' predicates.[33] Introducing the predicate 'grue' as applying to all things examined before some time t if and only if they are green and to all other things if and only if they are blue, Goodman first suggests that the inspection of any number of green emeralds before t will (on the assumption that hypotheses are confirmed by observed instances) confirm the hypothesis that all emeralds are grue just as well as it confirms the hypothesis that all emeralds are green. Now we can concede that this and similar paradoxical constructions conclusively refute any purely syntactical theory of confirmation. But the important further question is, what has to be added to a purely syntactical approach? What is it that makes 'All emeralds are green' better confirmed than 'All emeralds are grue'? The only answer that Goodman will allow is that 'green' is better 'entrenched' than 'grue', that is, basically, that it is 'a veteran of earlier and many more projections'.[34] He refuses to allow that 'green' and 'blue' are purely qualitative whereas 'grue' and 'bleen' are not, arguing that 'qualitativeness is an entirely relative matter', since if we had started with 'grue' and 'bleen' we would have explained 'green' and 'blue' in terms of them and a temporal term.[35] And his summing up is that 'the line between valid and invalid predictions (or inductions or projections) is drawn upon the basis of how the world is and has been described and anticipated in words'.[36]

If this means only that we can demarcate acceptable from non-acceptable projections by reference to the linguistic establishment, it may well be true. But it would clearly provide no answer to the problem of justifying some projections as contrasted with others. At the very least, the justification of our now projecting predications of 'green' rather than of 'grue' would have to be not merely

[33] N. Goodman, *Fact, Fiction, and Forecast*, chapters 3 and 4.

[34] Op. cit., p. 95. Goodman's account allows for several complications, so that a predicate which is itself new and unfamiliar may derive entrenchment from other related predicates, but in the end his appeal is to actual habitual projections alone.

[35] Op. cit., p. 79. 'Bleen', of course, applies to all things examined before t if and only if they are blue and to all other things if and only if they are green.

[36] Op. cit., p. 117.

that we have done so in the past, but that we have done so successfully; and this is not merely 'a function of our linguistic practices'.
But in any case it is just not true that qualitativeness is entirely
relative to language. It seems to me undeniable that different
things that are of the same shade of green are intrinsically alike in
colour whereas grue things which are, and are not, examined
before t are not alike. (The extended universal, green, covering
different shades, is a complication which we should not allow to
divert us from what is here at issue: we shall consider such items
later.) It is not possible to brush this aside as a prejudice arising
merely from our present language, nor is it tied to language as
such. Does anyone doubt that it would be considerably easier to
train a non-verbal animal to respond consistently to same-shade-
of-green things than to grue things? Or that a purely physical
green-detector would be a simpler piece of machinery than a
grue-detector? These are in the first place epistemological asym-
metries between 'green' and 'grue'. but they surely indicate an
ontological difference, that the one term records intrinsic resemblances where the other does not. And the same is true of analogues of 'grue' which avoid the use of an arbitrary temporal
term. Presumably we can find some purely qualitative predicate
'P' which is true of all emeralds that have so far been examined—
'P' may be some disjunction of ordinary terms 'A or B or ...'
Then we can define 'grue$_1$' as '(P and green) or (not-P and blue)'.[37]
Now 'grue$_1$', like 'green' and unlike 'grue', is a qualitative term,
and the hypothesis that all emeralds are (not green but) grue$_1$ is
not altogether unworthy of consideration. Perhaps it is only their
being P that has made the emeralds so far examined green. This
is a real possibility to be examined seriously, not a purely arbitrary
sceptical move; but it is still clear that grue$_1$, though qualitative,
is a more complex predicate than green, and the hypothesis that
all emeralds are green will have the usual advantages of simplicity
over the hypothesis that they are grue$_1$ until there is some evidence that positively favours the latter. However, it is not my
purpose at present to pursue the theory of confirmation, but
merely to repeat that if there is ontological nominalism involved
in Goodman's discussion, it is still utterly implausible, and should
not derive any credit from the valid points Goodman makes
against a purely syntactic approach to confirmation.

[37] This variant was brought to my attention by Jonathan Adler.

Still, we can understand why nominalism is attractive. Words, like concepts, seem to offer a way out of difficulty for those who are looking for things that can be universal but who reject, with good reason, both Plato's Forms and a substantial interpretation of Aristotelian universals. For words, like concepts, can be general in their signification; and not only type-words: a token-word too can be universal in that it is true of, and may in fact be applied to, indefinitely many particulars. Of course this is not so much an answer to our question as a reiteration of what is presupposed in it, but we can take it as a negative answer: words can be universal (in their signification) but nothing else is universal at all. But what constitutes this signification? Surely the intentions (perhaps the standard, conventional, rule-enshrined intentions) of their users. Nominalism can hardly help slipping into conceptualism here. But, what is more serious, it is not by being related directly (by users' intentions) to this, that, and the other individual that a general word is general in its signification. Anyone who uses the word 'man' uses it in a way different from that in which he uses the name 'John', no matter how many Johns he knows or knows of. The general signification of a common noun is parasitic upon the facts that it is associated with what Locke calls a nominal essence, and that the characteristics that make up this essence can be repeatedly instantiated, or at the very least that there are resemblances upon which the word's use somehow depends. Thus nominalism, like conceptualism, can supply entities that are in some sense universal only because the objective things obey either Aristotelian realism or the resemblance theory.

The main contenders, then, as basic accounts of objective universals are Aristotelian realism on the one hand and a resemblance theory with nominalist and conceptualist trimmings on the other.

8. *The resemblance theory*

According to the resemblance theory, the fact on which our use of general terms ultimately rests is that there are objective similarities or resemblances between things. But this statement needs amplification: what we have are not just resemblances but resemblances in certain respects. This seems, at first sight, to have the advantage of being more economical than the rival view: the

Aristotelian theory introduces a new, strange category of exis-
tents—characteristics, qualities, or whatever they may be called—
and so saddles itself with unnecessary problems about their criteria
of identity, how they can be in many places at once, and so on. If
the defender of the Aristotelian view protests that a universal is
not a *thing*, that all that is meant is, say, that this and that particular thing are both white in just the same way, that it is their
being white that is multiply reproducible, and that no questions
of numerical identity of characteristics arise, but only questions
of generic identity, such as the question whether these two things
are exactly alike in colour or not, then it may seem that the disagreement between the Aristotelian view and the resemblance
theory is purely verbal, that it is just a dispute about preferred
terminologies. One party likes to say that two things have a
property in common, the other party likes to say that the two
things resemble one another exactly in a certain respect, but since
there are no conceivable conditions in which one of these
expressions would be appropriate but the other not, it would
seem that once they are freed from misleading suggestions these
turn out to be two different ways of saying exactly the same
thing.

But not quite. For if we adopt the resemblance theory we make
the fundamental fact a relational one, one thing's being like
another in a certain respect, that is, a fact which presupposes the
existence of at least two things. Yet surely just one thing, by
itself, has characteristics or properties, and we can pick out its
intrinsic properties as those which it (logically) would have
whether or not there were any other things. In respect of these
intrinsic properties, it is of this, that, and the other sort whether
or not there are other things to form these 'sorts' with it. If each
of two things has thus, by itself, a certain property, then it is a
logical consequence that they will resemble each other in this
respect. And two things cannot have the relation of exact resemblance in a certain respect except as a logical consequence of each
one's having, on its own, a certain feature. What the Aristotelian
view draws attention to, each thing's having qualities on its own,
its just being as it is in several ways, is indeed the fundamental
reality. For every case of a thing's having a certain quality or
intrinsic property, we can think of possible worlds in which
this situation survives without any corresponding relations of

resemblance, but we cannot think of possible worlds in which a relation of resemblance survives without any corresponding situations of the thing-having-property form. As we have seen, we can admit the charge that the Aristotelian account, thus interpreted, offers the problem itself as a solution, but maintain that it is right to do so. Any conceivable reductive analysis of this fundamental reality will fail through circularity: we shall have to postulate items of this thing-intrinsically-of-a-certain-sort form among the data of any explanation we attempt to give.

9. *Universals and the work of the mind*

If we are right in thus preferring the Aristotelian account, we must conclude that Locke speaks misleadingly when he sets up his problem about abstract ideas and general terms by saying that 'all things that exist are only particulars'.[38] They are not only particulars; everything that exists has universal aspects as well. Each thing has that about it which something else could reproduce, something such that another individual could be exactly like it in this respect. Locke concedes that nature provides the similitudes of things; but he should have conceded more than this, that it provides intrinsic but essentially reproducible features which underlie these similitudes.

Yet we can largely agree with Locke's claim that 'the *sorting* of [things] under names *is the workmanship of the understanding*'.[39] Though, as Locke says, nature supplies the similitudes, it supplies far more of them than we use: it is by the work of the mind that some resemblances and not others are recorded in language. There are also, as Locke again admits, the clusterings of common features that constitute natural kinds; but these account for only a small part of the range of general terms. Even substance-terms often name artefacts and other things whose classification is determined by their functions, and hence by their relation to human uses and purposes rather than by intrinsic properties—consider 'bed', 'hammer', 'container', 'drink'—while what Locke calls mixed modes are also plainly determined by human interests.

Also, many general words refer to what I have called extended, rather than exact, universals. That is, many of our classifications

---

[38] III. iii. 6.   [39] III. iii. 13.

group together things that have no property or even conjunction of properties that is both common to them and distinctive of them as opposed to all other things. Even among colour-words we have no names for exact shades, and every ordinary colour-word like 'red' covers, in its standard use, many shades that have no qualities in common. Colours form a continuum in at least three dimensions, and the boundaries between named colours are somewhat variable and arbitrary. They are not indeed quite as arbitrary as is usually thought, and what human beings regularly perceive as varying degrees of resemblance between hues determine at least a number of natural foci for colour-words; but even their naturalness is a matter of (nearly universal) *human* experience.[40] (These considerations complicate the issue, raised by Goodman and discussed in Section 7 above, whether 'green' is a qualitative predicate or merely an 'entrenched' one, but they should not be allowed to obscure the fact that there are exact resemblances and objective common properties in comparison with which grueness is an artificial construct.) With many other general words also, their use is determined not by the possession of any distinctive common property or cluster of properties—even functional or relational ones—but by series of resemblances. As Mill says,

. . . new objects are continually presenting themselves to [people] which they are called upon to class *proprio motu*. They . . . do this on no other principle than that of superficial similarity, giving to each new object the name of that familiar object, the idea of which it most readily recalls, or which . . . it seems to them most to resemble. In this manner names creep on from subject to subject, until all traces of a common meaning sometimes disappear . . .

And Mill quotes from Bain the way the word 'stone' is 'applied to mineral and rocky materials, to the kernels of fruit, to the accumulations in the gall-bladder and in the kidney; while it is refused to polished minerals (called gems), to rocks that have the cleavage suited for roofing (slates), and to baked clay (bricks)'.[41] In all such cases what underlies the use of a general word is not an Aristotelian universal, an objective common property, but only

[40] Cf. B. Harrison, *Form and Content*, pp. 72–84, quoting B. Berlin and P. Kay, *Basic Colour Terms*.
[41] J. S. Mill, *A System of Logic*, Bk. I, Ch. 2, Sect. 5.

a network of resemblances and differences on the basis of which, in a way that is both complex and fairly arbitrary, we have formed concepts—habits of recognition and associated rules of naming. Also, as the example of colours shows, there are resemblances which we record as closer or more remote, which are ultimate, not reducible to or explained by the presence of common qualities.[42] For extended universals, then, a blend of the resemblance theory with nominalism and conceptualism holds, and it is appropriate to speak as Locke does of the workmanship of the understanding. But recognition of this fact should not blind us to the complementary truth that Aristotelian realism, interpreted cautiously without any attempt to treat universals as things, gives a correct account of the more fundamental exact universals. The inescapable basic reality has the form of each thing's being of a certain sort, or rather of several sorts, that is, its being in itself such that something else could exactly resemble it in this or that respect.

I conclude, then, that Locke was wrong in thinking that we need ideas to bridge a gap between the particularity of things and the generality of words. The basic explanation of how most words can be general in their signification is that things too are general as well as particular in that they have, intrinsically, repeatable features. But ideas, or the work of the mind, enter the account of general words in at least two important ways. First, there are, necessarily, mental processes involved in the annexing of words to the general features of things. It is quite appropriate for a philosopher to take some notice of them: this is not a reprehensible confusing of logic with psychology. The basic account which Locke gives of these processes, that they involve abstraction in the sense of selective attention, is correct as far as it goes, and while his account of the further processes by which we construct complex ideas cannot be defended if taken literally, it is possible to sketch a defensible reinterpretation of this which would harmonize with his basic theory. Secondly, although the intrinsic generality of things is what ultimately makes possible the use of general words, it is not this but an independent tradition of thought and language use that determines which common features, which resemblances, and which complex networks of resemblances and differences have words annexed to them. Indeed, as we have already seen with regard to real essences in

[42] Cf. Hume, *Treatise*, I. i. 7, footnote (Selby-Bigge p. 637).

Chapter 3 and to numbers in Section 4 of this chapter, and as we shall see in Chapter 6 with regard to personal identity, Locke's stress on ideas leads him to underestimate the complexity and indirectness of the ways in which the meanings of words are based on experiential elements.

5

IDENTITY AND DIVERSITY

1. *Locke's general theory of identity*

LOCKE sets out in Chapter xxvii of Book II to explain the ideas of identity and diversity. After sketching a general theory of identity he becomes interested in the controversial special topic of personal identity, and most of his chapter is devoted to this. I shall take up this special topic in Chapter 6; the subject of the present chapter is identity and diversity in general, which involve more problems than Locke realized.

Hume, as we shall see in Section 2, thought that the notion of identity is essentially connected with persistence through time. Locke, too, makes some remarks that would suggest this, but he also says firmly that at any one time any thing is 'the same with itself'. His real view, then, seems to be that the identity and diversity of things at any one time is unproblematic, and that it is only where things persist through time that identity becomes controversial enough to raise any issue or to require any detailed account. At one time each thing will be in some one place, and no other thing of the same kind can be in that same place.[1] But this is not as straightforward as Locke thought. In speaking of things of one kind, he meant particularly that no two bodies could be in the same place. Since 'spirits' were for him things of a different kind, this would not prevent a spirit from being in the same place as a body, but distinct from it. He does not explicitly consider whether a mind might be identical with a brain, though he raised something like this question in suggesting that matter may be able to think.[2] Some modern philosophers, however, have argued explicitly that minds are identical with brains, or sensations with brain processes, and have appealed to such analogies as the identity of a flash of lightning with an electrical discharge and of a gene with a DNA molecule. The question, 'Is this in the same place as that?' does not provide either a reliable or a readily usable criterion for deciding such issues. I shall examine this 'identity

[1] II. xxvii. 1.   [2] IV. iii. 6.

across kinds' in Section 5 below. But I shall turn first to the
questions that Locke found interesting: what are we saying when
we claim that something which exists at a later time t_2 is identical
with something which existed at an earlier time t_1, and how are
we ever justified in saying this?

Even this problem, Locke thought, is not really difficult once
we realize—though he does not put it quite in this way—that
identity is relative. The question to ask is always whether this is
the same x as that, where 'x' is some sortal term, that is, some
noun that indicates a kind of things that can be distinguished
from one another as individuals and perhaps counted. We must
ask about the same body, the same atom, the same tree, the same
horse, the same man, the same person, and so on. The noun in
question, the 'x', will determine what the relevant requirements
for identity are: the requirements for the sameness of an atom are
different from those for the sameness of a tree. On the other hand
Locke is not saying that the word 'same' is merely ambiguous, or
that it has as many different meanings as there are sortals: rather
his suggestion is that the requirements for the same x are determined systematically by the idea—whatever idea we have—of an
x. Locke's idea of an atom is of a continuous solid lump of
matter, not physically divisible or deformable. So an atom which
exists at t_2 is identical with one which existed at t_1 if and only if
there is a spatio-temporally continuous history of a solid lump
of matter of that shape joining the atom-occurrence at t_1 with that
at t_2. Locke's idea of a mass or of a body is that of a collection of
atoms in some spatial region, so a body which exists at t_2 will
be the same body as one which existed at t_1 if and only if there is
a continuous history of just that collection of atoms joining the
two body-occurrences. The atoms in the body can be 'ever so
differently jumbled,' and it will still be the same body, but if even
one atom is lost or added, it will not be the same body. But what
if one atom (or any number of atoms) is taken away and then that
same atom (or that same set of atoms) is brought back and reunited with the remainder? Locke does not explicitly say whether
it is the same body or not in this case, but I think that the consistent answer would be that it is not: there has not been a
continuous history of a united collection of atoms joining the two
body-occurrences. But since there has been a continuous history
of a sometimes-scattered collection of atoms joining them, we

could say that we have the same atom-collection at t_2 as at t_1. Our idea of an organism, a plant or an animal, Locke says, is not that of a mere parcel of matter, but of a certain organization of parts which contribute to and partake of a common life. It is for this reason that something will still be the same oak tree even though great quantities of matter are added to it and taken away from it, when it grows from a seedling to a large tree and when its branches are lopped: there is a continuous history of an organized vegetable life linking the earlier and later oak-occurrences, although that life is constantly being communicated to new particles of matter and withdrawn from others. Similarly, Locke suggests, our idea of an animal is that of something like a self-winding watch which keeps going while it is gradually being modified and repaired, and consequently we again have the same animal at t_2 as at t_1 if and only if there is a continuous animal life linking the two occurrences. And, Locke says, our idea of a man—though not of a person—is that of an animal of a certain sort, and the requirements for the same man are just like those for the same horse.

Thus Locke's general theory of identity through time is that x-occurrences at t_1 and at t_2 are occurrences of the same x if and only if there is a continuous x-history linking them. It is not, of course, important whether we accept his accounts of the ideas of an atom, a body, a plant, an animal, or a man; what matters is the thesis that *if* we use these ideas, *then* our requirements for the same atom, the same body, and so on will be determined accordingly. The sameness of a substance through time is constituted by the spatio-temporal continuity of a thing of the kind in question.[3]

A test case would be the identity of an artefact, say that of the watch with which Locke compares an animal. To be a watch, it does not need to be going, or even able to go, so there is still a watch there even if one or two essential parts are removed: such removals and replacements will not break the continuous line of watch-occurrences, and so we shall still have the same watch. But what if the watch is taken completely to pieces and then re-assembled? We should be inclined to say that after re-assembly it is the same watch: but was there a watch at all when it was all in pieces? Was it a watch in pieces or only a complete set of pieces

[3] II. xxvii. 3–8.

of a watch? To sustain Locke's thesis we must say the former, and perhaps we would. It is worth noting that we are more likely to call it a watch in pieces if we expect it later to be put together, and so, if it is actually put together again, we shall tend to say retrospectively that it was a watch in pieces, so that there was a continuous watch-history after all. But this is at least a borderline case, and there is some plausibility in the view that our requirements for the same watch are not quite so strict as Locke's general theory would suggest: we may be willing to speak of the same watch at t_2 as at t_1 even if there were times between t_1 and t_2 at which we would not say that there was a watch in this continuous line.

Locke's theory would enable him to deal neatly with an ancient problem about identity.[4] If a ship is continuously repaired over the years by the putting in of new planks, etc., until no single piece of the original ship remains, and all the discarded pieces are ultimately reassembled in the same order as at first, we have, eventually, two different ships: which, if either, of them is the same ship as the one with which we began? Let us call the one that has resulted from the constant repairs the seaman's ship, and the one which has been put together out of the discarded pieces the antiquarian's ship: indeed it is not likely to be anything more than a museum piece, whereas the other may still be seaworthy. Locke's theory would lead us to say that the seaman's ship is the same *ship* as the original one, since there is a continuous ship-history linking them, whereas the antiquarian's ship is only the same collection of ship-components as the original, since what links them is a continuous history of what has for most of the time been a dispersed collection of ship-components, and such a dispersed collection is not a ship—particularly when throughout much of this time a large part of this collection has formed part of something else that was undeniably a sea-going ship.

Locke's attempt thus systematically to relate 'the same x' to the concept of an x does, however, lead to some difficulties. A

<hr />

[4] Hobbes, *English Works*, ed. Molesworth, vol. i, pp. 136–7. The example is from Plutarch's *Lives*, 'Life of Theseus', where it is mentioned as having been discussed by the philosophers of Athens. Hobbes anticipates Locke's thesis of relativity: 'But we must consider by what name anything is called, when we inquire concerning the identity of it. For it is one thing to ask concerning Socrates, whether he be the same man, and another to ask whether he be the same body . . .'

daffodil bulb may divide spontaneously into two fairly equal parts: each of the two bulbs that exist at t_2 is then linked by a continuous vegetable life to the one bulb that existed at t_1; is each of the later bulbs therefore the same bulb as the original one? But then, since the two later ones are clearly two, in different places, the relation '. . . is the same bulb as . . .' cannot be both symmetrical and transitive, it cannot obey the usual logic of identity. Can we say that the continuity of vegetable life is broken at the point of division, so that neither of the later bulbs is the same as the earlier one? Yet if just after the division one half had been destroyed, we should probably have been happy to say that the surviving half is the same bulb as the original, just as, if the division had been markedly unequal, we would happily say that the larger resulting bulb is the same as the original one. So where the bulb divides equally and both halves survive, it may seem inconsistent to say that neither is the same bulb as the original; but of course it would be arbitrary to say that one is and the other not, and yet to say that both are the same as the original would violate the logic of identity.

This difficulty arises from a peculiarity in our ordinary concept of a persisting thing. When we think of a daffodil bulb, say, we are not thinking of a bulb-occurrence (or bulb-phase or bulb-time-slice), nor yet of a bulb-history. After the division, we clearly have two bulb-occurrences, and neither is identical with any earlier bulb-occurrence. Equally clearly we have one continuous though bifurcated bulb-history to which all the bulb-occurrences in question belong. There would be no problems about the logic of identity for either bulb-occurrences or bulb-histories. But there is a problem for us, just because we think of a persisting thing as neither a history nor an occurrence. In a straightforward case, where there is no division, we want to say that the whole bulb is present at t_1, and that the same whole bulb is present at t_2, even if it has grown or diminished in the interval. It is this that becomes awkward where there is an equal division.

It is worth reflecting on the nature of this awkwardness. In a way, there is no doubt about what has happened: the whole history of bulb division can be assumed to lie open to our view. (No doubt at any time there are details of which we are ignorant, and we could keep on learning more about the exact processes of cell-division and growth and so on; but we are reasonably confident that no learning of additional details will substantially modify the puzzle with which we are confronted.) Our problem is how to fit the concepts and the logic of identity and persisting things on to this adequately known but recalcitrant material. We are determined to say, after the division, where both halves survive, that these are two different bulbs. We want '. . . is the same bulb as . . .' to be symmetrical and transitive. So we cannot say that both later bulbs are the same as the original one. We want to avoid an arbitrary choice. So we cannot say that either of them is so. Yet we also want to accept a bulb that grows or diminishes as the same persisting thing, and it seems arbitrary to withhold this when half has split off but immediately perished. So, finally, we are left saying 'This (the sole surviving half) is the same bulb as the original, but it would not have been so if the other half had survived': the sameness in this branch of the bulb-history is not intrinsic, but is conditional on what happened in the other branch. This untidiness is not due to ignorance, but is an unavoidable result of the attempt to apply the concept of identity to a persisting but changeable thing. The concept of identity which Locke reports (or proposes) meets with no difficulty when it is applied to unchanging things like atoms or to mere united collections of atoms, but it encounters unexpected difficulties when it is extended, in a most natural way, to something whose unity is that of, say, a 'vegetable life'. This lends some plausibility to Hume's claim that identity is a *fiction*.

2. *Hume's account of identity*

It is not quite clear whether Locke thinks that he is merely reporting how we already handle the concepts of identity and diversity or would admit that he is recommending an improved way of handling them. But in either case he is prepared to endorse what he describes, and hence to say that the old oak is the same plant as the sapling: it meets the requirements for the sameness of plants, which are different from, but just as respectable as, the requirements for the sameness of atoms. Hume, on the other hand, thinks that when we ascribe a continued existence and identity to a changing object we are not merely following different rules but are making some kind of mistake for which a psychological explanation is to be found. But he seems to think that the position is even worse than this, that the very notion of identity rests on some confusion of thought.

'For', he says, 'in that proposition, *an object is the same with itself*, if the idea expressed by the word *object* were no ways distinguished from that meant by *itself*; we really should mean nothing, nor would the proposition contain a predicate and a subject. . . . One single object conveys the idea of unity, not that of identity.' But equally no multiplicity of objects can convey the idea of identity. Identity seems to be something in between unity and plurality; and yet there is nothing between them[5].

Hume therefore suggests that we should 'have recourse to the idea of time or duration'. He suggests that the notion of identity arises only from that of a thing's persistence through time. This is a different view from Locke's, for although Locke says that we get the ideas of identity and diversity by comparing a thing with itself existing at another time, he also says that a thing at any one time *is* the same with itself. As I have said in Section 1, Locke's view is that identity is to be found in any thing at one time, but that this is trivial: the interesting cases are of identity through time. But Hume is here arguing that only in the persistence of a thing through time can we make room for identity as opposed to mere unity. Hume is here anticipating a problem of Wittgenstein's: if identity is a relation, it must be between two things, and yet if it holds, there are not two things but only one. And Hume is appealing to a thing's persistence through time as a solution of this paradox, as supplying something intermediate between unity and plurality.

Yet Hume's actual account is more involved than this. Time strictly considered, he says, consists in a succession of unlike items, so an unchanging thing is not in time. It is already a fiction, therefore, to ascribe temporal difference to earlier and later phases of an unchanging thing; we create this fiction by a transfer from coexisting things which do exhibit a succession of unlike items. The idea of identity, therefore, is that of 'an object that remains invariable and uninterrupted through a supposed variation of time'.[6] But then by a further confusion we fail to distinguish something which changes gradually, like the oak, from something that persists without changing, and ascribe identity also to the former. Besides, where there is a '*common end* or purpose', as

[5] *Treatise*, I. iv. 2.   [6] Op. cit., I. iv. 6.

with the repaired ship, and where, as with plants and animals, there is a '*sympathy* of parts to their common end', and reciprocal causal relations between them, we are the more willing to ascribe identity to changing things, and we more readily tolerate changes of a degree and kind that are usual in things of the sort in question.[7] For Hume, then, identity is a nest of fictions.

But his account is open to several objections. First, there is no reason why an unchanging thing should not quite genuinely be in, or persist through, time. Secondly, although Hume has rightly seen that there is a puzzle about how identity can as it were hover between unity and plurality, his solution is too narrow. The general form of an identity statement is 'The X is (identical with) the Y': there are two introductions, but what is being said is that what is thus twice introduced is just one thing. The identity statement will be true if and only if the two descriptions 'the X' and 'the Y' refer to one individual: but the identity is not, of course, ascribed to the two descriptions but to what they describe. Identity is unity: to be the same is to be 'one and the same': but it is truly asserted under the name of identity, that is as a relation that something has to itself, only when the one thing is introduced or considered twice. The identity statement will be trivial if the two description tokens are of the same type, if it has the form 'The X is the X' (unless, of course, they contain indexical terms, as in 'This wire is the same as this wire', with two different pointings). It will also be trivial if, though of different types, the two description tokens have the same sense. Consequently where an identity statement is true but non-trivial we have the following curious combination of elements. The identity, being that of a thing with itself, is always necessary; but it is contingent that it can be stated in this particular way; and the contingent truth that makes this possible is that there is just one individual to which the two senses or contextually differential uses of the two descriptions each uniquely apply. What Hume has offered is a particular case of this general solution of the puzzle, where the two senses include how something is at different times. And this is too narrow, because while we can say truly that the clock Smith bought ten years ago is (identical with) the clock Smith now has in his dining room, we can also say truly that the immediate successor of ninety-six is identical with the only prime number in the

[7] Loc. cit.

nineties, where the two descriptions make no use of any time difference, and a telephone engineer, sorting out a number of lines, can truly say 'This wire is the same as that wire' (pointing to different parts of the same wire), where though there is a slight time difference, it is irrelevant.

Thirdly, it may be objected that Hume should not have said that the identity we attribute to changing (or even interrupted) things is fictitious. We are not saying falsely of the oak tree that it has not grown, but rather saying truly that it has gone on growing in the way an oak tree does. Even a watch that has been taken to pieces and reassembled with some new parts, or even (Hume's example) a church that has fallen in ruins and been rebuilt with new materials, may actually have the kind and degree of identity that we ascribe to it. Has Hume not confused the use of relaxed criteria, and hence a less stringent concept of identity, with an error or fiction?

But this will not do. The concept of identity is not one which can be made more or less stringent; identity is an all-or-nothing affair. Where there is room for relaxation and indeterminacy is in the individual concept to which identity is applied. If we join two lengths of wire by twisting the ends together, do we have *a* wire or do we still have two wires? We must decide what to say about this and we can decide either way. But what we say determines, with no nonsense, the correct answer to the question, 'Is this the same wire as that?' There cannot be a 'this wire' and a 'that wire' which are more or less the same.

Can we do the same with a watch and a church? Clearly we can with a watch-history or a church-history. We can take as an individual church-history the whole sequence of churches built, ruined, and rebuilt in one village, and we may find it most natural to do so if, as in Hume's example, there are never two churches in the village at one time, though even if there are sometimes two churches this need not destroy the unity of a church-history. And then, as with the wire, we can point somehow to different parts and say 'This is the same church-history as that'. But a church is not what I am here calling a church-history. Our concept of a church, as of any other persisting thing, is that it is all there at once, at any time when it exists at all. At the very least we must say that it is a strange sort of individual which is all there at t_1, and (the same individual) all there also at t_2, and yet which is very different at these two times. Hume may be wrong in saying that in calling it the same thing we are (falsely) denying that it has changed; but there would be some plausibility in saying that this sort of thing, a persisting yet changing individual, is a sort of fiction, an incoherent mixture of features taken from the church (which is there all at once but which ceases to exist when there is any alteration) and the church-history, which can indeed be one and the same through change and even across interruptions (across times when there is no church) and across times when there are two churches at once.

If we speak of the same church across times when there has been no church and times when there have been two, there is indeed a fiction: there is a clear conflict between the claim that some one church has persisted through t_3 and the admission that at t_3 there was no church or that there were two. But where at each relevant time there is just one church, though it changes qualitatively from one time to another, there is no outright conflict. Nor is it fair to say that this is a strange sort of individual, since it is the sort of individual most familiar to all ordinary people: a persisting but changing thing is the ordinary, central example of a thing. Yet, reflecting on the case of the divided bulb, we could draw a distinction between thing-concepts which are such that their ordinary identity-conditions automatically ensure conformity to the logic of identity and those such that special clauses are needed to secure this conformity. The concept of a number is of the first sort, and so is that of an unchanging persisting thing, and even Locke's concept of a body, that is, of a united collection of elements which do not change, though they may be rearranged. But (because organisms behave as they do) his—and our—concept of a living organism is of the second sort. The relations between the bulb-phases at t_1 and at t_2 which ordinarily allow us to speak of one bulb can hold between one bulb-phase at t_1 and more than one bulb-phase at t_2. So we can save the logic of identity only by writing in the special clause that (fairly) equal division, which can occur quite naturally, destroys a bulb if both parts survive. This is the element of truth in Hume's view that the identity of changing things through time is a fiction.

We can relate this to what I called Locke's general theory of identity through time, that x-occurrences at t_1 and t_2 are occurrences of the same x if and only if there is a continuous x-history linking them. This definition entails that '. . . is the same x as . . .' is symmetrical and transitive: but for some instantiations of 'x' it also allows that there should be two simultaneous x-occurrences of the same x, while for others it precludes it. A continuous organism-history allows this, whereas a continuous atom-history or atom-collection-history precludes it. Since we cannot allow two simultaneous (but spatially distinct) occurrences of the same x, this definition needs supplementation for such instantiations of 'x' as 'organism' but not for such as 'atom' or 'atom-collection'. We may say that the identity through time of xs of the latter sort, and also the identity of a thing at any one time, and of things that are not in time at all, is *automatic*, while the identity through time of xs of the former sort, such as organisms, is *specially secured*.

3. *Essences of individuals*

This account of identity should be related to a question which Locke discusses separately, whether an individual thing can be said to have an essence. In one place he says that nothing is essential to individuals.[8] Any individual considered simply as such just has whatever properties it in fact has, and perhaps different and incompatible properties at different times, but no property that it has is any more essential to it than any other. It is only when we bring in species or classes that we can distinguish essential from non-essential properties. The properties which are essential to men as such are those which constitute the nominal essence of man, those whose lack or loss would stop us from classifying the individual as a man; non-essential properties are those which something may be without but still count as a man. But this concerns only nominal essence. Locke admits elsewhere that an individual will have an internal constitution, which is what he has recognized, following Boyle, as a real essence, and hence that this is properly called the essence of an individual: '. . . in this sense [the word 'essence'] is still used when we speak of the *essence* of particular things, without giving them any name'.[9] But even in this sense Locke is reluctant to say that the essence belongs as such to an individual: '*essence, even in this sense, relates to a sort,*

[8] III. vi. 4. 　　　[9] III. iii. 15.

and supposes a *species*',[10] and the reason he gives is that this internal constitution is called a (real) essence because it is the source of the properties which constitute the nominal essence of some species of thing, and in principle explains this conjunction of properties. The words 'essence' and 'essential' suggest to Locke inseparable features, and even what goes to make up a thing's internal constitution is not inseparable from it considered only as an individual. It is inseparable from it only as a member of some species, in the sense that if the internal constitution were to change it would no longer be a thing of that sort.

This hint about inseparability would suggest that the essence of an individual would be that without which it would not be the same individual—which means, that without which *it* would not be there. But if Locke is right about the relativity of identity, 'the same individual' is vague and indeterminate; it is only when we put in some sortal noun, some species-term, that we get any precise issue. We must ask if there are properties without which something would not be the same body, the same man, and so on. Even in this sense, therefore, what is essential will relate to some species. Following Locke's account of 'the same *x*' in terms of a continuous *x*-history, we should say that the essence of an individual *x*, that without which it would not be the same *x*, is just spatio-temporally continuous existence as an *x*.

This answers the question 'In what circumstances, by the retaining of what features, does an individual *x* continue to be the same *x*?'. But we can ask a further, counterfactual, question: 'Among various unrealized possibilities, what would and what would not count as occurrences of the same *x* as this actual one?' What is thus counterfactually essential to an individual is whatever is such that if it had been lacking this individual would not have been there—or, briefly, that without which this would not have been there.

Locke does not even ask this question; yet he inadvertently drops a hint that would lead to the answer. 'That therefore that had one beginning', he says, 'is the same thing; and that which had a different beginning in time and place from that is not the same, but diverse.'[11] This holds also, though Locke does not notice this, for counterfactual possibilities. If we consider the possibility of something's having had a different origin, a different beginning in time, from this sheet of paper, then even if it is the possibility of its also having been a sheet of paper, qualitatively indistinguishable from this one, and of its having come to be here at this time, this possibility is one which, regarding it as unrealized, we describe as the possibility of a different sheet of paper's being here. We do not describe it as the possibility of this sheet of paper's having had a different origin. (The fact that if this possibility had been realized we should now be calling that other thing this piece of paper does not, of course, affect the present issue: the question is not about what we counterfactually would have called something, but about what we now call an element in some counterfactually possible situation, while regarding this possibility as counterfactual.) On the other hand, if we consider the possibility of something's having had the same origin as this sheet of paper, but then having been sent to a different place, used for a different purpose, and having been destroyed, say burned, before now, we describe this as the possibility of this sheet of paper's having had a different history. So what is counterfactually essential to this individual sheet of paper, what cannot be detached from it, even in counterfactually possible courses of events, if it is still to be referred to as *this* individual, is, as Locke hints, its beginning in time and place.

This is a thesis that has been put forward by Saul Kripke, particularly with reference to named human individuals.[12] Queen Elizabeth, he says, could not have had different parents from those she was in fact born of, whereas she might never have become a queen. It is epistemically possible that she was not in fact born of those whom we now believe to have been her parents; but given that she was born of them, she was necessarily born of them. Anyone not born of them, though she might have done everything that Queen Elizabeth has done since infancy, would not have been this woman. If we contemplate the possibility that there should now be, as Queen of England, a woman with different parents from those, whoever they may be, that produced the present queen, we describe this not as the possibility that this same woman, Queen Elizabeth, should have had a different origin, but as the possibility that a different woman should have become queen, even if we suppose her to have been substituted for the

[12] 'Naming and Necessity', pp. 253–355, esp. pp. 312–14.

present queen as a baby, and to have had exactly the same career from infancy as the present queen.

This Kripkean thesis holds for non-human as well as for human individuals, whether named or not. These necessities of origin, contrasted with contingencies of development, provide a counterfactual essence for individuals, over and above what is essential to an individual as a member of a species, as an x, and relatedly, what is essential for its continuing to be the same x. Necessities of origin yield counterfactual essences for individuals just as necessities of constitution yield, as we saw in Chapter 3, counterfactual essences for stuffs like gold.

We should, however, stop to consider the metaphysical status of these necessities and essentialities. They are non-epistemic, and Kripke speaks of *de re* necessity. This might suggest that they constitute something objectively necessary. But in fact they reside only in our ways of thinking and speaking. But although Kripke is much concerned with the use of proper names, it is not primarily or exclusively their use that matters. The origin of this sheet of paper is what is essential to there being the same sheet in various counterfactual possibilities, and her origin is counterfactually essential to Queen Elizabeth because without it there would not have been this same woman. The use of names depends upon the concept of the same individual, not vice versa. These necessities rest upon how we handle identity in relation to possibilities, especially unfulfilled possibilities.

As Kripke says, we have a characteristic way of stipulating counterfactual possibilities for this very individual. 'One is given . . . a previous history of the world up to a certain time, and from that time it diverges considerably from the actual course.'[13] The possibilities that we consider with respect to individuals are such divergences, and when we consider them we secure the identity of things and persons through the transition from the actual to the merely possible by the same continuities that, as Locke says, ordinarily secure such identity in the actual world.

It is worth nothing just what we do here, and inquiring why we do it. Let us take as an example some man, say Nixon—we shall be concerned only with him as the same *man*, the requirements for which are, as Locke says, just like those for the same

[13] Op. cit., p. 314.

animal; the special problems of *personal* identity will not arise. We
have a picture like that of Diagram (i).

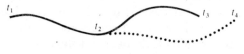

Diagram (i)

The actual career of Nixon is shown by the continuous line
from t_1 to t_3. The dotted line diverging from it represents things
that Nixon might have done and experienced from t_2 onwards,
including surviving after t_3 to t_4. This is a possible career *for
Nixon* because in this possible course of events there is a continuous man-history joining the Nixon-occurrences from t_1 to t_2
to the contemplated man-occurrences from t_2 to t_4, just as in the
actual course of events the Nixon-occurrences from t_2 to t_3 are
joined to those from t_1 to t_2.

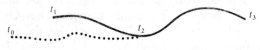

Diagram (ii)

But this diagram suggests another—Diagram (ii). That is, we
might consider possibilities which converge with actuality instead of diverging from it, or, what comes to the same thing, ones
that diverge from actuality as we go backwards in time. Here we
contemplate a possible man who is conceived at t_0, not at t_1,
whose career from t_0 to t_2 is different from that of the actual
Nixon, but whose actions and experiences from t_2 to t_3 are
exactly like those of the actual Nixon. To make this case as symmetrical as possible with that of Diagram (i), suppose that this
possible man's likeness to the actual Nixon from t_2 to t_3 goes
right down to the arrangement of all the molecules in his body.
Even so Kripke would say that this would not be Nixon, it
would not be the same man. Even if the actual and possible
careers from t_2 to t_3 were exactly alike, we should put in a dotted
line beside the firm one; our possible man never becomes Nixon,
so his career was not the possibility of Nixon's having had a
different origin. But though Kripke is, I think, right about our
actual way of describing these possibilities, it is clear that there
is an alternative, more liberal, view which would allow identity

to be preserved in backward as well as in forward divergences from the actual, letting us say that the man in Diagram (ii) is Nixon. There is also a third, less liberal, view, that even forward divergences destroy identity. This is what Leibniz held.[14] Though God might have made a man who had the t_1-t_2-t_4 career of Diagram (i), this man would not have been Nixon: this possibility is not correctly described by saying that Nixon might have done something other than he did after t_2, so in this diagram also we need a dotted line running alongside the firm one from t_1 to t_2. Thus our actual way of handling identity in relation to counterfactual possibilities, as correctly reported by Kripke, is intermediate between a more liberal view which preserves identity in counterfactually possible divergences both backwards and forwards and the Leibnizian view which denies identity in either case.

It is clear that we do not take the Leibnizian view, since we entertain the possibility that this very man might have done other than he did. If we believe in free will we think that some such actions are causally possible, but even if we are determinists we say that while it was not causally possible it was conceivable that this man should have done otherwise, without prejudice to his identity.

It is not quite so clear that we reject the more liberal view, that we should say confidently about the t_1-t_2-t_3 possibility in Diagram (ii) 'But that man would not be Nixon'. The truth is rather that we do not normally consider that sort of possibility. And this is not altogether surprising. It is not easy to see how men with the different earlier careers, t_1-t_2 and t_0-t_2, could have exactly the same memories or quasi-memories after t_2, or even how the same later pattern of molecular arrangements could causally follow either of two different antecedent sequences. Convergent causal processes are harder even for an indeterminist to accept than divergent ones. And this, I think, is the clue to an explanation of why we think and speak in the way that Kripke describes, that is, in a way that generates the necessities of origin and the counterfactual essences of individuals.

Let us consider a sort of diagram that has been used by Prior, von Wright, and Lucas.[15] In this small circles represent actual or

[14] 'Essais de théodicée' in *Die Philosophischen Schriften*, ed. Gerhardt, vol. vi. p. 363.
[15] A. N. Prior, *Past, Present and Future*, p. 127; G. H. von Wright, *Causality and Determinism*; J. R. Lucas, *A Treatise on Time and Space*, pp. 268–72.

possible states of the world, and the lines joining them represent causally possible developments. Time is represented as discrete, but this is a harmless simplification. In Diagram (iii), if the present state of the world is (a), it is causally possible that the next state should be either (b) or (c) and so on. If the present state is, (d), the lines from (a) through (c) to (g) and (h) and from (b) to (e) and (f) represent lost or defunct possibilities; they are what might have been but was not and now cannot be.

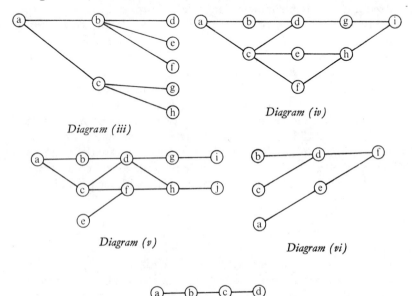

Diagram (iii)

Diagram (iv)

Diagram (v)

Diagram (vi)

Diagram (vii)

All these writers favour structures like that of Diagram (iii), a tree branching out towards the future. But we might consider such structures as those of Diagrams (iv), (v), (vi), and (vii). That is, we might allow for convergent as well as divergent possibilities, or for convergent ones only, or for neither convergence nor divergence. Determinism, in the sense that every event has preceding sufficient causes, would confine us to types (vi) and (vii), indeed traditional determinism would confine us to type (vii), denying that a total state of the world could have come from different antecedents. Libertarians favour type (iii), but why should they not also allow types (iv) and (v)? If causal laws allow alternative developments from the present state, should they not also allow a particular state to come from alternative antecedents?

However, there is a special reason why the sorts of possibility represented by Diagrams (iv), (v), and (vi) tend to be ignored. Even if it is causally possible for (d) in any of these to have come either from (b) or from (c), still there is just one immediately preceding state, say (b), from which it actually did come. The past is fixed, even if it is not causally fixed by the present. So if the top horizontal line in each diagram represents the actual course of events, (c), (a), and (e) in Digaram (vi) were never real possibilities, though they are causally possible sources of the actual state (f), whereas in Diagram (iii) if the present state is (a), all the others shown are still real possibilities, and if the present state is (d), then (c), (e), (f), (g), and (h) are real might-have-beens: it was at some time really possible that each of them should come about. Similarly (e) in Diagram (v) was never a real possibility. But some convergences represent real possibilities: for example, in (iv) or in (v) (d) really might have come from (c), though it actually came from (b).

We thus have an asymmetry between past and future possibilities, even if the causal possibilities as such are symmetrical. Though the present state causally could have come from more than one antecedent, it did come from just one, and the only way in which it really could have come from some alternative antecedent is by that alternative's being a possible outcome of some earlier possible divergence from actuality. Can we restore the symmetry by saying that it is equally true that though (given indeterminism) the present state causally could give rise to alternative subsequent states, there is just one state that will actually follow it immediately? The future, someone might say, is as metaphysically fixed as the past, even if it is causally open, just as, on this view, the past is causally under-determined by the present. But this logical fatalism, if separated from both causal determinism and divine foreknowledge, has seldom carried much weight.[16] In our ordinary thinking we suppose that, if the future is causally under-determined, more than one possibility is really open, whereas the past is closed, even if it is causally under-determined by the present.

[16] Cf. G. Ryle, *Dilemmas*, pp. 15–17; but contrast A. N. Prior's discussion of Diodorean modalities in *Past, Present and Future*, Chapters 2 and 3.

In fact our ordinary thinking, particularly about human action, is libertarian. We assume that there are causally and hence genuinely open alternative possibilities for the future, but not for the past. And this results from our combining of causal under-determinism with the view that the past is fixed just by having occurred. The basic element with which we work is a single line up to the present with possibilities branching out towards the future. Consequently we consider such possibilities as are represented by diagrams of type (iii), but not by those of types (iv), (v), and (vi), and we do not confine our thoughts to diagrams of type (vii).

This way of thinking, I suggest, is what underlies the handling of possibility and identity together in the way that produces the necessities of origin, the contrasting contingencies of development, and the counterfactual essences of individuals. But where, it may be asked, does identity come into the present story? It is not shown in the diagrams with which we have recently been working. Well, see what happens when we simply add persisting individuals to this scheme. If the present state is (a) in (iii), and it includes Nixon, then each of its successor states (b) and (c) can also include this very man. So when the actual course of events has run on through (b) to (d) we must say that the now defunct possible sequence through (c) to (g), if it included a man-history continuous with the Nixon-occurrence in (a), would also have included this same man, Nixon. It is not only a might-have-been, but also a might-have-been for Nixon. But since our ordinary way of thinking does not consider symmetrically convergent possibilities (except where these follow previous divergences), there are no unrealized possibilities of origin for Nixon. So, going back to our earlier diagrams, our ordinary ways of thinking provide that Nixon may, at t_2, pursue either the firm or the dotted line in (i), and consequently that, speaking at t_4, we can say that although he did follow the firm line he might have followed the dotted one. But they do not allow anything like (ii), though they do in principle allow for what is represented in (viii): he might have gone off the rails temporarily without this having any lasting effect.

Diagram (viii)

Thus the libertarian view of causal possibilities, conjoined with the view of the past as fixed and Locke's general account of the same *x*, would yield the main principles of our handling of identity in relation to what might have been. Admittedly these principles must be extended to apply to contracausal as well as merely counterfactual possibilities. But it is not surprising that we should so extend them once they have been formed in the context of causal under-determination. If we start to consider identity through contracausal possibilities, what could be more natural than to use as a model the ways in which we already handle identity through counterfactual possibilities?[17]

If this account is correct, the counterfactual essences of individuals, the fact that this sheet of paper could not have had any different origin from whatever origin (unknown to us) it actually had, though it might have been burned before now, are not a metaphysical mystery, but a consequence of our ways of thinking and speaking about identity in relation to possibility: these *de re* modalities are, in a very broad sense, *de dicto* after all, as are the necessities of constitution which, as we saw in Chapter 3, arise from the way in which we speak and think about kinds of stuff. Or, to put the point less paradoxically, these necessities, though formulated in a *de re* style, can be explained away linguistically in a manner that has been thought to belong exclusively to *de dicto* modalities. Contrary to what Locke thought, the names of stuffs can be, and are, annexed to real essences (even unknown real essences) rather than to nominal essences. It is evidence for this that we think of the same stuff, even in counterfactual possibilities, as being whatever has the same constitution. Similarly the names of individuals can be, and are, annexed to their origins (even unknown origins) rather than to the information through which we make contact with the individuals or recognize them. It is evidence for this that we think of the same individual, even in counterfactual possibilities, as being whatever persisting thing of that kind has the same origin. Our way of thinking and speaking about stuffs is itself contingent: we might have done otherwise. But it is not arbitrary or pointless. It is useful and fruitful just because the world contains many kinds of material whose

---

[17] In my article '*De* what *re* is *de re* modality?', on which the preceding discussion is based (*Journal of Philosophy*, vol. 71 (1974), pp. 551–61), this account is defended by criticism of some rival suggestions.

properties and behaviour are determined in systematic but complex ways by their internal constitutions. Similarly, we might have thought and spoken otherwise about persisting individuals, say in the liberal way or in the Leibnizian way. If there are metaphysical truths which underlie and give point to our actual practice, they will be the truths (if they are such) of causal under-determinism and of the differential fixity of the past as contrasted with the future.

4. *The relativity of identity*

Locke's theory of the identity of persisting things, which relates the requirements for the same x systematically to the concept of an x, both is intrinsically plausible and, as we have seen, works pretty well in many applications. However, it would seem to have the consequence that something we introduce as A may be the same x as something we introduce as B, and yet not the same y, even if A is a y, and perhaps B also. This seems to conflict with the basic principle that everything is identical with itself and with nothing else, so that either what we introduce as B just is A over again—and then if A is a y B must be the same y as A—or else B is not A over again—and then it cannot be even the same x as A.

But how do we deal with concrete examples? A certain man is also, at t_1, an official, say the station-master at Poole. If at t_2 he is no longer the station-master at Poole, and someone else has taken over this office, should we say that though we meet the same man at t_2 as we met at t_1, we are not meeting the same official? It seems more natural to say that we are meeting the same official, even though he no longer holds the same office, or perhaps any office. And if at t_2 we meet the new Poole station-master, it would not be natural to say that we are meeting the same official as we met at t_1, but merely that we are meeting the new holder of the same office. Again, suppose that a man is an officer in the army at t_1, that he is reduced to the ranks at t_2, but commissioned again before t_3, do we want to say that we meet the same man at t_3 as at t_1, but not the same officer? This would be entailed by Locke's theory as I have interpreted it, since though there is a continuous man-history joining the man-occurrence at t_1 to that at t_3, there is not a continuous officer-history uniting the two officer-occurrences. But here again the thorough relativization of identity is unnatural: because this is the same man, we will say also that this is the same officer, despite his ups and downs in military rank.

The dominant principle, then, seems to be that when we have once indicated a thing, we shall say that it is identical with itself under any description: we do not allow any A to be the same x as B but not the same y. Yet this does not refute Locke's form of the relativity thesis. We have still to decide, in raising any question of identity, about what kind of thing we are raising it. But 'kind of thing' here refers to some fairly basic category—number, atom-collection, organism. If the thing we are discussing is an organism, then it is the same thing as long as it is the same organism, and we shall not bother about any lack of continuity in its satisfying of more specific descriptions such as 'officer' or even 'man'. The choice of a kind of thing helps to determine what thing it is we are speaking about, and if it is a thing which persists through time we need Locke's rule to take us from the thing-occurrences to the unitary, identical thing. But once we have such a thing, we can adhere with respect to it to the principle that everything is identical with itself and only with itself. This principle carries with it the rule that if A is identical with B, A and B have all their properties in common, which is usually taken as the criterion of strict identity. (We need not restrict this to extensional or non-modal properties, for the sake of apparent failures of substitutivity of terms in 'referentially opaque' contexts within statements. Though 'Scott is the author of *Waverley*' and 'George IV knows that this man is Scott' do not together entail 'George IV knows that this man is the author of *Waverley*', this does not show that there is any sort of property that Scott has which the author of *Waverley* lacks.) The defensible form of the relativity of identity does not conflict with this requirement for strict identity.[18]

5. *Identity across kinds*

'Identity across kinds' looks like a contradiction in terms, since things of different kinds cannot be (strictly) identical. If A is identical with B, A must be of every kind of which B is. We can ask, however, whether something introduced by a description that belongs with one basic kind or category can be identical with

---

[18] This point is argued very fully in D. Wiggins, *Identity and Spatio-Temporal Continuity*.

something introduced by a description that belongs with another basic kind. The most controversial issues in this area are raised by various forms of the mind/brain identity theory, but there are other less difficult and more readily acceptable cases of what we may call identity across kinds, to which those who assert mind/brain identity commonly appeal. By studying these we may be able to establish principles that can guide discussion of the more controversial issues.

One important question is whether in handling identity across kinds we should introduce something less than strict identity, as defined above, which is yet worth calling identity. This question comes up in several ways.

For example, is an organism identical with the collection of all the atoms that compose it? It is constituted not, perhaps, by a mere atom-collection but by an atom-collection organized in a certain way, by these atoms together with the relations and interactions between them, and it is surely identical with what constitutes it. Where the organism is, there *is* nothing but these atoms and their relations and interactions. On the other hand the same organism is constituted by one organized atom-collection at t_1 and by a different organized atom-collection at t_2. If it is identical with either organized atom-collection it must be identical with both, and then the symmetry and transitivity of identity will require that these two different organized atom-collections should be identical with one another.

What has gone wrong? The trouble stems, once again, from the notion of the identity of a persisting but changing thing through time, which Hume regarded as a fiction and which I classed in Section 2 as 'specially secured'. There would be no difficulty in saying that an organism-occurrence is not only constituted by but also identical with an organized-atom-collection-occurrence, while a later, different, organism-occurrence joined to the earlier one by a continuous organism-history is identical with a different organized-atom-collection-occurrence, while the organism-history in question is neither identical with nor constituted by any organized-atom-collection-history; what constitutes it is made up of parts of many different atom-collection-histories. We get into difficulty because we are using the concept of an organism as a thing which is all there at once at t_1 (and therefore is identical with the organized atom-collection which is also all there at once at t_1) but which is equally all there at once at t_2 (and therefore is identical with the different organized atom-collection which is there at t_2). If we are to work with this concept, it seems that we shall have to introduce a qualified identity, identity-at-a-time. We could then say that the organism is identical-at-t_1 with one organized atom-collection, and identical-at-t_2 with another, but not strictly identical with either. This would defeat the paradox, but at the cost of introducing identity-at-a-time which is something less than strict identity.

But is this move really necessary? Or were we too hasty in agreeing that something is identical with what constitutes it? It is true that '... constitutes ...', or its converse '... consists of ...', is not the same relation as '... is identical with ...', since the latter is symmetrical while the other two are asymmetrical. But this leaves it possible that identity should hold wherever constitution holds. A stronger objection is that different descriptions may be appropriate for a constituter and what it constitutes. An atom-collection is presumably a set of atoms, but an organism is not a set. The atom-collection has the individual atoms as members, whereas the organism has them as parts. We may reply that we are thinking of the atom-collection not as a mere collection, not as the mathematical abstract entity, a set, but as something concrete which includes the relations and interactions between the atoms, and hence as something of which the individual atoms are parts, not members. But if this is how we are considering the organized atom-collection, can we not say that we have the same organized atom-collection at t_2 as at t_1, despite the fact that it has different atoms as its parts? Was not our reason for calling these different collections precisely that we were looking on each collection as a set, as something whose identity was determined wholly and simply by the identity of all the individual atoms that were its members? No doubt we can have a notion of constituting which does not amount to strict identity, and we can consider an atom-collection in such a way that it bears this relation to an organism. But if, instead, we take such a view of an organized atom-collection as will allow it not merely to constitute but also to be identical, even at a particular time, with an organism, we can identify it with what constitutes the same organism at another time, even if it no longer has the same component parts. If a constituter is identical even at a time with what it constitutes, it will have the same conditions for identity through time as what it constitutes, and so will be strictly identical with it. We have therefore no need for the notion of a qualified identity-at-a-time.[19]

But other examples raise further difficulties. A pint of water may be strictly identical with a collection of water molecules in certain relations with one another. Can we also say that its states are strictly identical with the corresponding states of the collection of molecules? Since a lump of ice, that is, frozen water, is constituted by and identical with a collection of molecules held by another in a certain space lattice, while the same water, before being frozen, was constituted by and identical with a differently organized collection of the same molecules, it is plausible to say that the water's being frozen is just the molecules' being held by one another in that lattice. Identity of states can thus be reduced to the identity of things in those states. But what about identity of properties? In view of the cautious interpretation of Aristotelian realism which I defended in Chapter 4, we must not treat properties as things. Some properties can be handled much as we have just handled states. The water's being at a temperature of 80° centigrade may be thus identified with its molecules' having a certain mean kinetic energy. It seems to be only a verbal awkwardness that we would not want to say that the mean kinetic energy is 80° centigrade.[20] It is not awkward to say that being at a certain temperature is having a certain mean molecular kinetic energy, and both of these can be ascribed both to the water and to the collection of molecules. On the other hand if we interpret a temperature as a dispositional property—a multiply-manifested disposition—it is not this but its ground that we can identify with mean molecular kinetic energy. Properties, we may say, are identical if and only if they could not come apart in any possible world. This test shows that if we take temperature as a disposition it is not identical with kinetic energy, whereas if we take it as the ground of that disposition it is: what is in fact the ground of that disposition just is, identically, kinetic energy, though this could not be known *a priori*.

Again, we want to say that a lightning flash is identical with an

[19] I owe this point to M. G. J. Evans.

[20] Cf. James Cornman, 'The Identity of Mind and Body', in *The Mind/Brain Identity Theory*, ed. C. V. Borst, pp. 123–9. The articles by Richard Rorty and Thomas Nagel in this collection are also particularly relevant to our present discussion.

electrical discharge, but if the flash is bright, is the discharge bright also? Or is this less than a strict identity, so that the two terms do not have all their properties in common? But this difficulty disappears when we detect an ambiguity in the phrase 'the lightning flash', and perhaps a corresponding one in the terms 'bright' and 'brightness'. What is bright as we see brightness is the flash as seen, the content of a visual experience; but this, being an intentional object, is not identical with the electrical discharge. What is so identical is the real external object, that which is seen as a flash. The sense in which this is bright is that it has the secondary quality of brightness, that is, the power to produce the sensation of brightness in us, and the discharge too is bright in this sense. Of course, if we make what Locke would call—rightly, as I believe—the mistake of construing secondary qualities as primary ones, of ascribing brightness as seen to the real external flash, then we might equally ascribe it to the discharge; or alternatively we might then equate the real external flash with some collection of properties that includes this brightness, but equate the discharge with some other overlapping but non-coincident collection of properties, but then we must say that the flash and the discharge are not identical but only partly coincident and partly causally linked. There are thus various possible coherent—if not all correct—ways of describing the situation, but for none of them do we need a notion of a less-than-strict identity: it is only if we mix these different treatments up in an incoherent way that we are tempted to say both that the flash is the discharge and yet that the flash is bright while the discharge is not.

A gene can be strictly identical with a DNA molecule, though being a DNA molecule is—or was until recently—no part of the meaning of the word 'gene'. This is possible because a gene is a substance; it is introduced in a genetic theory as that thing, whatever it is, that plays a certain part in the inheritance of characteristics. The term 'gene' is annexed to something which was initially identified only by way of its causal role, and which is therefore freely available for strict identification with something discovered and described in other ways. It might be objected, however, that a gene can be dominant or recessive; can a molecule be so? Yes, if it is the sort of molecule that is a gene. To be dominant or recessive is just to be such, in relation to its allelomorph, as to react in one way or another in the joint production of characteristics, and the relevant relations and causal powers can be ascribed to the molecule.

'Demoniacal possession is a form of hallucinatory psychosis.'[21] Is this a strict identity? We can look at it in either of two ways. We may take 'demoniacal possession' literally, as meaning 'having one's body occupied and controlled by one or more malevolent non-human personal beings', and then we shall say that there is really no such thing as demoniacal possession, but that what people used to believe to be demoniacal possession is a psychosis. Alternatively, we may take 'demoniacal possession' in the way in which we take the names of other disorders such as 'measles' and 'schizophrenia'.[22] That is, we may take the name to be annexed not to a set of symptoms nor yet to any particular supposed cause of those symptoms, such as the presence of non-human spirits, but rather to a kind of condition which is identified by way of some collection of paradigm cases and of paradigm non-cases, by specimens of the denotation and of what lies outside the denotation. Then since demoniacal possession will *be* this kind of condition, we shall say that it undoubtedly occurs and that it is— is strictly identical with—a form of psychosis. With either way of handling the term, we shall not be tempted to introduce any less-than-strict identity: we should be tempted to do so only if we mixed up these alternative treatments with one another.

The understanding that we have thus reached of less troublesome cases of what may be called, somewhat misleadingly, identity across kinds supplies a background against which the controversial mind/brain identity theses can be considered. I shall not, of course, be able to discuss them adequately, but only make some general but fairly crucial points.

First, our survey of the less troublesome cases gives us no encouragement to think of introducing any less-than-strict identity in the mind/body area.

Secondly, if minds and mental states and processes were introduced into our thought and discussion in the way in which genes, for example, are, then there would be no fundamental obstacle to mind/brain identity. Minds would be freely available for empirical identification with brains, just as genes are for identification with, as it has turned out, DNA molecules. Of course, it was epistemi-

[21] Cf. Richard Rorty in Borst, op. cit., pp. 187–213.
[22] Cf. Chapter 3, pp. 99–100 above.

cally possible that they should have been identified with something else: what precise identity holds in either case is a matter for empirical discovery. It is this line of thought, that mind can be defined as the inner cause of certain behaviour, that has been developed particularly by Armstrong.[23] The difficulty with it is that we seem to know more about minds than this, and the more that we know is an obstacle to this identification. One part of this obstacle is the intentionality of mental states. Someone's believing that p is a logically distinct state of affairs from the possible state of affairs which 'p' itself would describe: either can exist without the other. Yet his believing that p can be adequately described only by introducing into the description the statement 'p': the state of affairs which is the believing is descriptively parasitic upon the other, logically independent, (possible) state of affairs. It is hard to see what system of physical properties and relations could make one physical state thus descriptively parasitic on another. However, since this parasitism is something of a mystery on any view, it may be unfair to press it as a difficulty specially for physicalism.[24]

Phenomenal qualities in experience form another part of this obstacle; they also constitute a problem for Smart's treatment of the issue. If all that we know about having an after-image was adequately expressed by Smart's '*What is going on in me is like what is going on in me when* my eyes are open, the lighting is normal, etc., etc., and there really is a yellowish-orange patch on the wall'[25] then one's having of an after-image could be strictly identical with the occurrence of a certain process in one's brain. But again the difficulty is that we seem to be immediately aware of more than this: we know the respect in which the having of an after-image is like the seeing of a real orange patch, and more particularly that in which the image is like the orange patch as seen. In both there is a certain phenomenal quality, the colour as seen, a content of experience of the same specific sort in both, and the problem is how either to accommodate it in a physicalist account or to explain it away. It can indeed be reasonably

[23] D. M. Armstrong, *A Materialist Theory of the Mind*, especially Chapter 6.

[24] Armstrong has, of course, tried to deal with this problem both in *A Materialist Theory of the Mind* and in *Belief, Truth, and Knowledge*; I must leave readers to judge for themselves how satisfactory his explanation is. I have stated the problem more fully in 'Problems of Intentionality' in *Phenomenology and Philosophical Understanding*.

[25] J. J. C. Smart, *Philosophy and Scientific Realism*, p. 94.

predicted that all aspects of the experiencing state will eventually be correlated with neurophysiological occurrences; it is very likely that the mental state has a purely physical basis, so that any features that it has could be regarded as properties of a physical thing. But it would seem that the phenomenal qualities of the experiencing state are very different from most other properties of physical things: we seem to be left at least with a distinctive set of mental properties which, even if we *say* that they too are physical, are unlike other physical properties. A thoroughgoing physicalist would want to identify even these properties with other, indubitably physical, properties. But strict identity between properties here seems unattainable. We can think of possible worlds in which the phenomenal qualities are not associated with the physical properties on which they now rest. At this point we may be tempted to introduce some weakened variety of identity, say 'theoretical identity', according to which two occurrences (such as the presence of a certain phenomenal quality in experience and the presence of a certain neurophysiological condition) are theoretically identical if they have all the same causes and effects. But to say this is to abandon the substance of the identity thesis, to accept what many other thinkers have been prepared to accept under the name of correlation, and merely to *call* it identity. Alternatively, we might hope to 'reduce' the phenomenal qualities to neurophysiological ones. But just what could this reduction of qualities be? We know in principle what it is to reduce one theory to another, or one set of laws to another, when all the laws or theoretical statements of the reduced group are derived from laws and statements of the theory to which it is reduced with the help of some bridging principles or rules of translation. But this throws no light on a possible reduction of qualities. The one plausible method of reducing one quality to another is to explain away the first as a mere appearance of the second. We start by ascribing some colour as we see it to an external object. But then we may be persuaded by Boyle and Locke that colours are secondary qualities, that in the object there are only certain surface microstructures, the primary qualities of minute parts, which reflect light of certain frequencies. The colour as we see it is merely how these microstructures and light-frequencies look to us. But in thus explaining away the apparent colour-as-we-see-it quality of the external object we are, necessarily, retaining this how-it-looks as a feature of the content of our experience. Plainly this method of reduction cannot be successfully applied to the phenomenal qualities of the content of experience itself. It is useless to argue that appearances are mere appearances: this would leave them still there as appearances.

For example, it may well be that I feel pain when and only when my C-fibres are stimulated: can pain then be identified (strictly, not merely 'theoretically') with C-fibre stimulation? Well, we could conceivably use the word 'pain' in a way analogous to the second way explained above of using the phrase 'demoniacal possession' and then we could say that the pain just is the C-fibre stimulation. But this leaves untouched its phenomenal quality, how it feels to me, in fact its painfulness. Can we say that this is merely how C-fibre stimulation appears to me? Yes, but that is so appears is an unreduced and irreducible feature of the situation. If we annex the word 'pain' to this phenomenal quality, the physicalist is committed to something analogous to the first way of handling demoniacal possession, to saying 'What people now call pain is really C-fibre stimulation'.[26] But whereas we can easily explain away literal demoniacal possession as a mistaken explanatory theory, we cannot analogously explain away the painfulness. I may be mistaken in locating pain as I feel it in my toe, but I cannot be mistaken in feeling it as painful.

Thus it seems that the phenomenal qualities of the content of experience, once recognized, cannot be explained away: our only method of quality-reduction fails through circularity when applied to them. The only recourse for the thoroughgoing physicalist is to refuse to recognize them in the first place, and this is what both Smart and Armstrong, in slightly different ways, have done. But this seems utterly implausible, being in conflict with our most evident experience.[27]

6. *Answers and decisions*

To what extent, then, do questions about identity call for answers, and to what extent for decisions? How far are they questions of fact and how far matters of arbitrary choice?

[26] Cf. Richard Rorty in Borst, op. cit., p. 193.

[27] The need to modify Central State Materialism in order to allow for phenomenal properties is argued for example by Keith Campbell in *Body and Mind*, especially pp. 104–9.

No doubt it is in a very ultimate sense a matter of choice whether we use the concept of identity at all; but it is a fact that we have it and use it, and that we use the words and phrases that we do use to express it. Also it is a fact that our present concept of identity is in itself a clear and a strict one, with well-defined logical rules attached to its standard terms, especially the rules that each thing is identical only with itself and hence that if A is identical with B, B has all the same properties as A. There seems to be no good reason for altering or relaxing this basic logic of identity. The coherent way of speaking is to say that the relation between different features or descriptions of the same thing, or between different parts of the same thing, or between different occurrences, different time-slices, of the same persisting thing is not any qualified sort of identity but just diversity, mitigated only by the fact that they are related in the ways indicated to the same thing.

In the area of identity across kinds, it is always a factual question whether what we get at in one way is exhaustively constituted by, and hence identical with, what we get at in another way, or whether they are merely causally connected, or whether there is a partial overlap with something left over. These are not matters for decision, even linguistic decision. But where the items picked out by our terms used in one way, perhaps the currently standard way, are not identical, but, say, closely correlated or partially overlapping, there is always the possibility of explicit or implicit linguistic decisions which would change the use of either or both terms so as to make them both pick out the same (perhaps complex) item; but of course this will only mask the diversity that was previously recorded and that is still there, even if there is now no simple way of expressing it. Even if the word 'pain' came to be so used as to be annexed to whatever the phenomenal quality of painfulness is an appearance of, and so in effect to the neurophysiological basis, that phenomenal quality would still be different from all the obviously physical properties of that neurophysiological state.

In the area of identity through time, it is in a very fundamental sense a matter of choice whether we use the concept of the same persisting thing rather than the logically easier concepts of thing-occurrences (where thing-occurrences at different times are necessarily diverse) and of thing-histories (where thing-occurrences or time-slices are only parts of thing-histories). There is in principle a choice between an ontology of persisting things and one of events and concatenations of events. But this is a choice that has been made; it is the concept of persisting things that is familiar and enshrined in ordinary language and psychologically almost irresistible; the rival, logically easier, concepts seem artificial and we have to coin new words to express them. The latter are useful particularly in philosophical discussion, in order to clarify our handling of the familiar persisting-thing concept, but it is this that we shall go on using in most ordinary contexts. And it is clear that we shall do so because this concept is appropriate: the world as it is lends itself to description in these terms. The logically more difficult concept is epistemically prior to the logically easier ones, and perhaps necessarily so. We can pick out bulb-occurrences only through being able to pick out bulbs, and we pick these out by means of their persistence.

But given that we are going to speak about persisting things, there are further choices to be made about the sort of persisting thing we consider on any occasion. If it is to be an unchanging thing, or one like Locke's 'mass' or 'body', which can change only by jumbling of its parts, then the conditions for its identity are automatically fixed. But if it is to be something that can change in other ways, grow, absorb elements, shed parts, and so on, then its identity needs to be 'specially secured', that is, we need special provisions to ensure that the logic of identity is obeyed. But still it is not that this logic is being relaxed: rather when the concept of one thing of a certain sort is relaxed by allowing growth and so on, it needs to be somewhat arbitrarily restricted elsewhere in order that the resulting 'thing' should still conform to the strict logic of identity.

It is because there is this choice of a kind of thing to be made before any clear questions about identity through time arise that we can defend what I have called Locke's thesis about the relativity of identity; but I have rejected the more extreme relativity thesis that some one thing, A, could be the same x as B but not the same y as B. Once we have chosen a kind, that is a basic category, of persisting thing, the natural requirement for its unity and hence its identity will be the one I have ascribed to Locke, the spatio-temporal continuity of the corresponding thing-history, along with special clauses where required. These decisions carry with them implicit decisions about the essence of an individual in the sense of what is essential for an individual's continuing to be the same x. What is counterfactually essential to an individual rests upon a further choice which, I have argued, is implicit in our way of handling identity and counterfactual possibility together, but there may be metaphysical truths which make these ways of thinking and speaking appropriate.

Granted that there is this degree of arbitrariness about our choice of the thing-concepts to which the notion of identity is applied, do we, or could we, go further and see one and the same thing in a discontinuous series of thing-occurrences? Can, or could, the same thing exist at different times but exist intermittently and not persist? Nothing in the logic of the concepts would preclude this. Such identity would, of course, have to be 'specially secured', but so does the identity of some already respectable persisting things. But what would give point to talk about identity here rather than about a mere sequence of numerically diverse but qualitatively similar things? Only, I think, one of two possibilities. This identity might be parasitic upon the identity of some persisting thing—as, for example, we may speak of the same church when one has been destroyed and a replica built on the same site or at least in the same village. Alternatively, we might believe the successive intermittent occurrences to be not only similar but directly causally connected with one another across and despite the temporal gaps—but we have at present no reason to believe that any such form of causation occurs.

6

PERSONAL IDENTITY

1. *Locke and the unity of consciousness*

IDENTITY in general is a problem for logicians and philosophers, but the identity of persons is of much wider concern. Personal immortality, survival after bodily death, and the transmigration of souls have at all times been objects of religious belief, anxious doubt, and intensely interested speculation. Cases of changed or divided personality and loss of memory are prominent in imaginative literature as well as in popular psychology, and science fiction has introduced further fascinating or horrifying possibilities. Some of the actual or possible odd cases are not merely of private interest, but do, or might, call for legal decisions about penalties, responsibilities, duties, and rights. The philosophical problem of what constitutes the identity of a person is highly relevant to all of these. On the answer to it depends the very coherence of some of our hopes and fears as well as our understanding of and response to some of the things that do, or might, occur. It is not surprising, then, that it was to this problem that Locke devoted most of his chapter on identity and diversity, or that his answer, and the question itself, have continued to be keenly debated ever since.

Locke, in accordance with what we have called his principle of the relativity of identity, says that 'to find wherein *personal identity* consists, we must consider what *person* stands for', and answers that this is 'a thinking intelligent being that has reason and reflection and can consider itself as itself, the same thinking thing in different times and places'.[1] But Locke is rightly concerned not just with the word 'person' itself. He is using it as the noun that corresponds to all the personal pronouns. His question is, 'Wherein consists my identity, and hers, and his, and yours?'

His answer is that it is consciousness that constitutes personal identity, that makes me, for example, the same me, the same person, through and despite the passage of time. His argument is

[1] II. xxvii. 9.

that consciousness 'is inseparable from thinking', that when we perceive or meditate or will we know that we do so, and that it is by this consciousness that each of us considers himself as himself, as one persisting thinking thing. It is by this reflective consciousness that our different sensations and perceptions and thoughts and desires at any one time belong to one self, and, Locke thinks, the same principle must account for the sameness of the self at different times: 'as far as this consciousness can be extended backwards to any past action or thought, so far reaches the identity of that *person*: it is the same self now it was then, and it is by the same *self* with this present one that now reflects on it, that that action was done'.[2]

What this amounts to as a positive doctrine is not yet clear, but there are at least two views that Locke is plainly rejecting. First, in distinguishing the person from the man, and hence *the same person* from *the same man*, he is denying that bodily continuity, the persistence of the human organism, makes personal identity. The same living human body with its continuity of animal life constitutes the same man; but not necessarily, Locke holds, the same person. But secondly he is denying that to be the same person is to be, or to have, one persisting immaterial, spiritual soul-substance. Against this view he argues not by denying that there are spiritual substances but by saying that their identity does not matter. If there are soul-substances, then presumably these can be reincarnated: the present mayor of Queenborough may, for all that anyone knows, have what used to be the soul of Socrates; but if he has no consciousness from the inside of any of Socrates's actions or thoughts, no direct awareness of those experiences as his experiences, then he is not the same person as Socrates.[3] Again, if the same soul-substance carried two alternating sets of co-conscious thoughts, there would be two different persons with one soul. Locke uses parallel arguments to bring out the irrelevance to the identity of the person of both the living body and the

[2] II. xxvii. 9.

[3] II. xxvii. 14. I am assuming that 'one who was persuaded his had been the soul of *Socrates*' in this section is the mayor of Queenborough referred to as possibly identical with Socrates in Section 19. The description 'in the post he filled, which was no inconsiderable one, he passed for a very rational man' might well apply to a mayor, though 'the press has shown that he wanted not parts or learning' is contrary evidence, since there seems to be no record of publications by a mayor of Queenborough in the relevant period. Cf. query by R. H. in *Locke Newsletter*, No. 4 (1973), pp. 43–4.

supposed soul-substance. 'Could we suppose two distinct in-communicable consciousnesses acting the same body, the one constantly by day, the other by night ... I ask ... whether the *day-* and the *night-man* would not be two as distinct persons as *Socrates* and *Plato*'. Similarly, since we know that an 'immaterial thinking thing may sometimes part with its past consciousness and be restored to it again'—that is, there may be a total but temporary loss of memory—we can imagine in the same soul-substance 'these intervals of memory and forgetfulness to take their turns regularly by day and night', and then 'you have two persons with the same immaterial spirit, as much as in the former instance two persons with the same body'.[4] Conversely, if we had 'the same consciousness, acting by intervals, two distinct bodies', Locke argues that this would be the same person in the two bodies, just as you may have the same man in two different suits of clothes; and this still holds if there are also two distinct immaterial substances. Personal identity might be 'continued in a succession of several substances'; it might be 'preserved in the change of immaterial substances ... as animal identity is preserved in the change of material substances'.[5] Locke is using the analogy of the way in which the same vegetable or animal life is continued despite the metabolic processes that constantly replace the material components of an organism to argue that there could be a sort of spiritual metabolism, the same consciousness being passed on from one soul-substance to another.

Equally, it might be passed from one body to another: 'should the soul of a prince, carrying with it the consciousness of the prince's past life, enter and inform the body of a cobbler as soon as deserted by his own soul, everyone sees he would be the same person with the prince, accountable only for the prince's actions'. This example is used to drive a wedge between *the same man* and *the same person*; no one, Locke thinks, would say that this is the same man as the former prince.[6]

In these examples Locke introduces a method which has been taken over by many later contributors to this discussion, the construction of puzzle cases. The continuity of animal life in one body and a unified mental history or unity of consciousness normally go together, and the presence of a single immaterial

---

[4] II. xxvii. 23; cf. II. i. 11–12.   [5] II. xxvii. 23, 10, 12.
[6] II. xxvii. 15.

soul-substance was presumed by Locke's contemporaries normally to accompany these. But Locke has imagined a series of cases in which the identity and diversity of these three items, body, consciousness, and soul, do not all go together, but are separated and combined in various ways. In examples of the Jekyll-and-Hyde type the same body and the same soul are associated with two separate unities of consciousness, two mental histories not linked by mutual awareness. In Socrates and the mayor of Queenborough we may have the same soul but different bodies and disjoint consciousnesses. In the prince and the cobbler we have the same soul and the same consciousness successively in two different bodies. And so on. Locke claims that in all these various combinations it is plausible to say that we have the same person where and only where we have the same consciousness; the sameness of the living body is neither necessary nor sufficient to constitute the same person, nor is the sameness of a spiritual substance.

Locke makes out a strong case for both his negative theses, that personal identity is to be equated neither with the identity of a soul-substance nor with that of a man, that is, of a living human animal body. There is also considerable plausibility in at least the broad outline of his positive thesis, that personal identity is somehow to be equated with, or based on, the unity of consciousness. True, he could hardly claim, and he does not in fact claim, that everyone uses the phrase 'the same person' in accordance with his principles. He admits that 'in the ordinary way of speaking, the same person and the same man stand for one and the same thing'.[7] Rather what he is saying is that if we find three distinct meanings for the terms 'spirit', 'man', and 'person', we shall in consequence let the identity of persons be determined in the way that he suggests. He reinforces this claim by saying that 'person' is 'a forensic term, appropriating actions and their merit'. That is, the sameness of a person is intended to carry with it legal and moral responsibility for actions; that is why it 'belongs only to intelligent agents, capable of a law, and happiness and misery'. This personality 'imputes to *itself* past actions, just upon the same ground and for the same reason that it does the present. All which is founded in a concern for happiness, the unavoidable concomitant of consciousness: that which is conscious of pleasure and

[7] II. xxvii. 15.

pain desiring that that self that is conscious should be happy'.[8] This brings in another factor, one's concern for one's own future happiness. I have a peculiarly intimate, egoistic concern about my own possible future happiness or misery, quite different from any altruistic or sympathetic interest that I may have in the well-being of others: hardly anyone literally loves his neighbour as himself. Locke assumes that this forward-looking concern fits in with the reflective self-ascription of past actions: the future self for whose well-being I now have this special concern is the one which will impute to itself whatever I now do and which will remember my present experiences from the inside. If this is so, then it is peculiarly appropriate, especially on deterrent grounds, but also on some other views about punishment, to tie responsibility to such a two-directional unity of consciousness. If I know that the future self for which I have this special concern will be punished for my wrong actions (which it will remember and impute to itself), this gives me a reason for now refraining from wrong actions. But if I do not refrain, and that future self is punished for them, it will remember them and associate the punishment with them and so, through its like concern for a further future self, will be deterred from repeating those wrong actions. Backward-looking memory and action-ascription and forward-looking concern seem thus to go together, and in conjunction they supply the rationale for the use of the concept of an identical person as the bearer of responsibilities and rights. This is, I believe, the thought behind what Locke says here, though we have to read between the lines to find it.

2. *Objections and difficulties*

Locke, then, not only raised the problem of personal identity in the form in which philosophers have gone on discussing it, and introduced the method of constructing puzzle cases, but also proposed a solution which still has a great deal of force. Yet it must be admitted that his solution involves some obscurity and is open to a number of serious objections.[9]

[8] II. xxvii. 26; cf. II. i. 11.
[9] Many of the objections are stated by A. G. N. Flew, in 'Locke and the Problem of Personal Identity', *Philosophy*, 26 (1951), reprinted in *Locke and Berkeley*, pp. 154–78. Flew also acknowledges the merits of Locke's contribution.

First, we need some explanation of the noun 'consciousness' which will show how we can speak of the same consciousness. This must be based on the relation *being conscious of*. Being conscious of doing or experiencing something is quite different from awareness of material things and external events, or of what someone else is doing or experiencing; let us call the former, to distinguish it, consciousness of an action or experience from the inside. Also, there is a kind of memory which one may have of doing things and of having experiences, and which consists partly of a faint copy of fragments of the earlier experience, still seen from the inside. Locke is saying that in this way one can at one time be conscious of actions and experiences which occurred at an earlier time. He then slides from using 'consciousness' as an abstract verbal noun, meaning just one's being conscious of these various items, to the use of it as a concrete noun, so that he can speak of 'two distinct incommunicable consciousnesses'. The phrase 'the same consciousness' can be used in either way and facilitates the transition. But what does 'consciousness' as a concrete noun stand for? Presumably an entity consisting of someone's being conscious of a number of actions and experiences together. If Locke then wants to identify this someone, the person, with this consciousness, he can avoid circularity only by taking the entity in question to be the collection of co-conscious items themselves, that is, by anticipating Hume's thesis that a person is just a 'train of perceptions' held together by certain relations.[10] Alternatively, Locke could, and I think would, say that the someone that has the experiences and performs the actions is something other than the perceptions, but that a consciousness consists simply of this something other having a series of co-conscious experiences. He would thus leave room for a thinking subject, perhaps a spiritual substance, but still insist that the identity of the person is determined by the unity of a consciousness alone.

Now it is conceivable that there should have been well-defined units of consciousness, distinct consciousnesses, that is, separate mental histories, such that there was perfect co-consciousness within any unit and no co-consciousness between units, in other words, that any later phase of such a consciousness could remember, in this special way, from the inside, all and only earlier items belonging to that same unit, that is, that any earlier item could be

[10] Cf. *Treatise* I. iv. 6.

made co-conscious by memory with any later item in that same unit. Any such mental history could then have been plausibly said to be the history of a single identical person; and this suggestion would have been still more attractive if every earlier phase of such a history had included the special concern mentioned above for the well-being of every later phase of the same history.

But in fact things are not like this. Relations of memory and concern occur untidily, so that they do not mark off any well-defined units. The gallant-officer story of Reid (following Berkeley) is well known: an elderly general can remember capturing a standard as a young officer, but cannot remember being flogged as a boy for robbing an orchard, whereas the young officer could remember the flogging; so the general and the young officer should belong to one unit of consciousness, and again the young officer and the boy, but not the general and the boy. This difficulty remains even if we stretch the sense of 'could remember' to include what one could remember with the help of cues and reminders: however we construe this requirement, not only is any person's memory of the past conscious life of that same man extremely fragmentary, but the *could remember the experiences of* relation is non-transitive, and so does not define any units of consciousness. Similarly in the other direction the relation *feels special concern for* is non-transitive, and in any case it does not always fit in with *could remember*: it may well be that a middle-aged man remembers some of his experiences as a child, but the child was quite thoughtless about his well-being in middle age. Conversely, even if I knew that I was to enjoy total and permanent amnesia from tonight onwards, this would not make me indifferent to the possible sufferings tomorrow of the person who would be the same man as I.

In the face of this difficulty, there are three different lines that Locke, or a Lockean, might take:

One is to say that there are units of *potential* consciousness, that a person could in principle remember every conscious action or experience of his, even those that he cannot in fact be brought to remember by any stimulus. But what can this 'could in principle remember' mean? Surely only that those actions and experiences are his. If this suggestion is to avoid circularity, it must presuppose that there is some other criterion or constituent of personal identity; it tacitly abandons the Lockean theory in favour of some other view. The same results if the criterion suggested is that it is logically possible for the person to remember an item: for what makes this logically possible is that the item should have been an experience of *his*. (Yet there is something else that 'could in principle remember' might mean: this is related to a modification of the Lockean theory which I shall be suggesting towards the end of this chapter. If there is something—say the continued existence of the same central nervous system—that normally makes remembering possible, we might say that someone 'could in principle remember' where this normal basis of remembering was present, but where a special interfering cause, say a local brain injury, prevented the man from ever in fact remembering certain experiences, even with the help of cues and reminders.)

A second, much more plausible, suggestion turns the problem of transitivity into an advantage, by taking the unit of consciousness to be determined not by the relation *could remember*, but by its ancestral—that is, by the relation which is to *could remember* as *ancestor* is to *parent*. For example, since the general can remember the young officer's experiences, and the young officer could remember the boy's, the general's experiences and the boy's, as well as the young officer's, all belong to the same unit of consciousness, the same unified mental history.[11]

We may develop this proposal in more detail. Locke could have said that what makes me the same person from one moment to the next, while I am awake, is a genuine co-consciousness of experiences, an overlapping of specious presents. What I take to be happening now is not instantaneous, not confined within a knife-edge present, but fills some short stretch of time, and these nows overlap one another. For each now there is, we might say, an I-occurrence, and successive I-occurrences will similarly overlap and fade into one another: thus these I-occurrences build up into a continuous I-history. The single person, the I, is what is taken to be there, all at once, at each moment in an I-history. This constitutes my identity throughout any one waking day, any period throughout which I am continuously conscious. But to bridge gaps in this continuity, especially those between one day and the next where these are separated by periods of unconsciousness, of dreamless sleep, we bring in memory: what makes me today the

[11] This suggestion is developed into a theory of personal identity by H. P. Grice in 'Personal Identity', *Mind*, vol. 50 (1941), pp. 330–50.

same person as yesterday is that I remember from the inside at least a few of the items that belonged to yesterday's continuous consciousness. A network of overlapping specious presents and day-to-day memory bridges builds up what we now take to be a single consciousness: we can thus generate a relation *is the same person as* and another *belongs to the same person as* which are both transitive and symmetrical, despite the very fragmentary nature of what we can actually remember, even with the help of stimuli.

Such an account has several merits. It develops Locke's plausible initial suggestion that the sameness of a person is based somehow on co-consciousness of experiences and actions. Admittedly it does not strictly exemplify what I called in Chapter 5 his general theory of identity—x-occurrences at t_1 and at t_2 are occurrences of the same x if and only if there is a continuous x-history linking them—but it bears a close analogy to this: the overlapping I-occurrences during a waking day make up an I-history which has the sort of continuity that is appropriate to persons, though different from the spatio-temporal continuity of bodies and organisms, and the memory bridges joining me on one day to me on the previous day are a kind of substitute for continuous existence. Also what this account gives us coincides pretty well with what we ordinarily recognize as the same person, and obeys the standard logic of identity.

However, this is a revision, not an interpretation, of Locke's account. Not only does he not say this, he commits himself explicitly to a different view. He mentions the objection, 'Suppose I wholly lose the memory of some parts of my life beyond a possibility of retrieving them, so that perhaps I shall never be conscious of them again: yet am I not the same person that did those actions, had those thoughts that I once was conscious of, though I have now forgot them?' His answer is that 'we must here take notice what the word *I* is applied to, which, in this case, is the man only'.[12] That is, the person who did those forgotten actions is not the same person as I now am, though no doubt a series of memory bridges will have connected them. Again, 'as far as any intelligent being can repeat the *idea* of any past action with the same consciousness it had of it at first, ... so far is it the same *personal self*. For it is by the consciousness it has of its present thoughts and

[12] II. xxvii. 20.

actions that it is *self* to *itself* now, and so will be the same *self* as far as the same consciousness can extend to actions past or to come . . .'[13] We must take it that Locke means 'so far and no further'. For these remarks follow an explicit admission of the fragmentary nature of our memories and the interruptions of consciousness by sound sleep. These breaks in consciousness, he says, have raised doubts 'whether we are the same thinking thing, i.e. the same substance, or no'. He brushes this question aside, insisting that it is consciousness, not sameness of substance, that makes the same self. He should have recognized that fragmentary memories and interruptions of consciousness are as much a problem for his own theory as they are for the Cartesian view of a substance whose essence is thinking. But since with these difficulties fully in sight he repeated the assertion that personal identity extends as far as consciousness, he must have meant this literally: having identified a person at a particular time we are to take as belonging to that person all and only those past actions and experiences which he could now be brought to recollect, and, presumably, all and only those future person-occurrences for which he feels a concern somewhat like the special, intimate concern that one feels for one's present self.

It is this third line, then, that Locke actually takes with regard to the lack of well-defined units of consciousness: though he does not explicitly recognize this, he is committed to giving up the transitivity of personal identity. It is particularly because he sees persons as bearers of responsibility that he finds this extreme view appropriate. 'For whatsoever any substance has thought or done, which I cannot recollect and by my consciousness make my own thought and action, it will no more belong to me, whether a part of me thought or did it, than if it had been thought or done by any other immaterial being . . .'[14]

Locke defends this view against the objection that it would make a man, now sober, not responsible for what he did while drunk, if he really cannot remember doing it, and equally make people non-responsible for actions done while sleep-walking, whereas courts of law do not admit these excuses. He argues that human judicatures are reasonable in not admitting them, because they cannot be sure that such pleas are genuine. But, he is convinced, at the day of judgement God will hold each of us respon-

[13] II. xxvii. 10.   [14] II. xxvii. 24.

sible only for what he can remember, and he rules, by implication, that if a human court could be certain of the truth of a plea of amnesia, it should hold the accused non-responsible.[15] In a case of sleep-walking, we might well agree. With drunkenness, we may hesitate, but we might be able to reconcile our inclinations with Locke's principles by saying that the man was non-responsible for what he did while blind drunk, but responsible for getting drunk in circumstances in which he was then liable to do harm, for getting drunk is something that he embarked upon while sober, and he can presumably remember at least the earlier stages of the process. But do we also want to say, with Locke, that I am not now responsible for all those actions, good or bad, which were performed by the man that I am, and performed under normal conditions, while the man was sane, sober, and wide awake, but the memory of which I have in a quite ordinary way lost beyond recall? Can an artist no longer claim any credit for a work which he no longer remembers producing?

But perhaps the most damaging objection is this. Since a man at t_2 commonly remembers only some of his experiences and actions at t_1, whereas what constituted a person at t_1 was all the experiences and actions that were then co-conscious, Locke's view fails to equate a person identified at t_2 with any *person* identifiable at t_1. It is only a theory of how some items which belonged to a person identifiable at t_1 are appropriated by a person who can be identified as such only at t_2. It is therefore hardly a theory of personal identity at all, but might be better described as a theory of action appropriation. Locke seems to be forgetting that 'person' is not only 'a forensic term, appropriating actions and their merit', but also the noun corresponding to all the personal pronouns.

All these problems, and what I have called the three possible lines of thought with regard to them, with their difficulties, arise from the lack of well-defined units of consciousness, which itself results from our failure to remember all the actions and experiences of what is, in Locke's terms, the same man. Is there a converse problem about paramnesia, where someone remembers, or seems to remember, actions and experiences that were not his, either that never occurred at all or that were done by or happened to someone else? We should distinguish two kinds of case. First,

---

[15] II. xxvii. 22.

there is entirely illusory pseudo-memory—however sincere—illustrated by Russell's example of George IV 'remembering' his leadership at Waterloo and Flew's of 'those who press forward to claim sincerely but without factual foundation the discredit for committing the latest newsy murder', and also by cases where the 'remembered' events never occurred at all. Here we can surely say that the subject is merely imagining and not remembering the supposed actions. Genuine remembering is related causally to the experiencing or learning of what is remembered, and though there is some causal link between the actions of various men who really fought at Waterloo and the king's fantasies, and again between the real murderer's actions and the fantasies of those who confess, these causal links are of quite the wrong kind to help to constitute memory, since they go through oral or written reports, evidence left by the murderer, found by the police, and described in newspapers, and so on. Neither Locke's own theory nor the revision of it suggested above need be embarrassed by cases of this kind. But, secondly, it is conceivable that there should be cases where the consciousness of an action from the inside was passed directly from what we should at present call one mind to another, perhaps by some non-physical thought-transference, perhaps by some science-fictional electronic offprinting. It is to Locke's credit that he mentions and struggles with this difficulty. But he does not overcome it. He evades it, saying that it can 'be best resolved into the goodness of God, who, as far as the happiness or misery of any of his sensible creatures is concerned in it, will not, by a fatal error of theirs, transfer from one to another that consciousness which draws reward or punishment with it'.[16] That is, God just will not allow such direct transfers of consciousness to occur. But this will not do as a defence for Locke, for it presupposes that there is something else which really constitutes personal identity, which is the true bearer of responsibility, and which therefore needs to be protected from the unjust effects of a transfer of consciousness. But if, as Locke is maintaining, consciousness itself and nothing else constitutes the identity of the person, then in the imagined cases there would be no error, no injustice, that the goodness of God can be invoked to prevent. The actions of which someone thus became directly conscious would be as much his as anyone's past actions are in any normal

[16] II. xxvii. 13.

case. As Locke has insisted, it would not, on his theory, matter at all if these actions had been done by a different man or by a different spiritual substance.

Locke's inconsistency here is matched by a peculiarity of his treatment of the story of the prince and the cobbler.[17] Since he uses this to enforce the distinction between the same man and the same person, by arguing that after the change we have the same man as the former cobbler but the same person as the former prince, he can, and does, allow that what is transferred is not just the prince's consciousness but 'the soul of a prince, carrying with it the consciousness of the prince's past life'. With this description, as Locke says, 'everyone sees he would be the same person with the prince'. But if the example were to test Locke's own positive theory, it would have to be restated, leaving the prince's soul behind (perhaps in total amnesia) and transferring only the consciousness of the prince's past life to the cobbler's soul in the cobbler's body, the cobbler's own memories having been erased. But when the story is told in this way, there is much less general readiness to acknowledge that what now has the cobbler's body is the same person as the former prince, and Locke's own hesitation in Section 13 shows that even he would not in these circumstances be so confident about accepting the implications of his official theory.

Recent discussions of personal identity have often presented memory and bodily continuity as rival criteria, and it is sometimes argued that the memory criterion cannot stand on its own, but is parasitic upon that of bodily continuity.[18] The argument is that in order to exclude paramnesia we have to distinguish genuine memory, which is a criterion of personal identity, from merely apparent memory, sincere but false memory claims like that of George IV, and that we can do so only by saying that there is genuine memory only if (along with some other requirements) there is bodily continuity. But this is, I think, a mistake. It is true that we commonly use bodily continuity, or the lack of it, as evidence for or against the truth of memory claims; we take the fact that the man who became George IV was not present at

---

[17] II. xxvii. 15.

[18] e.g. S. Shoemaker, *Self-Knowledge and Self-Identity*, pp. 199–200; B. Williams, 'Personal Identity and Individuation', *Aristotelian Society Proceedings*, 57 (1956–7), reprinted in *Problems of the Self*, pp. 1–18.

Waterloo as decisive evidence against his 'memories'. But it is evidence only, not part of what is meant by calling something genuine memory; we have constantly to be on our guard against the use of the term 'criterion' to slur over this distinction. In fact it is rebuttable evidence: if one man not only made sincere memory claims about the earlier experiences of another man but was sufficiently accurate in ways that defied explanation in terms of lucky guesses, unconscious inference, indirect transmission by way of now forgotten reports, and so on, then I think that not only the man himself but others also would have to take seriously the possibility that he was really remembering, by some direct causal link, this other man's experiences. I see no reason for saying that it is part of the meaning of the words 'memory', 'remember', and so on that a man can remember only that same man's experiences; but if anyone maintains that it is we can easily introduce another term, say 'q-remember', which has the other requirements of genuine memory, such as a direct causal link between the earlier experience and the remembering (not by way of reports, etc.) but which does not have this alleged requirement of the sameness of the man; and then some account of a Lockean type, either Locke's own extreme view or our proposed revision, can be stated in terms of q-remembering instead.[19] We can still set aside as irrelevant spurious though sincere memory claims—that is, ones with no causal links or with causal links of the wrong sort, whether their content is accurate or not—but allow genuine q-memories, without bodily continuity, to constitute personal identity. While we are giving an account of what constitutes personal identity, we do not need to meet the challenge of saying how we could decide, in difficult cases, whether the requirements for genuine q-remembering were met. This concerns the question of evidence, not the question of what constitutes personal identity. Paramnesia, then, is no real problem.

As well as such particular difficulties there is a general objection put forward by Butler, that Locke's own theory rests on the confusion of what constitutes identity with evidence for it, on which I have just been commenting. Locke's account, Butler says, concerns our knowledge of personal identity, not what constitutes it: 'And one should really think it self-evident, that consciousness

---

[19] Cf. D. A. Parfit, 'Personal Identity', *Philosophical Review*, 80 (1971), pp. 3–27, esp. pp. 14–16.

of personal identity presupposes, and therefore cannot constitute, personal identity; any more than knowledge, in any other case, can constitute truth, which it presupposes.'[20]

The general principle to which Butler is here appealing is both sound and important: no genuine proposition can be made true by being known, and equally there cannot be any item which is constituted by awareness or consciousness of that very item itself; there cannot be any entity which exists in and by being known. If this principle had been thoroughly clarified and generally understood we should have escaped many confusions that have played a large part in modern philosophy. But the application of this principle to the present issue is more doubtful. Locke is not, I think, saying, and certainly he need not say, that what constitutes personal identity is consciousness of personal identity itself. Rather, his view is that what makes a certain past experience mine, that is, what makes it belong to the I that is here now, is that I remember it (or genuinely q-remember it), as I have put it, from the inside. This is a particular way of remembering an experience, but it does not include as a component the factual memory that it was I who first had that experience, that the original experiencer was identical with me. If it did, then indeed Locke's account would be viciously circular; but in fact it is not.[21] Admittedly the inference from this particular way of remembering an experience to the belief that it was I who had the experience is so automatic that it is hard to separate the remembering from the belief. But they are distinguishable, so that Locke's suggestion that such remembering (or q-remembering) constitutes personal identity is not viciously circular or trivial. Again, with an action, it is not that I remember that I did it, but rather the remark 'I did it' or 'I remember doing it' expresses a way of remembering the action that (if genuine) makes it mine.

Yet behind this unsound criticism there is an element of truth. We are reluctant to believe that our identity through time is constituted by this sort of memory, and are more inclined to regard the memory as evidence for an identity which is already there, constituted by something else and somehow making that memory possible. Though Butler cannot show Locke's view to be

[20] J. Butler, Dissertation I, 'Of Personal Identity', published with *The Analogy of Religion*.
[21] Cf. D. A. Parfit, op. cit.

incoherent, he could say that it is in conflict with a firm and natural belief.

Locke's device of constructing puzzle cases has been used with great enthusiasm and ingenuity by philosophers in recent years, and it would take a long time to follow all the twists and turns of their arguments. But an important central theme has been the problem of what to say about possible or at least conceivable cases of fission and fusion.[22] The problem of fission is formally similar to that of the daffodil bulb in Chapter 5. This difficulty arises for the view that memory is sufficient on its own for personal identity from the possibility that two apparently distinct persons should each remember, from the inside and in the required causally direct way, the experiences of some one earlier person. If bodily continuity were required as well, or if bodily continuity on its own were held to be sufficient for personal identity, the difficulty still arises, since it is conceivable that human organisms should divide as daffodil bulbs do. A somewhat less fanciful version of the difficulty is suggested by the fact that the most important part of the human body for these purposes is the brain. It is conceivable that a man's brain should be divided and the two halves successfully transplanted into two different bodies, each half carrying with it the man's memories and character traits. The two resulting individuals would each have as much memory continuity and as much brain continuity with the original man as there is in some undisputed examples of the history of a single person—people have survived well enough with only one half of their brains in working order. So if the continuity of body, or brain, or memory, or of some conjunction of these, is sufficient for personal identity, the possibility of the corresponding case of fission entails that either two apparently distinct persons are identical with one another, or personal identity is either non-symmetrical or non-transitive. Even more acute difficulties arise from possibilities of fusion, which can be set up in corresponding ways, because one of the two logically possible options is now even less plausible. We might allow that two apparently distinct persons, in different places at the same time, are really one person, because they have arisen from and are continuous, in whatever

---

[22] e.g. Flew, op. cit.; C. B. Martin, *Religious Belief*, pp. 97–105; B. Williams, 'Bodily Continuity and Personal Identity', *Analysis*, 21 (1960), reprinted in *Problems of the Self*, pp. 19–25; D. A. Parfit, op. cit.

way or ways are thought necessary, with some one earlier person. But we would hardly say that two persons, who at t_1 are as distinct from one another as two different persons ever are, are really one and the same person because at some later time t_2 they will merge into one.

3. *Conceptual analysis and evidence*

In the face of all these difficulties we may well feel that neither Locke's own rather extreme view nor our revised Lockean account is satisfactory, and yet that no other obvious solution—such as taking bodily continuity to constitute personal identity, and rejecting Locke's distinction between the same person and the same man—is any more attractive. In such an impasse it would be sensible to ask ourselves just what kind of solution we are seeking and to distinguish the different questions that we may be trying to answer.

First, there is the question of conceptual analysis. What do we mean by 'the same person'? What do we take to constitute that sameness? What am I asserting when I not only ascribe past actions and experiences to myself, to the me that is here now, but also identify with this me the person who was there then and did those actions and had those experiences? Secondly, there is the question of evidence. How does any of us know, or on what grounds does he believe, that he himself—the he that is here now —is identical with a person somehow indicated as existing at some previous time? On what grounds do we believe that some other person that is here now is identical with an indicated one who existed earlier? But thirdly, and in the end of the greatest importance, there is the question of factual analysis. What is the truth of the matter? What reality underlies our talk and belief about personal identity? How, if at all, is each of us really the same from one time to another?

There can be no doubt that bodily continuity occupies a special position in lines of evidential support for personal identity. It is not, indeed, that bodily continuity is our usual initial evidence for ascriptions of identity either to other people or to ourselves. We do not watch other people continuously, we hardly ever watch ourselves and we cannot watch ourselves during the times when we are asleep. The evidence that is immediately available to us and that we rely on in reidentifying other people, or, as it is more often, the cues to which we respond automatically and without explicit awareness of them when we recognize people we know, are similarities in appearance, what these people say, and how they respond to us and to what we say. Still, what this immediate evidence is in the first place evidence for is bodily continuity. What we primarily believe, on practically sufficient, though not absolutely conclusive, evidence, is that this is Richard Roe, the same man that we saw yesterday or ten years ago, and we then regard its being the same man as establishing an almost unrebuttable presumption that it is the same person. Even when the whole process of recognition is instantaneous, it would be most unnatural to say, 'Yes, this is Richard Roe, the same person; I wonder if it is the same man', or 'I wonder whether he has had a continuous bodily history since I last saw him': the bodily continuity is presupposed in the recognition of him as the same person. Bodily continuity would be taken by any ordinary court of law to be both necessary and sufficient for personal identity. If the Tichborne claimant had been able to establish that he was the same man as the Roger Tichborne who had disappeared years before, he would have acquired the title and the property, and he could not have acquired them without establishing this. No amount of apparent memory of Roger's childhood, even coupled with physical and psychological similarity (which in the actual case were so sadly lacking) would have given the claimant any legal rights except by showing that he was the same man as Roger Tichborne. Memory and character are not as evidence alternatives to bodily continuity; they serve, in law and in all ordinary cases, as evidence of personal identity only in so far as they are evidence of bodily continuity. Such continuity occupies a similar position as evidence even of my own identity as a person. Whenever and wherever in the past the same man as I am was conscious and active, I presume that it was I who was there and who did whatever this man did. I am quite ready to ascribe to myself innumerable actions and experiences which I do not now remember once I am satisfied of the bodily continuity of that person with me.

On the other hand, bodily continuity is not what we mean by personal identity. I can conceive that I should find myself with a body that is not organically continuous with this one, or even without a body at all. Millions of people have not only conceived but firmly believed that this sort of thing would happen, and millions still do. And though I could not hope to persuade a court of law to assign to me, in another body, any property or special rights that I have now, anyone who believed my story would feel that its refusal would not really be just.

It is this that gives Locke's account some plausibility as a conceptual analysis. But his own extreme view cannot be right as an answer to the question of meaning. The difficulties surveyed in Section 2 show this, in particular the failure of transitivity, the problems of fission and fusion, and the fact that it is, as I have put it, a theory of action appropriation rather than of personal identity. Our ordinary concept is, plainly, a concept of identity, obeying the logic of identity, and of identity between complete persons, and Locke's account does not meet these requirements.

Is our revised account adequate as a conceptual analysis? It incorporates Locke's plausible initial suggestion that the sameness of a person has something specially to do with co-consciousness, it coincides in all ordinary cases with our recognition of persons as the same, and it allows, as the analysis in terms of bodily continuity does not, for the conceivability of a person's surviving the death of his present body and finding himself with a different body or without one. It preserves the symmetry and transitivity of identity in all ordinary cases. Admittedly its conformity to this standard logic would break down in the imagined cases of fission and fusion of memory networks, but it is not clear that this matters. We can surely employ a concept of a certain sort of thing, and apply the notion of identity to it, in a world where what we take to constitute such a thing in fact gives us well-defined units, even if it is conceivable that it should fail to do so.

Yet this does not seem to be a correct conceptual analysis. I seem able to conceive that I should suffer total and permanent amnesia, and yet that *I* should still be there. Again, suppose that someone loses his memory completely on Tuesday night, so that on Wednesday he remembers nothing of his former life, but on Thursday he not only remembers, as well as we usually do, what happened on the previous day, Wednesday, but also regains his memories of what he did on Tuesday and earlier. That is, there are memory bridges between the man on Thursday and all parts of his earlier life, but on Wednesday there were no memory bridges linking the man on Wednesday with any of his earlier life. By our revised account, therefore, the man is in fact one person throughout. But if he had been killed on Wednesday night, he would have been a different person on Wednesday from the person he was at all earlier dates. But it is not compatible with our ordinary concept that whether the Wednesday man is or is not the same person as the Tuesday man should depend on what happens on Wednesday night. What we want to say is that if he had died on Wednesday night he would still in fact have been the same person on Wednesday as on Tuesday, though the proof of this, the Tuesday–Thursday and Wednesday–Thursday memory bridges, would have been suppressed. But we can say this only if we take our revised account not as an analysis of what, on our present concept, constitutes personal identity but as an account of something that reveals personal identity.

Neither Locke's own view, nor our revision of it, then, is correct as conceptual analysis, nor would be an account in terms of bodily continuity. And it seems that no combination of these criteria will be right either.

It is true that further revisions might cope with such specific counter-examples. Yet it seems unlikely that any account constructed out of these materials will be correct as an analysis of our present concept of personal identity. This thesis has been maintained by Richard Swinburne.[23] Calling any theory which analyses personal identity in terms of bodily continuity or continuity of memory and character or both an empiricist theory, he argues that no empiricist theory can be right as an account of what ascriptions of personal identity now mean. Our present concept is of something more absolute than any such analyses could achieve. We will allow the identity of a daffodil bulb to be, as I called it in Chapter 5, specially secured, but not the sameness of a person. It will not do to say that one survivor of a divided brain transplant operation counts as the same person as the original one if and only if the other half of the operation fails: our present concept requires that if this survivor is the same person as the original one, he must be so intrinsically: his identity cannot depend on something as extraneous as the success or failure of the other transplant. More generally, our present concept requires that there

[23] 'Personal Identity', *Aristotelian Society Proceedings*, 74 (1973–4), pp. 231–47.

must *be* some definite, non-arbitrary, right answer to the question whether this person is the same as that, whether or not we can in practice decide what the right answer is, and that the sameness of persons is not a matter of degree. But each proposed kind of continuity is a matter of degree. There could be any amount of continuity of consciousness from total recall to total amnesia. Also, there conceivably could be simultaneous replacement of any proportion, from zero to a hundred per cent, of a body (or of a brain). If any sort of continuity is to constitute identity, then perfect continuity of that sort will indisputably be identity and total discontinuity of that sort will be non-identity. But if there is a continuous gradation between these two extremes of continuity, it seems to follow either that identity too is a matter of degree, or that there is an arbitrary division between the degree of continuity that is just enough for identity and that which is just not enough. Our present concept of personal identity differs from our concepts of the identity of cars and of nations precisely in respects which make it resistant to analysis in terms of any empirical continuities.[24] We will allow that there are borderline cases with regard to the identity of cars or nations, where our concepts of such things give no clear rulings and we can decide fairly arbitrarily what to say, but our concept of a person is of something whose unity is in itself unequivocal, whether decidable or not. Swinburne, therefore, is right to conclude that what we mean by personal identity 'is something ultimate', as Butler and, less explicitly, Reid, also held.

Yet it would not be true to say that our ordinary concept of personal identity is of something that has nothing to do with consciousness. Suppose that I am the subject of a doubly successful divided brain transplant, so that there come to be two men each remembering my earlier life, each claiming to be John Mackie. In terms of our ordinary concept such a description leaves something out, and what it leaves out is how it is for *me*. There are various possibilities. I may have just ceased to exist. I may be unconscious. I may have died and gone elsewhere. I may be one of the two survivors, and know the other one to be an impostor,

---

[24] It is this that Butler recognizes but misdescribes when he contrasts a 'loose and popular sense' of 'same' which is applied to vegetables with a 'strict philosophical sense' which is applied to persons. As I have argued in Chapter 5, it is not that 'same' is used in different senses, but that we have different views about the sorts of thing to which it is applied.

though he alleges with sincere conviction that I am an impostor. Or I may be both of them, living indeed a double life, seeing the world from two different points of view at once, with a very thorough form of double vision. Could my two halves then be 'distinct consciousnesses'? I think not. Our ordinary concept will allow that the same person could be both Dr Jekyll and Mr Hyde, with alternating conscious states with no memory bridges between them, but not that I could be conscious at one time in two different bodies, in two different places, without the experiences of the two halves being co-conscious. Our ordinary concept of a person, then, is of a necessarily unitary subject of consciousness. But this phrase needs to be rather carefully interpreted. This subject can, of course, cease to exist. Even while it exists, it can be unconscious. Its successive conscious experiences need not be co-conscious. But all its simultaneous experiences must be co-conscious, because it is just one subject of consciousness at any one time. And its identity is automatic, like that of a Lockean atom, not specially secured like that of a daffodil bulb, not indeterminate like that of a car or a nation, not even potentially indeterminate as that of a person as defined by our revised Lockean account would be.

This, I think, is our present concept. This is what we mean by ascriptions of personal identity, and it is on this concept that our hopes, fears, and speculations are based. But are we justified in using it? Have we not come back precisely to the notion which, dressed up in the philosophical terminology of spiritual substances, Locke so rightly criticized and set aside? If we allow for a moment that there are such necessarily unitary subjects of consciousness, what ground have I, or has anyone else, for identifying one such subject with John Mackie throughout his life? Why should we take bodily continuity as such strong presumptive evidence for this other, ultimate, unity? Why should we be prepared to take memory as evidence of it if bodily continuity failed? Do we ever observe this ultimate unity going along with bodily continuity or memory? If we do, what is it that we then observe? If not, how can any observed continuities be evidence for it? Locke, indeed, concedes that 'the more probable opinion is that this consciousness is annexed to and the affection of one individual immaterial substance',[25] but why should this opinion be more probable? If

[25] II. xxvii. 25.

we are to admit immaterial substances, why is it not just as likely that there should be a whole series of them associated with each human body and with each network unity of consciousness? Above all, what ground have we for asserting the necessary unity of each subject of consciousness, not only at one time but also through time, so that its identity is unequivocal, non-arbitrary, and not a matter of degree, which are the features that most clearly divide this ordinary concept from all empiricist analyses? This would be a *de re* necessity of a kind that could not, like the necessities of constitution discussed in Chapter 3, Section 7 and the necessities of origin discussed in Chapter 5, Section 3, be explained as residing in our ways of thinking and speaking. It is not merely that, using the ordinary concept, we will accept as a person only something whose unity is clear cut, that we impose conformity to the standard logic of identity as a requirement, but that we believe that there are things which in themselves cannot fail so to conform. The problem is, what right have we to believe this? Swinburne thinks that the only reason for objecting to this ordinary concept is 'the verificationist principle that a proposition has no factual meaning if no evidence of observation can count for or against it', a principle against which he has argued elsewhere and which I agree with him in rejecting.[26] But while we can grant that ascriptions of personal identity in this ordinary sense are meaningful, we may still object that no reason has been given for making one such ascription rather than another, not merely in problem cases but even in those that we take to be uncontroversial.

4. *Factual analysis and reinterpretations*

In these circumstances Hume's thesis that personal identity is a fiction becomes attractive, indeed much more attractive than the corresponding thesis about identity in general. As we saw in Chapter 5, Section 2, all that could be defended of the latter was that the identity of organisms, artefacts, and the like is not automatic but specially secured, and that there is some arbitrariness in the choice of the relations that determine such units. But since most reasonable people will readily admit this, they can hardly be accused of falsely ascribing to such things an unequivocal identity

---

[26] 'Confirmability and Factual Meaningfulness', *Analysis*, 33 (1973), pp. 71–6; *Sense and Nonsense in Physics and Theology*; cf. Chapter 2, Section 5 above.

like that of a Lockean atom. The identity that we commonly ascribe to persons is of this unequivocal sort: if, as I have argued, such ascriptions regularly go beyond everything for which we have positive support, then they are fictional in a way that our more modest ascriptions of identity to organisms and artefacts are not. What, then, are we entitled to say? What concept of personal identity will best reflect the ascertainable truths in this area?

A fairly plausible suggestion is that we should adopt the revised Lockean account, openly admitting that it is not a correct analysis of our present concept, but proposing it as a conceptual reform and as a factual analysis, an account of all that is true and relevant in this area.[27] The merits of this account have already been stated, and it has been defended against the criticism that it could not stand on its own, but is parasitic upon bodily continuity.

But do we want what is one of the consequences of this account, that periods of total amnesia, with no memory bridges in either direction linking them with the rest of a man's network of communicating consciousness, are excluded from the life of this person? Do we want to say that in such a period though I, this man, was present, I, this person, was not? From a Lockean point of view there are two reasons why we should say this. Since 'I' and 'person' are used primarily with reference to a system of co-conscious items, it seems appropriate to exclude from their application what is quite cut off from this system. Also, it seems appropriate to hold someone non-responsible for actions performed during such a period of amnesia. But this second reason becomes less compelling when we reflect that there are several grounds on which we may want to hold someone non-responsible, or less than ordinarily responsible, for actions that were done not only by this man but also, in terms of the present proposal, by this person. We have to say 'He did it, but he was in a disturbed mental state' or 'He did it, but he is of such low intelligence that he cannot fully understand the character and implications of what he did'. Why should we not also say, 'He did it, but he does not remember doing it' rather than 'He does not remember, so it was not he that did it'? Is it not the mental disturbance of which it is a symptom rather than the amnesia itself that should modify our judgements about responsibility? It seems better to consider all

---

[27] A similar conceptual reform, rather than mere analysis of our present concepts, is, I believe, needed in ethics. I hope to discuss this topic in another book.

problems of non-responsibility and diminished responsibility together, rather than to deal separately with a special group of them under the heading of non-identity of the person.

The first reason mentioned above is also less compelling when we reflect that, as we noted in Section 2 above, forward-looking concern does not always match backward-looking memory. I would be specially, not just altruistically, concerned about the welfare of the same man as I am even in a period cut off by amnesia.

It may, indeed, be argued that such special concern is irrational. If I try to explain and justify it, I am tempted to say that what I am afraid of is that I, this same person, may suffer, but this seems to invoke the ordinary concept of personal identity which we have found grounds for rejecting. And Bernard Williams has shown how we can pass gradually from this case to one where it is more natural to say that it is not I but someone else who will suffer.[28] Contemplating the whole series of steps, we cannot decide with confidence at any step, even at this first one, whether it is really I who will be suffering, and this remains as undecidable after the event as before. It is arguable that something which, to us at least, will always remain undecidable cannot really matter very much to us. However, though I cannot thus explain and justify my concern, it is a hard fact that I feel it, and nearly everyone, when he contemplates the possibility of the same man as he is suffering pain during a period cut off by the lack of memory bridges at either end, will similarly feel this concern. And it is not surprising that evolutionary selection and our individual experience and traini   have produced and encouraged in us such a generally   ve directed to the well-being of this sam   is one of the factual data which we should   n reconstructing our concept of personal ident   argue that concern ought to match some othe   ined personal identity, we can require that what w   identity should match the hard facts of biologically and psychologically determined concern. In several respects, then, our revised Lockean account is not altogether satisfactory even as a conceptual reform.

A more extreme proposal has been put forward by Derek

---

[28] 'The Self and the Future', *Philosophical Review*, 79 (1970), reprinted in *Problems of the Self*, pp. 46–63, esp. pp. 55–6.

Parfit.[29] He argues against the common belief that a question about personal identity must have a definite answer: no one, he says, thinks this about nations or machines, and like Hume he holds that personal identity is in the same predicament. He therefore welcomes the puzzle cases where even when we know all the hard facts, everything on which we might have supposed identity to be founded, we still do not know what to say about personal identity. He particularly stresses the imagined possibilities of fission and fusion where the logic of identity threatens to break down. He admits that the Lockean concept of psychological continuity—in which he includes similarity of character as well as memory—is not quite suitable as a basis for a concept of identity, but he argues that none the less it is this continuity that matters. He contends for a notion of survival which does not imply identity, and which is therefore unembarrassed by the fact that I might survive in two different persons, or that two different persons might both survive in me. Even if our present concepts of remembering and intending make it logically true that I can genuinely remember only my own experiences, and that I can intend to do something only by intending that I should do it, we can introduce new terms which are free from these logical requirements but preserve all that is interesting and valuable about remembering and intending. Since 'what matters in the continued existence of a person are, for the most part, matters of degree', survival also admits of more and less. If fission and fusion did occur, then it would be more appropriate to speak in terms of survival than in terms of identity, since what matters would then cut across anything that could have the logic of identity. And though as things are we can speak of personal identity, it is illuminating to consider a possible alternative way of speaking, in which we 'redescribe a person's life as the history of a series of successive selves'. This will be particularly appropriate where there is some dramatic change of attitude and character, such as a religious conversion, and where in consequence the successive selves have different policies and conflicting interests—for instance, a generous young man may take precautions against the predictable meanness of his middle-aged self. But even in the ordinary course of events each of us as he now is will survive less and less as time goes on. In place of the religious believer's hope of im-

[29] 'Personal Identity', pp. 3–27.

mortality, and the ordinary materialist's expectation of abrupt extinction, Parfit offers to our present selves the assurance of gradual but inevitable disappearance even while our bodies stay alive.

Given that there is no factual basis for the employment of our present absolute concept, it cannot be denied that this alternative way of speaking is permissible. It has an important bearing on moral philosophy, especially in bringing out that there is no exclusive rationality about having an equal concern for all one's future selves—or, as we now put it, for oneself at all future times. However, I want to suggest a way in which, while avoiding the false claim of absolutism, we can still keep close to our present view of personal identity. This is based on a small but significant reinterpretation of the ordinary concept.

Swinburne writes as follows:

One comes to understand the meaning of 'same person' not by being provided with a definition in terms of body, character, and memory, but by being provided with clear examples of pairs of persons who are and pairs of persons who are not the same, and being shown the grounds on which judgments about personal identity are made. By being shown the evidence and clear cases where the evidence points one way rather than the other, we come to have an understanding of what is at stake. But there is no reason to suppose that the understanding is simply an understanding of the evidence (i.e., that we mean no more by personal identity than some conjunction or disjunction of the kind of features which lead us to make judgments ascribing it) . . .[30]

This is true and important. But the conclusion Swinburne wants to draw, that the personal identity we thus learn to speak about is something ultimate and unanalysable, does not follow. It is quite obscure how such an ultimate identity could be 'observable only by observing these'[31]—that is, the various empirical continuities. Surely this case is rather analogous to that of substance terms like 'gold'.[32] These too are learned with the help of examples, but Locke was wrong in thinking that all that we could thus learn to associate with the name 'gold' was the set of features which we observed in the examples, in short some nominal essence. As he saw (despite his disapproval) we intend to annex

---

[30] 'Personal Identity', *Aristotelian Society Proceedings*, 74 (1973–4), p. 241.
[31] Op. cit., p. 240.   [32] Cf. Chapter 3.

the name 'gold' to a real essence, a supposed inner constitution
from which the properties that serve, for different speakers, as
different nominal essences of gold are believed to flow. And contrary to what Locke thought, we can do what we intend. Similarly, it may be suggested, we intend to annex the terms 'I' and
'person' to whatever underlies and makes possible the co-
consciousness of experiences, and so to speak of the same person
just so long as whatever sustains this possibility over stretches
of time is still there. The unity of consciousness is, as it were, the
nominal essence of personal identity, and Locke is here making
the analogous mistake of thinking that words can be used in a
clear and precise way only if they are annexed to their nominal
essence. But the real essence of personal identity will be whatever
underlies and makes possible the unity of consciousness. It is to
this that we intend to annex this term: can we not succeed in
doing so in this case as with gold? Butler acutely pointed out that
when Locke defined a person as a thinking intelligent being, and
personal identity as the sameness of a rational being, he suggested
a better answer than the one he officially gives.[33] Personal identity
is the sameness of that which thinks, not the unity of the thought.
But Butler and Swinburne fall into an opposite error, which is
analogous to that of equating a real essence with a substratum
which is unknowable in principle. Rather, I would say that it is
an empirical question what makes co-consciousness possible, just
as it is an empirical question what inner constitution generates
the more readily observable properties of gold. And if it is an
empirical question, we now know at least the outline of the answer:
what makes co-consciousness possible is the structure of the
central nervous system and the persistence of that structure
through time.

We can link this answer with what has often been seen as a fatal
difficulty for views like that of Hume, that a person is really just
a train of perceptions held together by certain relations. Hume
himself quickly became dissatisfied with his account of personal
identity as a fiction, and while the account that he gives of the
difficulty he found in it is obscure, it is reasonable to suppose that
what he half saw is that his explanation of how 'we' falsely attribute identity to our different perceptions, 'because of the union
of their ideas in the imagination when we reflect upon them', pre-

[33] Butler, op. cit.; cf. II. xxvii. 9.

supposes some real unity of the thinking subject that is alleged to be deceived and to construct this fiction.[34] As Bradley put it: 'Mr Bain collects that the mind is a collection. Has he ever thought who collects Mr Bain?'[35] But such objections to the 'bundle theory' of the mind run together two criticisms, one sound and one unsound. The sound criticism is that we need some further explanation of how 'perceptions' can be related as we find that they are. There are not just the perceptions; something has to interact with the physical objects that are perceived, to store and reproduce information, and so on. But it is possible in principle, and in practice established beyond reasonable doubt, that what does all this is the central nervous system. The unsound criticism is an analogue of what I called in Chapter 3 the weak logico-linguistic argument for a substratum underlying all properties. It similarly demands something which while still spiritual, still essentially a thinker, is to be a substratum underlying all thoughts. The doctrine of a spiritual substratum, like that of a material substratum, is supported by too crude an insistence upon some of our ordinary ways of speaking: a mind *has* all its thoughts, as a thing *has* all its properties. And just as the material substratum is only a pseudo-explanation of the individuation and persistence of a physical thing, so the spiritual substratum is only a pseudo-explanation of the individuation and persistence of a person. If we reject the unsound criticism and adopt the sound one, we shall conclude that what collects Mr Bain is not a spiritual substratum endowed with a necessary unity, but rather a neurophysiological structure. And this conclusion will bring with it the corollary that some 'perceptions' that are not tied into the bundle by purely mental relations can still form part of, or belong to, Mr Bain.

In a way, then, personal identity, on the present view, would boil down to bodily continuity. But this comes about only indirectly and contingently. Bodily continuity is no part of what 'personal identity' ordinarily means, any more than having atomic number 79 is any part of the ordinary meaning of 'gold'. The concept of personal identity, as we are now interpreting it, is not the concept of bodily continuity, but it is the concept of something that turns out to be the continuity of the structure of a certain part of the body. It is conceivable that personal identity should have been the persistence of some immaterial substance, since it

[34] *Treatise* I. iv. 6, and Appendix.   [35] F. H. Bradley, *Ethical Studies*, p. 39.

might have been upon this that the possibility of the co-consciousness of experiences depended. We have no reason to suppose that it does: but it is an empirical, not an analytic, truth, that we do not survive bodily death.

This interpretation of the concept of personal identity is, of course, closely analogous to Armstrong's view of the mind as by definition the inner cause of behaviour, and hence, contingently, the central nervous system.[36] But it is a more satisfactory answer to this question because the awkward issue of property identity does not arise here. A materialist view of the thinker is less controversial than a materialist view of thoughts.

Could this be defended as a conceptual analysis, as what we ordinarily mean by personal identity? I think it brings out part of the ordinary concept, and I think this approach throws some light on what would otherwise be quite obscure, why we take the empirical continuities as evidence for a metaphysical unity: the latter is, in effect, an explanatory hypothesis. But it is not a good explanatory hypothesis: the neurophysiological one is much better just because it can be worked out and tested in detail. However, I do not think that the proposed interpretation will do as a complete analysis of our ordinary concept. I believe that this does include as well the notions which are expressed by such philosophical terms as 'immaterial substance' and 'necessarily unitary subject of consciousness', notions which would conflict with the equating of what makes co-consciousness possible with a neurophysiological structure. I would defend this interpretation, then, not as a conceptual analysis but as a conceptual reform, but one that builds on one part of our already existing concept, while rejecting another, in the light of what it is reasonable to take as the underlying facts.

This answer enables us to deal with the puzzle cases that have seemed so intractable. If the sameness of the person is the persistence of the relevant neurophysiological structure, then offprinting of memories from one such structure to another would not give us the same person. It would not give us what is now typically the object of biologically determined and psychologically reinforced concern. It could, I admit, be argued that it would give us something just as good: if such offprinting became common and reliable, then there is no reason why we should not come to

[36] D. M. Armstrong, *A Materialist Theory of the Mind*, esp. Chapter 6.

look forward to surviving in this way just as much as we now look forward to surviving by way of the ordinary metabolic processes. But it would need a further conceptual reform to extend personal identity to cover such cases: we can cross that bridge when we come to it. On the other hand, with only the reform I have proposed, a successful brain transplant would give us the same person. But if the two halves of my brain, each carrying a normal stock of memories and character traits, were successfully transplanted into two separate bodies, then I would survive in two different human beings. In this case we should have to speak, as Parfit suggests, about survival without identity, despite the fact that in a similar case if only one transplant were successful we would naturally go on speaking about identity. The identity of persons, on this view, is not automatic but specially secured: but this need be no more surprising than that the identity of daffodil bulbs is so. We can now endorse the decision suggested by our criticisms of the revised Lockean view, that a man remains the same person even through periods of total amnesia: the structure that normally makes co-consciousness possible is still there, even if a particular breakdown prevents the actual achievement of co-consciousness.

It is, then, a merit of this proposal that it makes the person that I am coincide with what is the normal object of my special concern, which includes not only the subject of actually co-conscious experiences but also whatever continuing human body is controlled by the structure that normally makes that co-consciousness possible. It is, understandably, this that is the beneficiary of the considerable measure of egoism that I owe to Darwinian if not to divine providence.

7

EMPIRICISM AND INNATE NOTIONS

1. *Realism versus empiricism*

WE have encountered at a good many points in the previous chapters at least apparent conflicts between realism and empiricism. The distinction between primary and secondary qualities is not given immediately in experience, and it is largely on empiricist grounds that Berkeley holds that it cannot be drawn at all, and Bennett that only a different, less speculative, distinction can be defended. Similarly, empiricism draws our attention to the contents of our experience, and sets up both the problem of meaning and the problem of justification for our claims about a further reality which those contents represent. Empiricism would tend to identify any substances of which we can have any knowledge with collections of readily observable features, and to confine the meanings of words to nominal essences; but scientific realism postulates inner constitutions of things, real essences which are not directly observed, and an unbiased view of the use of language shows that words can stand for these real essences. With regard to universals, concentration on our immediate experiences and their contents tends to foster Locke's blend of conceptualism with the resemblance theory, whereas for a coherent view we require a modest version of Aristotelian realism. Our ordinary notion of personal identity is in sharp conflict with any kind of empiricist theory, and I have argued that we can apply here too the contrast between real and nominal essence, showing that Locke and many of his successors have in effect equated personal identity with its nominal essence, whereas something like a real essence for it can, and should, be found. A more detailed survey would reveal other similar conflicts.

I have tried to show, then, that the apparent requirements of empiricism should in several cases be resisted, though Locke himself did not always find the right way to do this. But we may now, somewhat belatedly, consider the basic case for empiricism, and in particular for the kind of empiricism that seemed compelling to Locke, which turned upon the denial of innate ideas and principles.

2. *The case against innate notions*

Chapters ii, iii, and iv of Book I of the *Essay* are devoted to arguing that there are no innate speculative principles in the mind, such as the maxims 'It is impossible for the same thing to be and not to be' and 'Whatsoever is, is', and equally no innate practical, moral, principles, and again no innate ideas, such as those of impossibility, of identity, or of God. Locke's arguments are simple, even crude. Since children, illiterate adults, and idiots have no apprehension of the speculative maxims, these cannot be imprinted on all men's souls. Universal acceptance would not prove innateness, but non-universality disproves it. It is 'near a contradiction to say that there are truths imprinted on the soul which it perceives or understands not'.[1] Locke dismisses the reply that men assent to these truths when they come to the use of reason: this means only that they can discover these truths by reasoning; it makes no sense to suggest that reasoning can uncover something already imprinted in the soul, but concealed. In any case the very abstract maxims mentioned above are not grasped as soon as people become able to reason: people reason very well about more concrete matters long before they assent to these maxims, and indeed they are of little use, and many people never think of them at all. Again, the claim that they are assented to as soon as they are proposed and their terms understood would not prove them innate. Practical principles are no better off, indeed they are worse off. There is no universal agreement about moral rules. Though robbers keep faith and observe rules of equity among themselves, they practise them as rules of convenience, which are needed to hold their own communities together, not because they recognize any absolute authority in moral rules. No moral rules are self-evident; none can 'be proposed whereof a man may not justly demand a reason'; but any innate principles would be self-evident.[2] No adequate criterion of innateness has even been suggested.[3]

Principles cannot be innate unless the ideas that compose them

---

[1] I. ii. 5.   [2] I. iii. 4.   [3] I. iii. 27.

are so: but such ideas as those of impossibility and identity are very far from being clearly grasped or even thought of at all by most people: the many puzzles about identity show that this idea is very far from clear. The idea of God is not innate, since there are nations which are reported by travellers to have had no idea of God. The idea of God that many men have can be explained by their having thought about the causes of things, and traced things to an original cause.[4]

The doctrine of innate notions is, Locke thinks, pernicious as well as false, for it is used to persuade people to accept principles on authority. One really knows only what one works out for oneself and comprehends, not what one takes on trust from another: 'Such borrowed wealth, like fairy-money, though it were gold in the hand from which he received it, will be but leaves and dust when it comes to use'.[5]

But of course Locke's case against innate notions is not to be found only in Book I. His argument is that the appeal to such ideas and principles is not merely unfounded but also unnecessary: he claims to be able to explain the ideas and the knowledge that we have without relying on anything innate, to show 'how men, barely by the use of their natural faculties, may attain to all the knowledge they have, without the help of any innate impressions, and may arrive at certainty without any such original notions or principles'.[6] He begins Book II by remarking '. . . what I have said in the foregoing book will be much more easily admitted when I have shown whence the understanding may get all the *ideas* it has . . . for which I shall appeal to everyone's own observation and experience'. We can, Locke thinks, prove the existence of God and of things outside us, and demonstrate morality as plainly as mathematics: since we can do all this with empirical materials, we have no need to appeal to anything innate.[7]

3. *The established opinion that there are innate principles*

The crudity of most of Locke's arguments in Book I presupposes a matching crudity in the views against which they are directed. Commentators have sometimes wondered whether any-

---

[4] I. iv. 10.   [5] I. iv. 24.   [6] I. ii. 1.
[7] II. i. 1; IV. x. xi; IV. iii. 18–20.

one held such views. But Yolton has shown that there undoubtedly
was, as Locke says, 'an established opinion amongst some men
that there are in the *understanding* certain *innate principles*, some
primary notions, κοιναὶ ἔννοιαι, characters, as it were, stamped
upon the mind of man, which the soul receives in its very first
being and brings into the world with it'.[8] Yolton quotes many
seventeenth-century English writers on morality and religion who
say just this (without even Locke's qualifying 'as it were'); moral
principles and the idea of God are stamped or imprinted upon or
engraved in the human soul by God himself. These writings also
include stock answers to some of the objections that Locke makes.
Even if a few people lack these notions, that will not disprove
their innateness, just as it is still natural for men to have two
legs even if some are born with only one. Also, Yolton distinguishes a 'dispositional' from a 'naïve' form of the doctrine:
though many writers just said firmly that these principles are born
with us, many others admitted that they were only implicit in the
soul, and require experience to elicit them. However, Locke has
arguments against the dispositional as well as against the naïve
version: '. . . it will be hard to conceive what is meant by a principle imprinted on the understanding implicitly, unless it be this,
that the mind is capable of understanding and assenting firmly to
such propositions'.[9] In other words, the dispositional view col-
lapses into the claim that the human mind has, by its nature, a
power of achieving knowledge of whatever truths are in question,
which Locke would not deny. However, writers like Henry More
are saying more than this: More claims that actual knowledge is
implicit in the soul, not like stars in the firmament to our outward
sight, nor like red letters in an almanac, but in the form of 'an
active sagacity in the Soul, or quick recollection as it were,
whereby some small businesse being hinted unto her, she runs
out presently into a more clear and larger conception'. Such knowledge is latent as memories commonly are: the mind needs only
to be 'jogg'd and awakened by the impulses of outward objects'.[10]
What we have innately is something like memories, not a mere
ability to find things out. Locke argues against the suggestion that

[8] I. ii. 1; J. W. Yolton, *John Locke and the Way of Ideas*, Chapter 2.
[9] I. ii. 22.
[10] Henry More, *An Antidote against Atheism* (1653), Bk. I, Ch. v, pp. 13–14,
quoted by Yolton, op. cit., p. 40.

innate ideas can be 'in the memory' on the ground that if I re-member something I must recognize it as something I had known before.[11] But this is a bad argument, an *ignoratio elenchi*: it shows at most that the ideas in question are not actually remembered, but this would not stop them from being in the mind in just the way in which latent memories are. A more serious difficulty is this: how could we distinguish between actual but latent innate knowledge that is merely awakened by experience, and an inborn mere power of arriving at knowledge by observation and reasoning? But the discrimination will depend upon the detailed account that is to be given of the process by which we arrive at this ex-plicit knowledge. If a plausible hypothetical description can be framed of the required steps of observation and reasoning, and if this hypothesis can be itself confirmed by observation, then it will be reasonable to speak only of an innate power of learning; but if the knowledge in question cannot be accounted for in any such way, if it contains elements for which no source can be found in observation or in any describable processes of reasoning, then this will support the rival hypothesis that these elements are latently innate. More (like Plato) argued on just these lines: against this view Locke's case depends essentially upon the suc-cess of his detailed account of the acquisition of ideas and know-ledge in the later books of the *Essay*.

In one form or other, then, the doctrine of innate knowledge was widely accepted in England in the seventeenth century, and such knowledge was held to be the necessary foundation of both religion and morality. The hostile reaction to the *Essay* was due largely to its attack on innate notions, which was seen as a dan-gerous challenge to established morality and religion.[12] Of course Locke himself did not accept this description of his work, since he claimed that the existence of God could be proved, and that morality was 'amongst the sciences capable of demonstration'.[13] However, his arguments for God's existence are very weak. They invoke such principles as that nonentity cannot produce any real being, and that it is impossible that things wholly void of know-ledge should produce a knowing being, which Locke treats, without warrant, as *a priori* truths, and which could not be ade-quately supported on empirical grounds. His argument also incorporates a fallacy of equivocation on the statement that '*some-*

---

[11] I. iv. 21.   [12] Yolton, op. cit., Chapters 1, 2.   [13] IV. x; IV. iii. 18–20.

thing must be *from eternity*'.[14] Similarly, his programme for the demonstration of morality appeals to the analyticity of such a proposition as *Where there is no property there is no justice* on the assumptions that the idea of property is that of a right to anything, and that the idea of injustice is that of the invasion or violation of such a right. This proposition is thus made equivalent to the statement that where there is no right to anything there is no invasion of a right to anything.[15] But of course no number of such analytic truths will add up to any moral system which will lay down duties or rules of action. Despite Locke's intentions, then, the conclusion that might reasonably be drawn from his work is that religion and morality cannot be established without the foundation of innate notions. As his critics said, the general tendency of the *Essay* is sceptical with regard to theism and to objectively prescriptive morality (as opposed to those 'rules of convenience' that even thieves and outlaws observe among themselves). This is, therefore, the hard core of the doctrine of innateness: long after the rest of the doctrine had fallen into disrepute, there survived some belief in an inborn moral conscience and natural religious inclinations.

4. *Interpretations of the empiricist programme*

But how does the purely negative thesis that there are no innate notions connect with those apparent requirements of empiricism which, as we noted in Section 1 above, make difficulties for realism? These arise from the positive side of the doctrine: if ideas and knowledge are not innate, they are, presumably, derived from, and based on, experience. But just what does this mean?

One thing that it could mean, and that hostile critics of the British empiricists have sometimes taken their doctrine to mean, is that all our ideas are images, fainter and in general imperfect copies of sense-impressions—or of impressions of reflection (introspection) construed simply as an internal analogue of sense-perception—and that our knowing consists simply in our having some collections and trains of such images. This interpretation does indeed have the advantage of making empiricism very easy

[14] IV. x. 3, 5, 8. The equivocation is between 'At no time was there nothing' and 'Some one thing has existed at all times'.

[15] IV. iii. 18.

to criticize; but it has the disadvantage that neither Locke nor any of his main successors held any such view.

Secondly, the empiricist theory might add to this account of a quasi-photographic reception of the elements of knowledge a description of some limited range of operations which the mind or understanding performs upon these materials. The mind, on this view, is passive in receiving image-style ideas, but it is active in bringing them up from the memory store and attending to them, comparing them with one another, discerning them, separating received complexes of ideas into their simple components (that is, abstracting), putting them together into new combinations, associating ideas with one another and in particular associating words with ideas, using words and ideas to represent other ideas, perceiving relations between ideas, and building up chains of reasoning out of such perceived relations. Now this is, in outline, Locke's theory.[16]

But thirdly, the empiricist may, and Locke does, recognize that even the reception of ideas in perception is not wholly passive, but includes a considerable element of (unconscious) interpretation: '. . . the *ideas we receive by sensation are often* in grown people *altered by the judgment*, without our taking notice of it'.[17] It is this fact that Locke uses Molyneux's problem to illustrate. If in looking at, say, a white sphere we were only passively receiving visual data we should see just a circle variously shaded; but in fact the impression we get immediately is of a solid convex object, a sphere.[18] And of course this is only one example of a very pervasive and complex sort of activity.

But even if we include this third factor in our interpretation of the empiricist thesis that all ideas and knowledge are derived from, and based on, experience, it will still have the phenomenalist tendencies which gave rise to difficulties. Further extensions are needed to leave room for realism.

For example, in Chapter 2, Section 6, in dealing with the meaning side of the veil-of-perception problem, I had to insist that the contents of our experiences are seen as real things without (that is, outside) us. I argued, indeed, that 'real' and 'outside us' are not positive terms, introducing further features that would need special explanation, but only deny any downgrading from simply

---

[16] See especially II. i. 23–5; II. xi; II. xxxiii; II. ii; IV. i.
[17] II. ix. 8.   [18] Cf. Chapter 1, Section 4 above.

being there to being merely how things look. Still, this does seem to be an interpretation which is built into the contents of our experience, something at variance with the passive or quasi-photographic view. Also, while it is reinforced by learning, by the acquisition of the skills which we use, still largely unconsciously, in distinguishing how things are from how they look, it seems likely that this interpretation is not, like those illustrated by Molyneux's problem, wholly a learned one: we may well have an innate propensity to see things realistically.

Again, Locke admitted that 'there is another *idea* which would be of general use for mankind to have, as it is of general talk as if they had it; and that is the *idea of substance*, which we neither have nor can have by *sensation* or *reflection*'.[19] This idea, then, might well have been innate: but in fact, he says, it is not, and so we have no clear idea of substance at all. But the ideas we have of substances are based on the sort of experience I illustrated in Chapter 3, Section 2, by speaking about our noticing a collection of instantiated cat-features going around together. However, do we just notice this sort of thing or are we naturally on the look-out for it from the start? There is no implausibility in supposing that we are innately predisposed to respond to certain sorts of regularity, this sort among others. Similarly, I have argued elsewhere that an infant may have some inborn reluctance to interpret what it sees as disorderly sequences, and will consequently be predisposed to take some patterns of repeated impressions as impressions of persisting things, and others as impressions of recurring processes of the same type.[20] We might not want to call such interpretative propensities innate ideas of identity and individuation, substance and process, but they would be something innate that contributes to our actual knowledge of the world.

Similarly, in explaining our concept of causation, which is important in many ways for our knowledge of the world, I have argued that there is at the core of it the notion expressed by a counterfactual conditional, the notion of what would have happened if this had not, and I have argued that this notion arises primitively from imaginative projection and analogizing: our tendency to do this and hence to think causally may well be another inborn propensity.[21]

[19] I. iv. 19.   [20] *The Cement of the Universe*, pp. 115–16.
[21] Op. cit., pp. 55–7.

The same may be true of our ability to learn from experience, our tendency to reason inductively, and to take imperfect regularities as indications of more perfect ones that are wholly or partly unobserved. We form expectations on the basis of observations in ways which if developed into explicit, formal arguments would include among their premises some variant of the principle of the uniformity of nature. We use this not only for direct projections of past experience by simple enumerative induction, but also more subtly and indirectly, assuming that where two fairly similar antecedent situations have had different outcomes there must have been some relevant difference between the antecedents, and hence looking out for, and paying special attention to, such differences.

It is to principles of these sorts that we have appealed in earlier chapters in order to relax the apparent requirements of empiricism. If the thesis that ideas and knowledge are derived from, and based on, experience is so interpreted as to allow for such principles and propensities the conflicts with realism will largely disappear.

5. *Leibniz's reply to Locke*

It may seem, however, that this relaxation does away with all that is distinctively empiricist, and concedes all that a rationalist would demand. For example, Leibniz develops the dispositional form of the doctrine of innate notions, using the analogy of a block of marble from which a sculptor produces a statue of Hercules. On Locke's view, the mind is like a uniform block of marble, which has indeed this statue potentially within it, in that it *can* be carved into this shape, but equally has any number of alternative statues potentially within it: being uniform, it can be equally well carved into any shape that will fit within its boundaries. Correspondingly, the mind has, as Locke admits, an innate capacity of knowing, but what it comes to know depends wholly upon what experience supplies: it has no inbuilt preference for one belief rather than another. Leibniz, on the other hand, thinks that the mind is like a block of marble in which the figure of Hercules is already marked out by internal veins or cracks, surfaces within the block along which it will split more easily than than any others. The sculptor still has to work to reveal this hidden form, to clear away the unwanted portions and smooth the surfaces thus exposed: but it is this figure and not any other that was preferentially latent within the block. Correspondingly, Leibniz thinks, the mind is innately predisposed to some beliefs rather than others.[22] Of course, this is only a simile; but some of the propensities I have suggested in my last interpretation of the empiricist programme might well serve as a literal description of what Leibniz intends.

But this is not all that Leibniz is saying. He also uses the doctrine of innate ideas to explain how we can know necessary truths in arithmetic and geometry, and know them to hold universally, whereas sensory perception could inform us only about particular examples and induction from them could never establish a necessary, universal truth. We also know necessary truths, he maintains, in theology and moral philosophy. Indeed he warmly commends most of the demonstrations which Locke has offered in these areas, and which I have criticized, though he detects the fallacy of equivocation pointed out in note 14 above.[23]

Leibniz replies to Locke's argument that specific differences between things are more primitively known and more fundamental than such abstract maxims as the principle of contradiction. We often argue in enthymemes—for example, 'this is a man, so he is mortal'—leaving out the major premiss on which we are none the less implicitly relying. Similarly, Leibniz suggests, when we realize that a square is not a circle, or that to be yellow is not to be sweet, we are implicitly relying upon and applying the principle of contradiction without explicitly formulating it.[24] But he admits that the doctrine of innate ideas is sometimes used to justify dogmatism and credulity, and he endorses Locke's condemnation of this use of it; the rationalist no less than the empiricist can insist that men must think and find things out for themselves.[25]

A much weaker point that Leibniz makes is that Locke, in recognizing ideas of reflection as well as ideas of sensation—that is, in admitting that the mind takes notice of its own operations—has in effect admitted that there are innate ideas.[26] If 'innate' meant no more than non-sensory, this would be true; but then the doctrine of innate ideas would be trivialized: to say that God has

[22] *New Essays*, Preface; Bk. I, ch. 1.
[23] Op. cit., Preface; Bk. I, ch. 1; Bk. IV, ch. 10.
[24] Op. cit., Bk. I, ch. 1.   [25] Op. cit., Bk. I, chs. 2, 3.
[26] Op. cit., Preface.

put these ideas into our minds but left them latent would be no more than to say that we have, by nature, the powers of perceiving, doubting, believing, and so on together with the ability to be self-conscious about their exercise. Of course, Locke, and everyone else, concedes this. But this concession will not support what is distinctive in the doctrine of innate notions, in particular the claim that we know necessary truths in mathematics, theology, and ethics, and the explanation of how we can know them. Nor is there any plausibility in the suggestion that the principle of contradiction is used implicitly in our recognition of specific differences. But granted that there may well be various innate propensities, the important outstanding issue is whether these are needed to explain, and whether they could explain, some knowledge that we have of necessary truths.

We have noted Locke's failure to supply valid demonstrations of morality and of the existence of God; but since it is questionable whether we have any knowledge, let alone necessary knowledge, in these areas they give no initial support to Leibniz's views. Mathematics, then, is the crucial example. Locke's attempt to analyse reasoning in arithmetic and geometry into chains in which each link is a perceived agreement or disagreement between ideas is hardly more successful than his proofs of God's existence. Reasoning in any system of geometry, such as Euclid's, relies upon axioms, for example that 'two straight lines cannot enclose a space'. But the mere idea of straightness as such does not disagree with that of enclosing a space, or, what comes to the same thing, meeting twice. If we use as our 'idea of straight lines' some complex of ideas that does so disagree, it will be a synthetic and surely empirical question whether any actual items that we recognize as straight lines by other criteria (such as rays of light, stretched strings, or the intersections of surfaces whose flatness is defined by mechanical procedures) conform to this complex of ideas.[27] Though what Locke says about geometry is wrong, the correction of his mistakes does not help Leibniz's case. In so far as geometrical truths are necessary, they are analytic; what is synthetic, namely the conformity of any specified material to this or that geometrical system, is also empirical; whereas only if we had truths which were at once synthetic and necessary would there be

[27] Cf. E. Nagel, *The Structure of Science*, Chapter 8; also my 'Proof', *Aristotelian Society Supplementary Volume* 40 (1966), pp. 23-38, and Chapter 3, Section 8 above.

any call for the sort of explanation that Leibniz offers. The
of arithmetic is more controversial, though I have argue
where that it is analogous to that of geometry.[28] The mo.
can say is that there might be, in arithmetic, synthetic but ne
sary truths which it would be difficult for an empiricist to accou.
for. We can inquire whether, if there were, anything like Leibniz's
view could account for their necessity. I shall come back to this
question in Section 8, but I want first to consider some general
questions about the possibility of innate ideas and knowledge.

6. *The possibility of innate knowledge*[29]

Locke plainly treats the question whether we have innate knowledge and innate ideas as an empirical question, to be settled by
evidence about how people think and speak, including children
and illiterate people and idiots, and about the beliefs of foreign and
savage nations. But we are often inclined to take a stronger line,
to say that there could not be innate ideas or knowledge. It seems
obvious that someone who had been blind from birth could have
no ideas of colours, that someone born without either the sense
of sight or that of touch could have no ideas of shapes. To many
thinkers it seems almost equally obvious that although we can of
course know, having learned from others, about things of which
we ourselves have no experience, no synthetic truth can be known
by anyone unless someone has had experiences that are evidence
for it.

But should we be so sure of either of these? A contrary argument seems to show that for any ideas and any knowledge that
anyone actually has, it is at least logically possible that someone
should have those same ideas or that same knowledge innately.
Whatever occurrent or dispositional state of a person constitutes
his having such and such an idea or concept, or such and such an
item of knowledge, it must be at least logically possible that a
relevantly similar state should either be present in an individual
person from birth or develop in him automatically, by a process
of maturation, without needing to be fed in from the outside. No

[28] In 'Proof', referred to in note 27.

[29] Much of the argument in this section is taken from my paper of the same title
in *Aristotelian Society Proceedings*, 70 (1970), pp. 245–57, which in turn was based
partly on Peter Unger's paper 'Experience and Factual Knowledge', in *The Journal
of Philosophy*, 64 (1967), pp. 152–73.

prior experience can be logically necessary for any specific cognitive state. In the face of this argument we might well ask why so many of us are so sure that this logical possibility is not realized, and that Locke's arguments against it, whether sound or not, are superfluous. Let us examine this question, taking separately the theses of concept empiricism, that no ideas or concepts are innate, and of judgement empiricism, that no authoritative judgements which could qualify as items of knowledge are innate.

The concept empiricist, thus challenged, might fall back to either of two positions. He might say that even if someone who was blind from birth had, in some strange way, ideas of colours, if he could imagine red and blue and green things as well as we can, we could never tell that he had such ideas. Since he would be unable to employ his innate colour-ideas in recognizing objects presented to his senses, he would be unable to correlate these ideas with our words, and in consequence we could never discover what ideas he had. But of course this is a weaker thesis than the one empiricists commonly endorse. Alternatively, the concept empiricist might say that having ideas or concepts is not just a matter of purely private, internal perceptions such as it must be logically possible that a blind-from-birth man should have of colours, but that to have an idea of, say, red is partly constituted by the ability to recognize red things, to discriminate them in favourable conditions from blue or green ones, and so on, and perhaps even that it requires competence in the use of the appropriate fragment of some public language. However, such abilities and such competence could conceivably be innate, in that someone might begin to display them immediately upon being confronted with opportunities for their exercise, with no period of gradual learning.

The concept empiricist must then abandon the thesis that there *could not be* innate ideas of, say, colours, and retreat to the weaker, inductively supported, thesis that there *are* not. We know quite a lot about how we now acquire new ideas and concepts, that is, either by having new kinds of perceptions (as with Locke's example of learning the taste of a pineapple[30]) or by combining or otherwise working on concepts that we already have, and it is reasonable to infer that our ideas of all sensible properties at least came in the first place from sensory experiences. But however

[30] III. iv. 11.

reasonable this is as a general account, and particularly of those concepts that can be readily related to sense-perception, it would be powerless to refute the suggestion that some special ideas or concepts are innate, and in particular those for which it is difficult to find an adequate sensory (or introspective) source.

The judgement empiricist can reply in stronger terms. He might argue that there could not be innate knowledge, because although whatever occurrent or dispositional states now constitute knowledge logically could have come into existence without their possessor's having had any relevant prior experience, these states would not then constitute knowledge. If a belief, however confident and however true, simply arose in a person as something like an instinct, whether as a result of evolutionary processes or by what Locke's contemporaries called being implanted or imprinted or inscribed in the soul by God, that person could not properly be said to know whatever he thus truly, instinctively, believed. He would not have good reasons for believing as he did; he would not be authoritative about it; he would not be epistemically justified; he would have no 'right to be sure'.

Yet there is a plausible argument on the other side. We want, indeed, to distinguish knowledge from mere true belief, but it has seemed to many thinkers that the distinctive requirement for knowledge is that it should not be an accident that the belief is true. If A knows that p, A's believing that p must depend somehow either on the fact that p or on something which is itself connected with that fact. If I know that there is a ladder outside this window because I have seen it, or because I have been told that there is by some reliable person who has seen it, then the presence of the ladder is causally responsible for my believing as I do, and if it had not been there I would not, in what were otherwise the present circumstances, be believing this. If I know that there will be an eclipse tomorrow, then though the eclipse itself is not causally responsible for my believing as I do, the earlier positions and the regular behaviour of the sun, earth, and moon will both have ensured that the eclipse would occur and, by way of the work of astronomers, helped to bring about my believing. In both cases I have non-accidentally true beliefs. Now true innate beliefs could meet this requirement. God might have implanted certain beliefs in men's minds because things are, or perhaps because by divine *fiat* things will be, as those beliefs will hold them to be.

God will have given us beliefs that are useful because they are true. If the facts had been, or were to be, otherwise, then God would have implanted suitably different beliefs. Again, suppose that evolution by natural selection has made us inductive animals, simply because the less inductive cousins of our remote ancestors did not survive, and did not survive because they were less inductive. Then there would not have evolved a race with the innate tendency to believe that there are detectable regularities in the course of events if there had not been such detectable regularities while the race was evolving. A part of the fact that there are such regularities has been a significant causal factor in the production of the corresponding instinctive belief. Thus if knowledge is defined as non-accidentally true belief, innate beliefs, whether developed by evolution or divinely implanted, could be knowledge.

It seems, then, that whether there could or could not be innate knowledge depends on what we take to be the criterion that distinguishes knowledge from mere true belief. But now the issue is in danger of becoming trivial. We have noted two variants of the criterion, and there may well be further possibilities. For example, we might distinguish, within the sense of 'knows' which requires that the knower should be epistemically justified, a sense in which someone knows only if he can defend his belief and a sense in which someone knows if he has, say, once made sufficient relevant observations or calculations but has now forgotten them. Does Newton still know a proposition he has himself proved when, some years later, he has forgotten how he proved it?[31] Similarly, we may draw further distinctions within the sense in which someone knows provided that it is not an accident that his belief is true. Thus we might require that there should be some actual connection, capable, at least in principle, of being discovered or further explained, between the believing and what makes the belief true. Or we might be satisfied with the bare fact that if what is believed about had been otherwise, the believing would have been at least likely to have been otherwise too, even if we thought that this was unexplainable even in principle. For example, if someone consistently predicts the result of some random process, such as the tossing of a coin, with, say, ninety per cent accuracy, can we admit, in the end, that his performance is

[31] Cf. IV. i. 9.

in principle unexplainable but still say, on some occasion when he has correctly predicted heads, that he knew this, on the ground that if it had not been going to be heads he would probably not have predicted heads? Or should we refuse, in this case, to say that he knew, but allow that the farmer who predicts the next day's weather, again with, say, ninety per cent accuracy, knows (when he gets it right) what the next day's weather will be, because we think that though neither we nor the farmer can tell how he tells this, there are fairly reliable causal connections between the recent and present weather conditions and, on the one hand, tomorrow's weather and, on the other, what the farmer feels—that is, that earlier weather conditions are a partial cause both of the prediction and of what is predicted? Surely we simply have two senses of 'know' here; one in which the coin predictor and the farmer both (when they get it right) know what will happen, and another in which the farmer knows but the coin predictor does not. (It might be objected that these two are not different senses of 'know', but a single sense—knowledge is true belief whose correctness is causally supported—differentiated by varying views of causation. On a pure Humean view of causes, the coin predictor's rightness is causally supported. But it will be convenient to speak throughout of different senses of 'know'.)

If there is such a spectrum of possible senses of 'know', a range of more or less stringent criteria of knowledge as opposed to true belief, it will be idle to dispute which analysis of knowing is correct. It is likely that competent speakers of English use the word 'know' sometimes in one sense, sometimes in another, and often with a sense that is indeterminate between several distinguishable precise senses. In most ordinary paradigm cases of knowing, all the senses apply equally well. But it may still be worth while to distinguish the senses, and particularly those at the extreme ends of the range, and to see what point there is in using them.

Consider, for example, the minimal sense, which requires only non-accidentally true belief. The currently orthodox pattern of analysis of knowing—A knows that p if and only if A believes that p, and p is true, and A's belief that p is (in some sense) justified—is somewhat misleading. It suggests that the commentator, the person who says that the cognizer (possibly but not necessarily someone else) knows something, first finds the belief, then learns that it is true, and only at the last that it is justified. It may well happen the other way round. The commentator may first decide that the cognizer's belief is justified, and thence infer that it is probably true. The minimal sense of 'know' covers just those cases where there is something about the cognizer's believing which would justify the commentator in inferring that the belief is likely to be true, even if he had no independent information on the subject. The notion of epistemic justification enters even into this minimal sense of 'know', though it is here justification for the commentator, not for the cognizer.

At the other end of the spectrum we have the concept of authoritative, autonomous, knowledge, the knowledge of the man who himself has the epistemic justification, the right to be sure. This does not, of course, exclude knowledge that rests partly on the testimony of others: I can still be authoritative about information thus received if I have somehow established for myself the reliability of the witness, or have established the probability of what I am told by independent witnesses by having checked for myself that they are indeed independent. But I do not have authoritative knowledge if I merely accept information from someone else without myself establishing his reliability, even if he happens to be reliable and the information happens to be true.

Having drawn these distinctions, we can see that while there could be innate knowledge in the minimal sense, it would not, as innate, be authoritative. Consider in how weak a position men would be if they had true beliefs implanted by God or developed by natural selection, but had no independent way of justifying them by any appeal to their own observations or calculations. Their beliefs would be true, but they could not defend them if they were challenged; if any sceptical doubts arose in their own minds they could do nothing to overcome them. We could indeed describe them as cognitively healthy: their believings on these matters would tend to be correct. But these men would be in a state of intellectual servitude. It might be a comfortable state, as long as sceptical doubts did not arise, but it would be servitude none the less.

This weakness of the position of men thus provided with innate beliefs had been brought out, even before Locke wrote, by Samuel Parker:

But suppose that we were born with these congenite Anticipations, and that they take Root in our very Faculties, yet how can I be certain of their Truth and Veracity? For 'tis not impossible but the seeds of Error might have been the natural Results of my Faculties, as Weeds are the first and natural Issues of the best Soyles, how then shall we be sure that these spontaneous Notions are not false and spurious?

The only means of gaining such certainty is to test these truths by experience.[32] Locke makes a logically analogous point about possible revelations:

Reason must be our last judge and guide in everything. I do not mean that we must consult reason and examine whether a proposition revealed from God can be made out by natural principles, and if it cannot, that then we may reject it; but consult it we must, and by it examine whether it be a *revelation* from God or no; and if *reason* finds it to be revealed from God, *reason* then declares for it as much as for any other truth, and makes it one of her dictates.[33]

Similarly, if Descartes or Leibniz, say, could demonstrate that our innate beliefs had been given to us by a benevolently veracious God, then those beliefs would become, for him, items of authoritative knowledge. But they are not so merely in so far as they are innate, and they would not be so for men who lacked this philosophical demonstration. And if this demonstration itself rests upon an innate idea of God or upon innate knowledge of his existence, then it will be viciously circular, and we shall never be able in this way to achieve authoritative knowledge either of God's existence or of the content of any other divinely implanted beliefs.

In the same way someone in whom true beliefs had been developed by evolution might be able to turn these into authoritative knowledge by showing that the evolutionary process that had developed them was very likely to have fostered true beliefs. But in all cases it is not simply as innate that such beliefs constitute authoritative knowledge. A further rational validation is required, and whether the appeal is to God or to evolution care is needed to ensure that this validation is not circular.

It is, then, not impossible that there should be innate knowledge in the minimal sense of 'knowledge'. It is not impossible even that

[32] Samuel Parker, *A Free and Impartial Censure of the Platonick Philosophie* (1666), p. 56, quoted and reported by Yolton, op. cit., pp. 44–5.
[33] IV. xix. 14.

there should be innate authoritative knowledge. But innate knowledge could be authoritative only if there were independent confirmation of the reliability or veracity of whatever it was that had made these beliefs innate. It is this insistence on independent empirical confirmation as a requirement for authoritative knowledge that is the strongest point in the judgement empiricist's case.

7. *Actual innate knowledge*

If these are the possibilities, we can turn again to the question whether we actually have any innate knowledge. It is very plain that we do not have innate knowledge of the kinds which Locke's contemporaries were most concerned to assert, knowledge of morality and of the existence of God. There is no empirical evidence of innate religious beliefs. No doubt men have a variety of inborn behavioural tendencies, including some that favour social life, though many of them, not surprisingly, are such as would have helped human communities to survive in the conditions that prevailed when these instincts were evolved, but are less helpful or positively harmful in the modern world. But nothing of this sort constitutes moral knowledge or authoritative rules of conduct: we must look elsewhere for the foundations of morality.

There are, however, two areas in which it is at least plausible to speculate about actual innate knowledge. One of these includes the topics mentioned in Section 4 above: possible innate propensities to see things realistically, to interpret impressions as impressions of persisting things or of repeated processes rather than to accept disorder as ultimate, to reason inductively, and to make the sorts of projection that contribute to our concept of causation. The other area is that of the forms of language, where Chomsky has argued that all human natural languages share specific structures, and that this general form of grammar is innate in that infants tend to interpret the linguistic data they encounter as conforming to it, and so acquire a grasp of the grammar of whatever particular language is spoken around them more readily than they otherwise could.

I shall not discuss the empirical question whether Chomsky's innateness hypothesis is correct. But if it is correct, we could say that children know innately that the languages they encounter have a certain general grammatical form, in so far as they automatically interpret data as having this form, and are right to do so, and are right not accidentally but in virtue of causal links between inborn psychological structures and the structures of actual human languages. But this is, for two reasons, a very minimal sense of 'know'; first, because this is just a matter of being non-accidentally right, and secondly, because the children presumably have no explicit beliefs that these languages have this grammar, but only behave in ways that would be rational in the light of such beliefs. Children do not have authoritative knowledge of the structure of these languages until they have found that these automatic interpretations work, that having learned the language in accordance with these predispositions they can use it successfully for communication with those who already speak it. If, alternatively, the innateness hypothesis about grammar is incorrect, we have to explain language-learning as just one application among others of our general principles of learning, some of which were mentioned in Section 4. It will be a reasonable speculation that human beings have such innate general learning strategies, whether or not they have specific grammatical ones as well. And again we can speak of innate knowledge in a very minimal sense of 'knowledge', in so far as we interpret data as conforming to such categories as persisting things, repeated processes, causation, and natural laws or uniformities. But once again such knowledge, as innate, will not be authoritative: we acquire authoritative knowledge only in so far as we confirm, in experience, that things actually fit into the categories in terms of which we are predisposed to interpret them.

Our conclusion, then, is that empiricism can, while still insisting on the need for an empirical basis for authoritative knowledge, interpret the thesis that ideas and knowledge are derived from experience in a way that allows for the more complex procedures suggested in Section 4 and, in consequence, leaves room for realism.

8. *Innateness and necessity*

We must, finally, take up the question whether anything like Leibniz's view could account for synthetic necessary truths in arithmetic. There could be synthetic propositions which we very firmly and innately believe to hold universally for whatever material we take our interpreted arithmetic to be true of. An example might be the Associative Law, that $(a + b) + c = a + (b + c)$, which is appealed to implicitly in, for example, Leibniz's proof that $2 + 2 = 4$.[34] Innate beliefs of this kind could hardly have been engendered by natural selection: it is only as divine implantings that they could plausibly be held to be innate. As such, if we can escape the circularity mentioned at the end of Section 6, they could conceivably amount to authoritative knowledge. But would they, on this account, be necessary truths? Surely the most that could follow from these premisses is that they would be necessary for us, that they would describe ways in which we could not help ordering things. Even this is dubious. If we were able to see that these propositions were synthetic, we should be able to see how things could fail to conform to them. Their necessity would be, at best, analogous to the necessities discussed in Chapter 3, Sections 7 and 9, and Chapter 5, Section 3 above, which derive from contingent facts about how we think and speak about individuals and kinds of stuff. Even if we make the greatest possible concessions to Leibniz, then, about the possibility of dispositionally innate notions, of belief-propensities which might count as knowledge, we must conclude that his approach fails completely to show even how truths about fully objective matters could be at once synthetic and necessary, let alone how anything innate could constitute knowledge of such synthetic necessary truths.

I have criticized Locke's optimism with respect to the possibilities of demonstrative knowledge in theology, ethics, geometry, and (in principle) in angelic chemistry and medicine.[35] It is on these subjects that we find the strongest rationalist tendencies in his thought. By contrast, I have defended what is perhaps the core of his empiricism, the insistence that authoritative knowledge of synthetic truths requires empirical support. But I have argued that this principle does not preclude the recognition that not only innate capacities but also innate propensities, anticipations of specific structures, and even what we can call in a minimal but quite respectable sense innate knowledge, may well make signifi-

---

[34] Op. cit., Bk. IV, ch. 7. The notion of interpreted arithmetic is explained in my 'Proof', referred to in note 27.
[35] Cf. Section 3 above, and Chapter 3, Section 8.

cant contributions to our learning about the world. I have argued also that what is defensible in empiricism does not commit us to those restricted views, about how ideas and knowledge and meanings are derived from the immediate contents of experience, which at several points in Locke's own thinking made difficulties for realism.

'Nature has given us not knowledge, but the seeds of knowledge.'[36] We have been selectively bred as learners, not as knowers. This is a thesis which Leibniz and Locke would both accept, though for rather different reasons. But just what seeds of knowledge are there; exactly how do they contribute to our learning; and to what kinds of knowledge do they therefore give rise? These are the controversial issues. In trying to settle them I have made some concessions to the defenders of innate notions, but have come down mainly on the empiricist side.

[36] 'Natura semina scientiae nobis dedit, scientiam non dedit.' Seneca, *Epistolae ad Lucilium*, cxv.

BIBLIOGRAPHY

BIBLIOGRAPHY

Including only works mentioned in the text, and showing the editions referred to or quoted.

AARON, R. I. *John Locke*. Oxford, 1955.

AMMERMAN, R. R. *Classics of Analytic Philosophy*. New York, 1965.

ANSCOMBE, G. E. M. 'The Intentionality of Sensation: a Grammatical Feature'. In *Analytical Philosophy*, 2nd ser., ed. R. J. Butler. Oxford, 1965.

ARISTOTLE. *De Anima* and *Metaphysics*.

ARMSTRONG, D. M. *Belief, Truth, and Knowledge*. Cambridge, 1973.

—— *A Materialist Theory of the Mind*. London, 1968.

AYER, A. J. *Language, Truth and Logic*. London, 1967.

—— *The Central Questions of Philosophy*. London, 1973.

AYERS, M. R. 'The Ideas of Power and Substance in Locke's Philosophy', *Philosophical Quarterly*, 25 (1975), 1–27.

BENNETT, J. F. *Kant's Analytic*. Cambridge, 1966.

—— *Locke, Berkeley, Hume: Central Themes*, Oxford, 1971.

—— 'Substance, Reality, and Primary Qualities', *American Philosophical Quarterly*, 2 (1965). Reprinted in Martin and Armstrong.

BERKELEY, G. *Philosophical Works*, ed. M. R. Ayers. London, 1975.

BORST, C. V. (ed.) *The Mind/Brain Identity Theory*. London, 1970.

BOSTOCK, D. *Logic and Arithmetic: Natural Numbers*. Oxford, 1974.

BRADLEY, F. H. *Ethical Studies*. Oxford, 1927.

BOYLE, R. *Works*. London, 1772.

BUTLER, J. 'Of Personal Identity'. In *The Analogy of Religion*, ed. J. Angus. London, undated.

CAMPBELL, K. *Body and Mind*. London, 1970.

CORNMAN, J. 'The Identity of Mind and Body', *Journal of Philosophy*, 59 (1962). Reprinted in Borst.

DUMMETT, M. *Frege – Philosophy of Language*. London, 1973.

FLEW, A. G. N. 'Locke and the Problem of Personal Identity', *Philosophy*, 26 (1951). Reprinted in Martin and Armstrong.

GEACH, P. T. and BLACK, M. (eds.) *Philosophical Writings of Gottlob Frege*. Oxford, 1952.

GOODMAN, N. *Fact, Fiction, and Forecast*. London, 1954.

GREGORY, R. L. *Concepts and Mechanisms of Perception*. London, 1974.

GRICE, H. P. 'Personal Identity', *Mind*, 50 (1941), 330–5.

HARRISON, B. *Form and Content*. Oxford, 1973.

HEMPEL, C. G. 'Problems and Changes in the Empiricist Criterion of

230   BIBLIOGRAPHY

Meaning', *Revue internationale de philosophie*, 4 (1950). Reprinted in Ammerman.

HOBBES, T. *English Works*, ed. Molesworth. London, 1841.

HUME, D. *A Treatise of Human Nature*, ed. L. A. Selby-Bigge. Oxford, 1960.

KÖRNER, S. (ed.) *Observation and Interpretation in the Philosophy of Physics*. New York, 1957.

KRIPKE, S. 'Naming and Necessity'. In *Semantics of Natural Language*, ed. D. Davidson and G. Harman. Dordrecht, 1972.

LEIBNIZ, G. W. *Die PhilosophischenSchriften*, ed. Gerhardt. Hildesheim, 1965.

—— *New Essays*. New York, 1896.

LOCKE, D. *Perception and Our Knowledge of the External World*. London, 1967.

LOCKE, J. *Works*, London, 1812.

—— *An Essay concerning Human Understanding*, ed. J. W. Yolton. London, 1965.

—— *An Essay concerning Human Understanding*, ed. A. D. Woozley. London, 1964.

LUCAS, J. R. *A Treatise on Time and Space*. London, 1973.

MABBOTT, J. D. *John Locke*. London, 1973.

MACKIE, J. L. '*De* what *Re* is *De Re* Modality?', *Journal of Philosophy*, 71 (1974), 551–61.

—— 'Locke's Anticipation of Kripke', *Analysis*, 34 (1974), 177–80.

—— 'Proof', *Aristotelian Society Supplementary Volume*, 40 (1966), 23–38.

—— 'Self-Refutation: a Formal Analysis', *Philosophical Quarterly*, 14 (1964), 193–203.

—— 'The Possiblity of Innate Knowledge', *Proceedings of The Aristotelian Society*, 70 (1970), 245–57.

—— 'What's Really Wrong with Phenomenalism?', *Proceedings of The British Academy*, 55 (1969), 113–27.

—— 'Problems of Intentionality'. In *Phenomenology and Philosophical Understanding*, ed. E. Pivcevic. Cambridge, 1975.

—— *The Cement of the Universe*. Oxford, 1974.

—— *Truth, Probability, and Paradox*. Oxford, 1973.

MALEBRANCHE, N. *De la recherche de la vérité*. Paris, 1965.

MARTIN, C. B. and ARMSTRONG, D. M. (eds.) *Locke and Berkeley*. London, 1969.

MARTIN, C. B. *Religious Belief*. New York, 1959.

MILL, J. S. *A System of Logic*. London, 1889.

MORE, H. *An Antidote against Atheism* (1653): extract quoted in Yolton, *John Locke and the Way of Ideas*.

NAGEL, E. *The Structure of Science*. London, 1961.

NAGEL, T. 'Physicalism', *Philosophical Review*, 74 (1965). Reprinted in Borst.

O'CONNOR, D. J. (ed.) *A Critical History of Western Philosophy*. London, 1964.

PARFIT, D. A. 'Personal Identity', *Philosophical Review*, 80 (1971), 3–27.

PARKER, S. *A Free and Impartial Censure of the Platonick Philosophie* (1666): extract quoted in Yolton, *John Locke and the Way of Ideas*.

PAUL, G. A. 'Is there a Problem about Sense-Data?', *Aristotelian Society Supplementary Volume*, 15 (1936). Reprinted in *Logic and Language*, 1st ser., ed. A. G. N. Flew. Oxford, 1968.

PLATO. *Parmenides*.

—— *Phaedo*.

—— *Republic*.

PLUTARCH. *Lives*.

POPPER, K. R. *The Logic of Scientific Discovery*, Second English edition. London, 1972.

PRIOR, A. N. *Past, Present, and Future*. Oxford, 1967.

—— 'Berkeley in Logical Form', *Theoria*, 21 (1955), 117–22.

R. H. Query in *Locke Newsletter*, 4 (1973), 43–4.

RORTY, R. 'Mind-body Identity, Privacy and Categories', *Review of Metaphysics*, 19 (1965). Reprinted in Borst.

ROSS, W. D. *Plato's Theory of Ideas*. Oxford, 1951.

RUSSELL, B. *The Problems of Philosophy*. Oxford, 1948.

RYLE, G. *Dilemmas*. Cambridge, 1954.

—— *The Concept of Mind*. London, 1949.

—— 'John Locke on the Human Understanding'. In *Tercentenary Addresses on John Locke*, ed. J. L. Stocks. Oxford, 1933. Reprinted in Martin and Armstrong.

SENECA, L. ANNAEUS. *Ad Lucilium Epistolae Morales*. London, 1917.

SHOEMAKER, S. *Self-Knowledge and Self-Identity*. Ithaca, 1963.

SMART, J. J. C. *Philosophy and Scientific Realism*. London, 1963.

SWINBURNE, R. G. 'Confirmability and Factual Meaningfulness', *Analysis*, 33 (1973), 71–6.

—— 'Personal Identity', *Proceedings of the Aristotelian Society*, 74 (1973–4), 231–47.

—— *Sense and Nonsense in Physics and Theology*. University of Keele Inaugural Lecture, 1973.

UNGER, P. 'Experience and Factual Knowledge', *Journal of Philosophy*, 64 (1967), 152–73.

VON WRIGHT, G. H. *Causality and Determinism*. New York, 1974.

WIGGINS, D. *Identity and Spatio-Temporal Continuity*. Oxford, 1967.

WILLIAMS, B. A. O. *Problems of the Self*. Cambridge, 1973.

—— 'Bodily Continuity and Personal Identity', *Analysis*, 21 (1960). Reprinted in *Problems of the Self*.

—— 'Personal Identity and Individuation', *Proceedings of the Aristotelian Society*, 57 (1956–7). Reprinted in *Problems of the Self*.

—— 'The Self and the Future', *Philosophical Review*, 79 (1970). Reprinted in *Problems of the Self*.

YOLTON, J. W. *John Locke and the Way of Ideas*. Oxford, 1956.

—— *John Locke and the Compass of Human Understanding*. Cambridge, 1970.

INDEX

INDEX